THE PROVOST'S HANDBOOK

THE PROVOST'S HANDBOOK

The Role of the Chief Academic Officer

James Martin, James E. Samels & Associates

Johns Hopkins University Press
Baltimore

© 2015 Johns Hopkins University Press
All rights reserved. Published 2015
Printed in the United States of America on acid-free paper
9 8 7 6 5 4 3 2 1

Johns Hopkins University Press
2715 North Charles Street
Baltimore, Maryland 21218-4363
www.press.jhu.edu

Library of Congress Cataloging-in-Publication Data

Martin, James, 1948 January 14–
  The provost's handbook : the role of the chief academic officer / James
Martin, James E. Samels & Associates.
    pages cm.
  Includes bibliographical references and index.
  ISBN 978-1-4214-1625-0 (hardcover : alk. paper)—ISBN 978-1-4214-1626-7
(pbk. : alk. paper)—ISBN 978-1-4214-1627-4 (electronic)—ISBN 1-4214-1625-5
(hardcover : alk. paper)—ISBN 1-4214-1626-3 (pbk. : alk. paper)—
ISBN 1-4214-1627-1 (electronic) 1. Education, Higher—United States—
Administration. 2. Deans (Education)—United States. I. Samels, James E. II. Title.
  LB2341.M295 2015
  378.1'01—dc23   2014024711

A catalog record for this book is available from the British Library.

Special discounts are available for bulk purchases of this book. For more
information, please contact Special Sales at 410-516-6936 or
specialsales@press.jhu.edu.

Johns Hopkins University Press uses environmentally friendly book materials,
including recycled text paper that is composed of at least 30 percent post-
consumer waste, whenever possible.

Contents

Preface

The chapters that follow provide a fresh look at the role of chief academic officer. Our research on this topic over the past decade confirms that most CAOs still spend the bulk of their time addressing traditional academic leadership concerns like strategic planning, faculty development, and budget design. In fact, when more than three thousand provosts and academic vice presidents were asked by editors of the American Council on Education's *CAO Census* what their two top priorities were, "promoting academic quality" and "setting the academic vision for the institution" were the most frequent answers.* At the same time, many CAOs agreed with us that their primary responsibilities are expanding and that a comprehensive set of best practices are needed, especially in areas traditionally less examined or even overlooked, such as accountabilities with departments of athletics; strategies to achieve higher institutional rankings; and new models of partnership with offices of advancement, admissions, institutional research, and student life.

Several chapters that follow provide original contributions to the field:

- An exclusive interview with the vice president for publications of *The Princeton Review* about the roles a CAO now needs to play in raising institutional rankings

- A tested model to ensure accountability in working with college and university athletic programs

* Peter D. Eckel, Bryan J. Cook, and Jacqueline E. King, *The CAO Census: A National Profile of Chief Academic Officers* (Washington, DC: American Council on Education, 2009), 9.

- The elements of a national orientation and training program for CAOs from the president of the Council of Independent Colleges

- A new admissions partnership model developed by a university president and a three-time head admissions officer and author of the best-selling guide, *College Admission: From Application to Acceptance*

- Multiple sidebars in almost every chapter by authorities in that field, along with lessons learned by the contributors to an earlier, related volume by Martin and Samels, *First Among Equals: The Role of the Chief Academic Officer,* who were asked, "As a CAO, what is the most important thing that you wish you had known when you wrote your original chapter?"

Chapters are grouped into two principal sections: "The Academic Agenda" defines the key responsibilities for a CAO in implementing the mission of the institution with the faculty and academic leadership team; "Essential Partners" broadens this discussion by offering best practices for working with the other institutional vice presidents and their operational areas.

"The Academic Agenda" opens with a chapter by Martin and Samels that updates the national conversation on the roles and responsibilities of the chief academic officer begun in their book *First Among Equals: The Role of the Chief Academic Officer* more than fifteen years ago.

In chapter 2, Bryan J. Cook, former director of the Center for Policy Analysis at the American Council on Education, provides an insider's view of the making of *The CAO Census: A National Profile of Chief Academic Officers,* including emergent trends now shaping the roles of CAOs.

Richard Ekman, president of the Council of Independent Colleges, believes formal training programs for CAOs have become a necessity. In chapter 3, he discusses the design and elements in the training program he recommends to the academic leaders in his 700-member association.

R. Michael Tanner, chief academic officer and vice president at the Association of Public and Land-grant Universities, offers a blueprint for the most effective relationship among provosts, presidents, and trustees in chapter 4.

Linda McMillin follows this discussion by expanding on her 2011 article in *The Chronicle of Higher Education,* "Through the Looking Glass: Faculty to Administration," with a set of guidelines for CAOs when working directly with members of the faculty.

In chapter 6, John Simon, provost at the University of Virginia, focuses on the responsibilities a CAO must assume for an institution's strategic planning process and its office of institutional research. Prior to his position at Virginia, Simon coordinated strategic planning for Duke University.

Robert Groves, provost at Georgetown University, builds on his weekly "Provost's Blog" with the elements of a strategy to address the most difficult decisions CAOs face regarding curricula and how they finally determine what is taught on their campuses.

Lon Kaufman, provost at the University of Illinois, Chicago, and his colleague at the university, Saul Weiner, extend this conversation with examples of how to lead by engaging faculty comprehensively in curriculum development and assessment initiatives.

As executive director of the United States Distance Learning Association and Executive Dean at Nova Southeastern University, John Flores serves as national spokesperson for new instructional technologies. In chapter 9, he details how these technologies are enhancing the classroom experience for professors and their students and what best practices a CAO needs to know to about curriculum, faculty expertise, and new resources.

The first section concludes with a conversation between Jim Stellar, former provost at Queens College, CUNY, and Michael Baer, vice president at Isaacson, Miller higher education search consultants, entitled, "Academic Governance: The Art of Working with People."

In Part II, "Essential Partners," contributors address the responsibilities of the CAO in working across the broader institutional community. This section begins with an action plan to achieve stronger, more transparent collaboration between a provost and the CFO by James Gandre, president of Manhattan School of Music and former provost of Roosevelt University, and Miroslava Krug, CFO at Roosevelt.

Bradley Bateman, president of Randolph College and formerly provost at Denison University, and Julia Houpt, vice president of institutional advancement at Denison, have conducted workshops on partnering the offices of academic affairs and advancement for the Council of Independent Colleges. In chapter 12, they illustrate how to design and achieve shared goals that can be benchmarked with specific outcomes.

In chapter 13, Penny Rue, vice president for campus life at Wake Forest University, and Suresh Subramani, CAO at the University of California, San Diego, follow with best practices for CAOs in working effectively with the Office of Student Life.

In chapter 14, Robin Mamlet, consultant at Witt/Kieffer Executive Search and former dean of admissions at Stanford and Swarthmore and author of the best-selling guide, *College Admission: From Application to Acceptance;* David Pershing, president of the University of Utah; and Sheila Murphy, consultant at Witt/Kieffer, explain new strategies for CAOs to work more closely and effectively with offices of admissions.

William Scott Green, dean of undergraduate education and senior vice provost at the University of Miami, and George VanderZwaag, director of athletics at the University of Rochester, provide fresh thinking and a tested model for CAOs to achieve greater accountability in working with departments of athletics, coaches, and student teams in chapter 15.

Martin and Samels follow in chapter 16 with a review of new developments in higher education law over the past decade as well as updates on several areas of specific concern such as intellectual property, personnel decisions, and various forms of institutional liability.

The volume closes with a look off campus at the new bridges that provosts need to build through their offices of external relations by Mark Lapping, former provost and now senior professor at the Muskie School of Public Service at the University of Southern Maine.

The authors would like to thank several individuals for key contributions to the final form of this book. Richard Ekman and Ginny Coombs at the Council of Independent Colleges and Bryan J. Cook, then of the American Council on Education, all provided valuable information about CAOs from a national education association perspective. Jean Dowdall, partner at Witt/Kieffer Executive Search, offered two suggestions late in the book's development that were instrumental.

We would also like to thank Arlene Lieberman of Samels Associates, Attorneys at Law for her useful contributions to chapter 16. Finally, we would like to acknowledge the work and wisdom our original editor, Jacqueline Wehmueller, who guided us through the development of an earlier volume with the Press, *First Among Equals: The Role of the Chief Academic Officer,* and that of our new editor, Greg Britton, who persuasively moved this book well beyond its original vision and goals.

I

The Academic Agenda

CHAPTER ONE

New Skills, Old Skills, and Leading the Academic Community

James Martin and James E. Samels

Most chief academic officers spend the bulk of their time engaged in the traditional activities of academic leadership such as designing and guiding curriculum, shaping budgets, and developing faculty. As responses to the latest *CAO Census* from the American Council on Education confirm, provosts' agendas are filled with many of the same issues their predecessors faced, and for that reason, most of the contributors to this volume consider at least one of these major issues in designing a new set of best practices for that operational area. However, in our research over the past five years and more, we have also identified a new group of challenges that earlier CAOs did not face:

- Pressures to raise institutional rankings

- Unprecedented student loan default

- Growing dependence on technological resources, platforms, and specialists

- Greater needs for academic accountability in athletics

- Higher levels of plagiarism among both students and faculty

- The impact of social media on academic life.[1]

Over the past two generations, colleges and universities have continued to grow in organizational complexity, and for provosts to lead these enterprises "as successful not-for-profit businesses, *and* as engines of local and regional development, *and* as world-class academic institutions— calls for a wide range of skills and experience."[2] Couple this with the fact that almost half of all CAOs spend their entire administrative

careers at one institution, and even those who move typically make one—
or at most two—changes in a lifetime, and one can see the wisdom of
Richard Ekman's proposals in chapter 3 for national training programs
for both new and veteran provosts.[3] Spending so much time at a single
institution, these individuals may not be gaining the breadth of experience necessary to lead a multigenerational workforce arrayed across more
than fifty professional disciplines.

Whether such programs will become the norm or not, it is clear to
many faculty members and administrators that campus life and the business of higher education are visibly changing and that chief academic
officers need to prepare for even more demands on their time, fewer
chances to study issues in depth, and persistent conflicts between their
origins as faculty members and their responsibilities as administrators.
These tensions and strategies to address them are considered in the chapters that follow, and they are also reflected in the five ways administra-
trative roles, faculty priorities, and student expectations are evolving
discussed below.

The Changing Environment in Which CAOs Must Lead

1. As student consumers decide more quickly, higher education
responds more slowly

Carrying over $1 trillion in student debt, undergraduates and young
alumni are becoming known as "generation Groupon" as they struggle
to overcome a shifting job market and lowest-rung positions lacking benefits.[4] It is not surprising that high school students and their parents are
considering long-term alternatives to traditional bachelor's degrees,
whether at a community college, a for-profit institution, or simply via a
decision to delay and re-think original plans. CAOs are observing how
new technologies and social media accelerate the pace of student decision making, while their models of new program design, approval, and
implementation lag behind—sometimes well behind—this curve.

Increasingly, students are attending college not to reflect and synthe-
size but rather to acquire the skills necessary to obtain a career foothold
immediately upon graduation. Many parents are now focusing on gainful employment opportunities during their child's associate or baccalaureate years, and CAOs are expected to integrate career development opportunities and regional employment trends into academic master
planning and student recruitment materials. As the authors of *The College of 2020: Students* observe, "The traditional model of college is changing, as demonstrated by the proliferation of colleges . . . hybrid class
schedules with night and weekend meetings, and, most significantly, on-

The Changing Environment in Which CAOs Must Lead: Five Examples

1. As student consumers decide more quickly, higher education responds more slowly
2. Administrative bloat has diminished faculty engagement and loyalty.
3. Tuition increases need to be explained and defended—in detail.
4. Budgets must be managed more skillfully.
5. Academic leadership expectations are in conflict.

line learning. The idyll of four years away from home—spent living and learning and growing into adulthood—will continue to wane."[5]

Provosts cannot put aside their need to address traditional academic responsibilities, but pressures from students, parents, trustees, and local employers for new majors with immediate career connections are forcing their way to the center of their planning and budget agendas.

2. Administrative bloat has diminished faculty engagement and loyalty

Administrative bureaucracies have gradually expanded, creating an environment that is "deleterious to a sense of academic community and generally to the faculty's traditional involvement in academic governance."[6] As campus bureaucracy stifles faculty influence, one result is that professors' participation in key areas of academic life has been reduced or squeezed out altogether. After analyzing cost ratios in higher education over a twenty-year period (1987–2008), Robert E. Martin confirmed that overhead costs grew faster than academic costs and institutions economized in their use of tenure-track faculty. In the process, faculty members' influence on campus priorities has shrunk, while the number of non-academic staff members has proliferated.[7]

As full-time faculty members retire, they are increasingly being replaced by adjuncts which also results in less overall engagement and fewer forms of loyalty to the college or university. In fact, as the number of administrators in higher education has almost doubled in proportion to the number of tenure-track teachers, provosts are gathering, managing, and assessing more raw information than in prior decades with the need to assemble it into new models of reporting for presidents and trustees.[8] As the director of the Center for International Higher Education summarizes, "Assessment exercises and other accountability measures require a lot of time and effort to complete. The pressure to assess academic productivity of all kinds is substantial, even if much of that work is in fact quite difficult or impossible to accurately measure. . . . The power of the professors, once dominant . . . has declined in the age of accountability and bureaucracy."[9]

3. Tuition increases need to be explained and defended—in detail

Regularly, CAOs are being told by their presidents, trustees, and legislative delegations to justify tuition increases with multiple rationales and to link them to accompanying increases in employment opportunities for new graduates. Worried parents are not the only constituency asking for this; students themselves are starting their senior years by asking their universities, "Have you done enough for me to find a job now?" In January 2014, the *Wall Street Journal* reported on the impact of escalating debt: "Today's average student debt of $29,400 may not sound overwhelming, but many students, especially at private and out-of-state colleges, end up owing much more, often more than $100,000. At the same time, four in ten college graduates, according to a recent Gallup study, wind up in jobs that don't require a college degree. Students and parents have started to reject this unsustainable arrangement, and colleges and universities have felt the impact."[10]

From his former perspective as Director of the Center for Policy Analysis at the American Council on Education, Bryan Cook adds, "With the costs of college and student debt both continuing to rise, policymakers have become increasingly interested in students' return on investment. Specifically, policymakers are focusing on graduation rates, student learning outcomes, and job placement. One of the biggest challenges facing chief academic officers will be figuring out how to increase their graduation and student job placement rates against a declining budget."[11]

For CAOs, the question is becoming a simple one: Will this tuition increase result in more employment opportunities for my graduates? Even if the answer to that question is yes, however, it may be met by skepticism and anxiety, and current provosts will need to defend it with a new depth of data and details.

4. Budgets must be managed more skillfully

Higher education critics are now finding themselves in unusual partnership with many college and university presidents who are calling for more skillful budget management by their chief academic officers, particularly the courage to eliminate dated, under-enrolled programs, to terminate faculty members who are not performing at necessary levels, and to redefine institutional missions in more professionally focused ways. Simply said, CAOs will spend more time studying, preparing, and executing their budgets, and they will be asked to work more transparently with chief financial officers in this process. As noted in chapters 3 and 11, the Council of Independent Colleges has been proactive in recommending formal leadership development programs to provide CAOs with the financial management expertise to partner effectively with their chief financial officers (CFOs).

In interviewing and speaking with several hundred provosts and deans for this book as well as our earlier book, *First Among Equals: The Role of the Chief Academic Officer,* we asked many what they viewed as their top three responsibilities. Most answers were similar: mentoring young faculty members, developing new programs, or increasing retention, as examples. Rarely, if ever, did we hear a CAO say, "Prepare the budget," or "Learn more about the budget." In fact, in our experience, even seasoned provosts can still be timid budget-makers.

Mary Jo Maydew, who served as CFO at Mount Holyoke College for twenty-four years as well as a term as board chair of the National Association of College and University Business Officers (NACUBO), believes that too many provosts know too little about their own budgets and that this is hurting their institutions. In her view, a thorough understanding of the budget "is critical for CAOs if they are to play an effective role in planning and priority setting for the college or university. The CAO is responsible for overseeing one of the largest and most complex parts of the institution, a responsibility that cannot be adequately performed without extensive knowledge of how the academic budget is developed and how it relates to other parts of the institution."[12] Failure to master the budget, she says, represents a significant risk to the long-term success of a CAO as well as to the institution as a whole. CAOs who lack sufficient information about their own budgets can acquire it through a mutually supportive relationship with the CFO.

5. Academic leadership expectations are in conflict

This final environmental change revisits a core question facing every chief academic officer: "Who is actually in charge of your college or university?" On one side, the CAO needs to work collaboratively across disciplines as the "first among equals," listening and building steadily toward consensus. On the other side, these individuals must also plan and decide among presidents, vice presidents, trustees, and legislators who often view the exercise of authority on campus through a different lens. As one higher education author warns, "We expect and desire leaders who will get out front, be courageous. . . . We don't applaud leading in

Something I Very Much Wish I Had Known on
My First Day as CAO

■ True loyalty among your staff will be rare.

the middle."[13] This call for powerful, even aggressive action runs counter to the more collaborative leadership styles of many CAOs.

In recent years, exercising academic authority has become an increasingly complex and nuanced process for a provost among faculty members who are less powerful and harmonious, among students who have declining interest in traditional elements of campus life, and among administrators who have grown in number but not comparable authority. Some observers simply explain that the academy itself has changed, and CAOs now need to change with it: "The expectations and standards of a rigorous education have yielded to thinly disguised professional training, while teaching and learning have been . . . subjugated to enrollment management, winning teams, bigger and better facilities, [and] more revenue from sideline businesses."[14]

As provosts lead their institutions into the future, it will be more necessary for them to stay ahead of workforce trends, no matter how elite their reputations may be. Faculty senates, trustee committees, parents, and, of course, presidents will be expecting them to set directions for new program development, outcomes assessment, and student retention, to name just three of the highest priorities. Effective provosts may choose to work quietly or boldly, but whatever their professional style, it will need to be adaptable, intuitive, and produce results, as the chapters that follow will confirm.

NOTES

1. Peter D. Eckel, Bryan J. Cook, Jacqueline E. King, *The CAO Census: A National Profile of Chief Academic Officers* (Washington D.C.: American Council on Education, 2009), 11.

2. Robin Middlehurst, "Investing in Leadership Development: The UK Experience," *International Higher Education* 67 (Spring 2012): 16.

3. Eckel et al., *CAO Census*, 52.

4. Joseph P. Kahn, "Generation Broke," *Boston Globe*, 29 May 2012, 12g.

5. Martin Van Der Werf and Grant Sabatier, *The College of 2020: Students* (Washington, DC: Chronicle Research Services, 2009), 5, 3.

6. Philip Altbach, "It's the Faculty, Stupid!—The Centrality of the Academic Profession," *International Higher Education* 55 (Spring 2009): 15, 16.

7. Robert E. Martin, "College Costs Too Much Because Faculty Lack Power," *Chronicle of Higher Education*, 5 August 2012, http://chronicle.com/article/College -Costs-Too-Much-Because/133357/.

8. Ibid.

9. Altbach, "It's the Faculty, Stupid!" 16.

10. Glenn Harlan Reynolds, "Degrees of Value: Making College Pay Off," *Wall Street Journal*, 4–5 January 2014, C-1.

11. Bryan J. Cook, e-mail to James Martin, 31 July 2012.

12. Mary Jo Maydew, e-mail to James Martin, 22 August 2012.

13. Stephen J. Nelson, "Balance Wheels: College Presidents in the Crucible of the 1960s and the Contests of Today," *Bridgewater Review* 31, no. 1 (June 2012): 26.

14. Richard P. Keeling and Richard H. Hersh, "Where's the Learning in Higher Learning?" *Trusteeship* 20, no. 4 (July/August 2012): 19.

CHAPTER TWO

New Realities and Lingering Stereotypes: Key Trends from the National CAO Census

Bryan J. Cook, Christopher J. Nellum, and Meredith S. Billings

Higher education is drastically changing in the United States. Federal and state governments are pushing for more accountability while cutting sources of funding, technology is disrupting the way colleges and universities deliver knowledge, and growing numbers of media stories are questioning the value of a college education. The ability of a college or university to navigate these and other challenges successfully rests largely on the shoulders of its senior leadership and their ability to embrace and adapt to change.

Given the nature of many of the changes facing higher education, it could be argued that the position most responsible for successfully achieving them is the provost, or chief academic officer. As college presidents increasingly are asked to manage external relationships and serve as primary fundraisers, CAOs are more and more becoming the day-to-day managers of many higher education institutions. In addition to overseeing academic programs and faculty, CAOs may be responsible for addressing accountability questions, for budgeting and financial management, and for managing student issues and development. As provosts play a bigger role in running colleges and universities, it is clear that they are a major factor in the success of any higher education institution.

In an effort to learn more about this crucial position, this chapter provides an overview of findings from the first-ever national survey of chief academic officers conducted by the American Council on Education (ACE). Known as *The CAO Census,* this study presents a profile of the individuals serving as CAOs as well as the nature of their work.[1] In what follows, we share key findings from the ACE report on how CAOs spend their time, how they see their roles, who they have effective and ineffective relationships with, and their long-term career aspirations.

Whereas the position of chief academic officer has been described as "one without structure," the contemporary role of the CAO involves managing much of the internal day-to-day operations of colleges and universities.[2] The role of the CAO now rests not only on his or her own academic expertise but also on their ability to understand and manage the core functions of teaching, research, and service. Recognizing the diversity within the CAO position, this chapter will also highlight noteworthy differences in the role of a chief academic officer across institutional types (e.g., research universities, minority-serving institutions, and associate's degree–granting colleges), as well as racial and ethnic groups.

How CAOs Actually Spend Their Time

By tradition, CAOs are the academic leaders of the college or university and are charged with maintaining the academic vision as well as supervising and evaluating the faculty. However, their role has broadened considerably since the 1990s, now to include administrative duties such as strategic planning, in-depth budget management, and overseeing the institution's technology plan. Given this expanding and changing role, how are CAOs actually spending their time? To assess how much time CAOs allocate to academic and administrative duties, respondents were asked to select the top three activities that consume most of their time. The most common choices were curriculum and academic programs (65 percent); supervising and managing personnel (57 percent); and accountability, accreditation, and assessment (47 percent). From these choices further indication emerges that the role of the CAO has evolved and now encompasses administrative responsibilities that consume significant amounts of attention.

While most CAOs reported spending the bulk of their time on academic and administrative responsibilities, key differences highlighting the diverse experiences of CAOs, depending on the sector of the institution, also emerged. For instance, CAOs at two-year colleges reported spending more time on enrollment management than their colleagues at four-year universities. Given the ongoing budget cuts affecting higher education, many colleges have reduced enrollments, so it is likely that CAOs at community colleges continue to spend significant amount of time on enrollment management. In addition, CAOs at two-year colleges reported spending more time on student development issues than CAOs at four-year universities. This does not suggest that CAOs at four-year university are not concerned with student development, but it is probable that CAOs at two-year colleges spend more time on these issues because their population tends to be nontraditional students and are often in need of remediation and college integration courses.

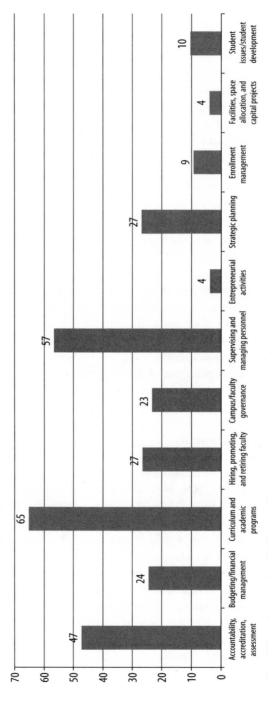

Most Time-Consuming CAO Activities

Top Three Time Commitments as Ranked by CAOs

1. Curricula and academic programs
2. Supervising and managing personnel
3. Accreditation and assessment reports

Whereas CAOs at two-year colleges reported that enrollment management and student development issues consumed more of their time, CAOs at four-year institutions reported two activities that required more attention than their peers at two-year institutions: budget management and strategic planning. A major trend that has influenced most major universities in the last decade is the decline in state appropriations to higher education as a result of the recent recession. As the primary overseers of short-term decisions for the university, it may be that CAOs of four-year institutions are increasingly forced to come up with creative ways not only to promote the academic mission of their institutions but also to maintain the administrative functions with fewer resources.

Our findings from the *CAO Census* also provide evidence that the CAO's role has expanded beyond the core academic functions of the university and now includes more administrative duties. New CAOs are expected from their first day to have knowledge of a much broader array of administrative functions and a comprehensive view of faculty relations and governance. Thus, it is easy to see why some scholars have concluded, "There is a growing consensus that the position of chief academic officer can no longer be defined by a succession of skilled amateurs rotating out of their faculties for short periods of time."[3]

What's Important: How CAOs See Their Value to the Institution

Even though the role of the CAO has expanded into more administrative duties, what do CAOs report as the top priorities of the position? In the *CAO Census,* more than half of CAOs chose promoting academic quality and setting the academic vision of the institution as the most important priorities. These top duties were consistent, regardless of how long CAOs have served in their positions and which type of institution that they were working in.

While the previous section suggests that CAOs spend increasing amounts of time on administrative responsibilities, when asked directly they still consider their primary value to the institution as its academic leader. As such, it seems that many would prefer to spend their time

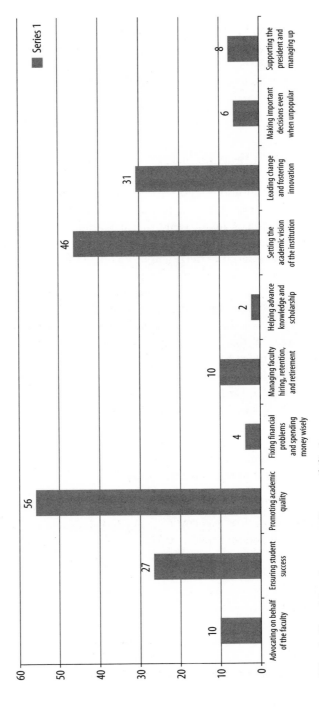

What Is Your Most Important Responsibility?

Series 1

- Advocating on behalf of the faculty: 10
- Ensuring student success: 27
- Promoting academic quality: 56
- Fixing financial problems and spending money wisely: 4
- Managing faculty hiring, retention, and retirement: 10
- Helping advance knowledge and scholarship: 2
- Setting the academic vision of the institution: 46
- Leading change and fostering innovation: 31
- Making important decisions even when unpopular: 6
- Supporting the president and managing up: 8

promoting activities central to the academic mission such as quality teaching, fostering innovative research, and increasing academic rigor. Other examples of a commitment to their academic role while serving as the CAO include teaching courses, conducting research in their academic discipline, and writing for scholarly publications.

Although most CAOs place more value in the academic dimensions of their job, those who are persons of color expressed slightly different responsibilities to their institutions. In addition to viewing themselves as the academic leaders, CAOs of color across all institutional types were more likely than their white counterparts to emphasize ensuring student success as one of their top priorities. Martin and Samels have suggested that students are now playing a more active role in their education by expressing increased expectations for their collegiate experience and thus holding administrators more accountable.[4] It is reasonable to think that because of their own experiences in higher education, persons of color serving as CAOs may be more cognizant of the struggles students face on their campuses, thus influencing the emphasis they place on ensuring that all students persist to graduation.

Friend or Foe: Faculty and the CAO

In general, the CAO of a college or university must represent the interests of the faculty and the administration, even if they think of themselves as faculty first. Yet, given the increased emphasis on certain aspects of the job such as budgeting and assessment, the CAO is increasingly required to make administrative decisions that may prove to be unpopular among their faculty colleagues. Such tension between the CAO and faculty members surfaced in the *CAO Census*. Although the CAO is sometimes viewed as a "first among equals," 30 percent of CAOs indicated that faculty relationships present their most challenging issue, often because of resource allocations.

It is also important to note, however, that there are slight institutional differences with regard to the nature of the relationship between the

Key Skills Necessary for CAO Success

- General managerial ability
- Interpersonal skills
- Budget development experience
- Strategic planning ability
- Accreditation and assessment management experience

faculty and the CAO. For instance, the relationship appears to be less strained at four-year minority-serving institutions (MSIs) than at comparable predominantly white institutions (PWIs). Perhaps the intentional collaboration among faculty at some MSIs has contributed to a more positive campus climate and relationships between the CAO and other faculty members.[5] Although the tension between CAO and faculty may vary by institutional type, in general it exists on some level. As a result, it is ever more important for the CAO to walk the fine line between advocating with respect to the central role of the faculty in student learning and fulfilling the administrative needs of the entire campus, especially those that shape the college or university mission.[6]

CAOs and the Presidency: Intentions and Trajectories

The ability to move up in the profession is a common ambition among working professionals. Indeed, within the higher education community the CAO position is one that traditionally leads to a college presidency. While this is increasingly the case, some institutional leaders have predicted a large number of retirements among college presidents in the next five to ten years.[7] Data from the most recent CAO census will equip administrators with critical insight that will assist with recruitment strategies as campuses look fill presidential vacancies over the next few years.

In general, many CAOs expressed no aspirations to seek a presidency (45 percent) or were undecided about seeking a presidency (25 percent). In fact, the longer a provost served a university in this capacity, the less appealing ascension to a presidency became.[8] Despite the apparent uncertainty or lack of interest in a presidency, an ongoing cohort of those in a CAO positions assume a presidency following their tenure as CAO. Thirty-four percent of presidents come from a senior leadership position in academic affairs, primarily the provost or CAO position.[9]

Among administrators at two-year colleges, the intentions of CAOs to pursue a presidency are of special concern because of a "rapidly approaching crisis" in community college leadership.[10] The crisis refers specifically to the majority of community college presidents who intend to retire in five years or sooner and will need to be replaced. Despite overall low aspirations expressed by CAOs to assume a presidency, more CAOs at two-year colleges than four-year institutions intend to seek a presidency (37 percent compared with 27 percent). This should be especially positive news for administrators and recruiters looking to fill presidencies at two-year colleges over the next few years.

Still, facing an unprecedented number of retirements by two-year college presidents, many have begun to ask where these institutions will find the next cohort of administrative leaders, and it seems that the answer

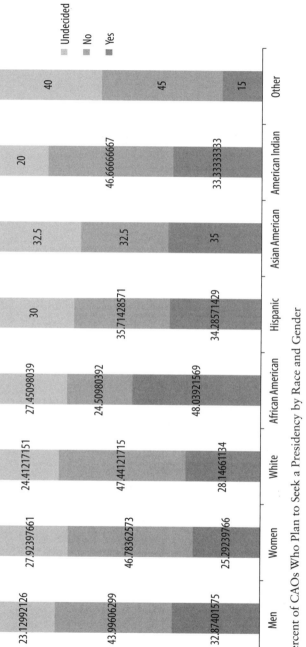

Percent of CAOs Who Plan to Seek a Presidency by Race and Gender

Legend:
- Undecided
- No
- Yes

Men: 23.12992126 / 43.99606299 / 32.87401575
Women: 27.92397661 / 46.78362573 / 25.29239766
White: 24.41217151 / 47.44121715 / 28.14661134
African American: 27.45098039 / 24.50980392 / 48.03921569
Hispanic: 30 / 35.71428571 / 34.28571429
Asian American: 32.5 / 32.5 / 35
American Indian: 20 / 46.6666667 / 33.3333333
Other: 40 / 45 / 15

for many colleges is to look within their own sector when filling presidential vacancies. Specifically, when compared to their four-year counterparts, more CAOs who served previously at a two-year college move into a presidency at their own or another two-year college. This finding corresponds with the literature on administrative turnover at two-year colleges and signals a major shift among those in leadership.[11] It is also true that even qualified candidates typically do not become the president of a four-year institution following a CAO position at a two-year college, giving rise to questions for some about structural inequities and hierarchy in postsecondary education administration.

Presidential aspirations among CAOs at four-year minority-serving institutions and among persons of color serving as CAOs at predominantly white institutions should draw the interest of those seeking to diversify the upper-level administrative ranks of America's colleges and universities.[12] For example, a higher proportion of CAOs at four-year minority-serving institutions expressed interest in pursuing a presidency than their peers at predominantly white institutions. This is important to note because, in general, administrators at MSIs also tend to be persons of color. Interestingly, when looking only at PWIs, more persons of color also had intentions to pursue a presidency than their white peers. These statistics suggest an abiding opportunity to target and mentor CAOs who are persons of color to remain in the administration and ultimately assume a presidency.

Related to the issue of diversity among institutional leaders, fewer CAOs from four-year MSIs advance to assume a presidency than CAOs at four-year PWIs. This is troublesome because CAOs at MSIs tend to be persons of color. Though we are unable to determine the trajectory of CAOs of a given racial or ethnic background,[13] taken together, the findings above suggest a likely but uneven pathway to a presidency. On one side, there are potential structural issues with the pipeline itself, including a lack of mentoring of persons of color who intend to seek a presidency. On the other hand, persons of color serving in CAO positions often lack critical elements of professional preparation such as diverse responsibilities, broadened administrative portfolios, and the sustained relationships necessary to be competitive candidates for presidencies.[14]

Concluding Thoughts: Conflicts and Rewards for the Future CAOs

As higher education undergoes significant change, so do the scope and the depth of the role of chief academic officer. Specifically, this role increasingly includes the management of activities that now extend be-

Three Emerging Trends

- CAOs need to demonstrate enhanced managerial ability from the start of their service.
- CAOs now spend increasing time on additional administrative tasks such as grants and development, technology planning, and budget management.
- The pressures to spend greater time on these tasks creates a mismatch between the expectations of some aspiring CAOs and the realities of the position they eventually achieve.

yond the traditional functions of a college or university. As a result, CAOs must increasingly demonstrate new skills, including the management of nonacademic areas, interacting with donors, and developing greater budget and strategic planning expertise. As this expansion of duties has created a broader set of roles for the CAO, they can also present challenges in identifying faculty members, specifically deans, who aspire to the expanded CAO position. As an additional deterrent, some critics now believe that the chief academic officer's role of promoter and protector of academic quality has become diluted and fragmented.[15]

Nonetheless, the provost's primary responsibility remains the academic mission of his or her institution. Each is charged to support quality teaching and research, maintain academic rigor, and ensure the comprehensiveness of curricula. However, as they are confronted by limited resources and competing priorities, many CAOs must spend more time in new administrative roles, such as balancing the budget, building a technology plan, or partnering with an advancement office to seek alternative sources of funding. Some CAOs view their administrative duties as a necessary evil for their success as an academic leader. Yet going forward, we expect CAOs will continue their dual academic and administrative roles and most likely will be asked to expand those duties from current levels.

Overall, we project that CAOs will spend more time on administrative duties such as strategic planning and technological adaptations that reflect the needs of the twenty-first-century campus. Future CAOs will also have to make hard decisions that could significantly influence the work of their faculty colleagues, particularly as it relates to student learning outcomes. The extent to which these decisions are made with transparency and faculty involvement will directly affect provost's ability to lead an institution as its chief academic officer.

NOTES

1. Peter D. Eckel, Bryan J. Cook, and Jacqueline E. King, *The CAO Census: A National Profile of Chief Academic Officers* (Washington, DC: American Council on Education, 2009).

2. G. O. Moden, R. I. Miller, and A. M. Williford, "The Role, Scope, and Functions of the Chief Academic Officer," paper presented at the annual forum of the Association of Institutional Research, Kansas City, MO, May 1987 (ERIC Document Reproduction Service No. ED293441).

3. James Martin and James E. Samels, "First Among Equals: The Current Roles of the Chief Academic Officer," in *First Among Equals: The Role of the Chief Academic Officer,* ed. James Martin, James E. Samels, and Associates (Baltimore: Johns Hopkins University Press, 1997), 3–20.

4. Ibid.

5. Damon William, Joseph Berger, and Shederick McClendon, *Toward a Model of Inclusive Excellence and Change in Postsecondary Institutions* (Washington, DC: Association of American Colleges and Universities, 2005).

6. Roy Austensen, "First Among Equals: The Current Roles of the Chief Academic Officer," in *First Among Equals,* ed. Martin, Samels, and Associates, 21–40; Ann Ferren and Wilbur Stanton, *Leadership through Collaboration: The Role of the Chief Academic Officer* (Westport, CT: American Council on Education/Praeger Publishers, 2004).

7. Marybelle C. Keim and John P. Murray, "Chief Academic Officers' Demographics and Educational Backgrounds," *Community College Review* 36, no. 116 (October 2008).

8. Eckel, et al., *CAO Census.*

9. Bryan Cook and Young Kim, *The American College President—2012* (Washington, DC: American Council on Education, 2012).

10. Keim et al., "Chief Academic Officers' Demographics and Educational Backgrounds."

11. Ibid.

12. Peter Schmidt, "Survey of Chief Academic Officers Raises Concerns about Diversity and Longevity," *Chronicle of Higher Education,* 12 June 2009, http://chronicle.com/article/ Survey-of-Chief-Academic-Of/1518.

13. We were unable to track demographic statistics because information about CAO's trajectories was provided by the previous CAO's immediate successor.

14. Eckel et al., *CAO Census;* Schmidt, "Survey of Chief Academic Officers Raises Concerns."

15. L. Paradise and D. Kimya, "New Peril for the Provost: Marginalization of the Academic Mission," in *About Campus* 12 (April 2007).

CHAPTER THREE

Professional Development Programs for Chief Academic Officers: A Key to Effective Leadership

Richard Ekman

On the surface, almost all chief academic officers appear to have had approximately the same prior experience when they began their new duties as CAOs, but that is not the case in reality. Most new CAOs who are drawn from other positions at the same institution assume that they already know what they need to know about the institution they are to lead, but they quickly learn otherwise. Moreover, many CAOs who have moved to their new positions at new institutions also assume too much transferable knowledge. Indeed, although the role of chief academic officer is generic across institutional types in some respects, any false sense of self-assurance is quickly dampened when CAOs who have previously followed widely varying professional careers recognize that they need professional development opportunities in their new positions. In our experience, differences among institutional types account for only some of a new CAO's gaps in professional knowledge.

Different Paths, Different Needs

Chief academic officers come to their positions mainly through promotions from other institution-wide academic administrative positions—perhaps as associate dean or assistant vice president. More than 50 percent of CAOs enter their positions from other academic administrative positions. At large public universities, the number is closer to 79 percent.[1] Curiously, only in the small-college world does one find a high percentage of individuals who have previously served as the chief academic officer of another institution (19 percent).[2] The small colleges also account for a comparatively large percentage (more than 20 percent) of new CAOs whose previous positions were department chairmanships or other roles with a mainly faculty perspective.[3] In this respect, small colleges are joined by private research universities.

One can assume that the majority of chief academic officers have come up through the ranks of the academic divisions of the institution and already know something about curriculum planning, faculty personnel matters, and students' academic performance. Yet even this assumption now needs to be tempered. The principal academic issues that form a CAO's daily fare are in constant flux these days. For example, a new CAO may know something about evaluating students' academic performance but surprisingly little about recent trends and advances in outcomes assessment and regional accreditation. The new CAO may know about the tenure system but little about retirement incentives for faculty members with "uncapped" retirement ages. Disciplinary background can also play a role. For a business professor-turned-CAO, for example, the biggest gaps in knowledge may be issues in the sciences or in a professional field with which the new CAO has insufficient expertise. Some of this new knowledge can be acquired by talking with colleagues at the same institution, and there will also be occasions when talking with the specialized accreditors or deans of graduate programs is essential. However, this should not be confused with the professional training required to lead a complex academic operation with a budget of, for example, $50–100 million annually.

These are the easier of the lessons that need to be learned—of gaps in knowledge that need to be filled. At least one lesson is more difficult for the new CAO: understanding that the new role is more than being a representative of aggregated faculty interests. Thinking "institutionally" is often a new experience for chief academic officers because it requires them to balance the competing interests of different academic departments with one another as well as with other nonacademic units of the university or college and its external interests.

In allocating resources, a new CAO must fully grasp the institution's mission and its plans for change as formulated by the trustees

Challenges for a CAO in Learning to Think "Institutionally"

- Fully grasping an evolving institutional mission
- Learning that any pie can only be sliced in a finite number of ways
- Realizing that departments within the college or university will contradict and compete with each other for budget, space, personnel, and student recruitment

and president. The simple part of this lesson is that the pie can be sliced in only so many pieces. The much more difficult part is learning that the interests of one department can seriously contradict the interests of another department. A proposed life-sciences building, for example, may conflict with plans for a revenue-generating residence hall or a promised soccer field. In response, the new chief academic officer needs to do more than simply learn the intricacies of different disciplines and the needs of separate departments; instead, he or she must immediately consider the institution as a whole. Hugh Heclo's *Thinking Institutionally* is a wise place to begin.[4] Help can also be found from professional associations that run orientation programs for new CAOs, such as the one-day workshops sponsored by the Council of Independent Colleges (CIC).[5]

Until recently, the average tenure of a chief academic officer was longer than that of a college or university president, and it was possible for the CAO to think of him- or herself as a defender of the permanent interests of the institution. Presidents, meanwhile, with a greater number of pressing priorities, were more likely to come and go with greater frequency. Today, however, the average tenure of a CAO is actually shorter than that of a college president (4.3 years versus 7.1 years).[6] While some posit that the working conditions of a typical CAO's employment have had the combined effect of shortening the average tenure, it seems clear that the nature of the job itself has changed. The CAO's role now encompasses much more than the academic affairs of the institution. For many new CAOs, this is a welcome surprise and a mind-expanding professional experience. For others, it serves as a dose of harsh reality and a reminder that some, perhaps many, of the reasons that he or she entered the academy originally have disappeared from the CAO's role. Their new duties may include planning new facilities and supervising their construction, raising money from reluctant donors, and representing the college to dozens of alumni groups. Even the anticipated responsibility for making decisions that affect academic departments and their instructional rigor can be so far down the list of daily decisions that they receive minimal time and focus.

Three New CAO Roles

- Planning (and supervising) campus construction schedules
- Raising money from (reluctant) donors
- Meeting with (dozens of) alumni groups

Accessing National Networks and Their Support

The rapid onset of the realities of serving as a CAO today make the honeymoon period for a new CAO very short. During the first year the new CAO gets oriented, often simply by time and circumstance, identifies what he or she needs to know, and becomes aware of the help available to him or her through professional development programs and services. To some extent, the help that is needed by a CAO beginning in the second year of service stems from the list of needs that was developed in the first year—a list that can require three or even four years to address on some campuses. Staying abreast of new developments in all of the standard areas of the CAO's responsibility can itself become a part-time job. Reading widely in the *Chronicle of Higher Education, Inside Higher Ed, University Business* magazine, and higher education titles issued by Jossey-Bass, Johns Hopkins University Press, and other publishers is almost essential to keep the big picture in mind. The Council of Independent Colleges has offered an annual Institute for Chief Academic Officers for more than forty years, and it is now by far the largest annual gathering of college and university CAOs. The American Association of State Colleges and Universities runs an Academic Affairs Summer Meeting that attracts almost all of its member CAOs.[7] Regional consortia and many statewide associations of private, public, and combined public and private institutions also bring together the CAOs of institutions with common interests to talk about their concerns. Among the best developed and most generously funded are those operated by the Great Lakes Colleges Association, the Associated Colleges of the Midwest, and the Associated Colleges of the South. The Council for Higher Education Accreditation also sponsors conferences to help CAOs and others learn more about assessment policy and procedures, and the Association of American Colleges and Universities plays an important role in piloting new curricular topics.

Over time, observers of the career trajectories of CAOs have made it possible to identify the persistent challenges that many CAOs are likely to encounter at different stages in their tenure. Once identified, these ongoing challenges can sometimes be addressed by the services of professional organizations. The Counsel of Independent College's Institute for Chief Academic Officers, for example, always includes a workshop on budget fundamentals for CAOs who have little prior experience in budgeting. Since 2000, many specialized and regional accreditors have tried to help CAOs understand their growing responsibilities for assessment and educational accountability. CAOs who do not have first-hand experience in working with the existing regulations can be overwhelmed by the additional paperwork and requirements that this new emphasis has caused. Fundraising is another responsibility that former faculty members tend to avoid in their first years as CAO. The Council for Advancement and Support of Education (CASE), the main national organization for development and advancement, runs workshops for academic officers to learn the rudiments of this increasingly important dimension of leading a college.[8]

The Department Chair: A Critical Link in Academic Affairs

BY VIRGINIA M. COOMBS

Department and division chairs occupy a pivotal role in the administrative structure of a college or university. The chair of a department or division is called upon to perform several roles simultaneously, such as to conduct searches for new faculty members; to evaluate faculty members for reappointment, tenure, and promotion; to mentor and provide counsel to colleagues; to resolve conflicts; to advocate on behalf of the department or division to senior administrators; and to communicate and explain decisions reached beyond the department or division level to their peers. At the same time, department or division chairs are expected to fulfill the traditional faculty roles, including teaching and advising students as well as maintaining their scholarly activities. Whatever the activity, chairs lead from the middle of the campus organizational hierarchy.

Most chairs come into their positions with little training for leadership responsibilities or experience cultivating a wider view of campus challenges. In order to be effective in their administrative roles, chairs need professional opportunities to develop their administrative skills. Among the opportunities currently available to chairs at independent colleges and universities are workshops such as the CIC's Workshops for Department and Division Chairs, offered annually since 2000.* Such workshops focus on four principal areas of administrative skills development:

1. *Academic Management Budget.* Normally, faculty members do not have extensive experience with budgets and how particularly the department's resources may fit into the larger institutional budget plan. As the individuals responsible for developing and overseeing a department's budget, chairs should be able to navigate many the types of budget information that are routinely distributed to them, including good practices:

■ Understanding how campus budgets function as strategic planning documents through matching campus priorities with available resources
■ Asking the CAO and CFO questions about budget line items that are not immediately obvious

(cont'd)

■ Communicating the budgeting process as transparent and accessible to departmental colleagues

■ Asking regularly for participation in budgetary decisions from departmental colleagues

2. *Collecting and Using Data.* Chairs should know what type of information the college or university collects on a regular basis and how to access it:

■ Much of the enrollment data is accessible through the registrar's office or the institutional research office.

■ Normally data on the assessment of student learning outcomes are generated in the department but may be collected and stored by an assessment office.

Department chairs use data to inform decision making principally in these areas of operation:

■ New content areas for the curriculum that may require additional resources

■ Alignment of curriculum with external benchmarks such as regional accreditation criteria or professional association standards

■ Choice of delivery systems and instructional practices for the curriculum

■ Factors related to student retention and satisfaction

■ Assessment of learning outcomes[†]

3. *Academic Personnel Planning.* Department chairs are responsible for a variety of personnel actions that can include orchestrating the hiring process for full-time and adjunct faculty members, participating in the annual evaluations of faculty performance, and dealing with colleagues and student complaints. Best practices in this area include the following:

■ Follow the campus hiring policies and procedures as stated in the Faculty Handbook.

■ Observe the budget considerations and timeline for submitting requests for a new position or replacement.

■ Know the chair's role in the hiring process.

■ Enlist the assistance of the human resources office to schedule an orientation for pertinent faculty members to review the search process policy.

■ Stress the need for absolute confidentiality of candidate information

■ Manage the final details of the search process.

4. *Evaluation of faculty performance.* The chair's role in the evaluation of faculty colleagues is frequently one that they are less comfortable in performing because they view themselves as peers. However, as chairs, they hold these responsibilities:

■ Follow the policies and procedures outlining the chair's role in the Faculty Handbook

- Include only relevant information such as past reviews and authorized materials in the evaluation decision
- Provide secure access to tenure and promotion files only to the departmental faculty committee
- Conduct a fair and honest assessment of the individual's performance according to the designated categories, i.e. teaching, scholarly activity, and service
- Refrain from using email to communicate personnel decisions
- Maintain confidentiality.

When You Become a Department Chair: Ten Best Practices

Faculty members who are considering a move to becoming a department or division chair should be able to ask questions about the chair's duties, the dean or chief academic officer's expectations of the chair, and the expectations of faculty colleagues. A well-written description of the department chair's duties might be a part of the Faculty Handbook. Some institutions have also developed a Department Chair's Handbook that contains practical information about policies, deadlines, and campus resources.

Experienced chairs are excellent resources for new chairs and can provide mentoring in many areas to complement the description of the department chair's duties in the Faculty Handbook. Ten best practices were offered by experienced chairs to their new colleague chairs at a CIC workshop in 2012:

- Tell the truth
- Communicate clearly and frequently
- Be timely
- Be consistent
- Do not surprise the provost
- Document everything and leave a program memory for the next chair
- Do not overuse email
- Get to know peer chairs
- Delegate projects and tasks as appropriate
- Distinguish between productive projects and those that are headed nowhere.[‡]

Virginia M. Coombs, until her retirement, was vice president for annual programs at the Council of Independent Colleges. In this position, she facilitated CIC's annual national gathering of chief academic officers and its many annual workshops for department chairs.

[*] The strategies and suggestions are taken from actual presentations at the CIC Workshops for Department and Division Chairs.
[†] Dr. Stuart Sigman, Provost for the College of Arts & Sciences at American Jewish University, produced this list.
[‡] Compiled from participants at the 2012 CIC Workshops for Department and Division Chairs.

Help is available from a wider range of national organizations than many deans and CAOs realize. For example, the Association of College and Research Libraries (ACRL), which is an excellent organization for librarians, also occasionally runs programs that draw CAOs into its orbit. While the ACRL's goal may be to enlist their attention and support for the cause of libraries, CAOs should think of these opportunities as a way to learn about complicated aspects of the college or university that are very hard to understand on one's own and are sometimes difficult to discuss in a neutral way even with one's own campus library director. Even more than in the case of libraries, the problem of receiving objective information is particularly acute in relation to the rapidly changing area of technology on campus. Often a CAO is the one required to make a big-ticket decision about purchase or lease of new technology. Neither individual vendors of hardware and software nor the campus's own CIO can provide as wide a knowledge of options or as neutral a perspective on the available choices and on the norms for expenditures as an organization such as EDUCAUSE can.

I do not mean to suggest that, once getting past the steep learning curve of the first year, service as a CAO remains essentially the same. There are stages in a career of a CAO. Often toward the end of the first year, the CAO will announce a set of priorities that covers a period of three or four years. As the end of that initial period draws near, he or she will need to define the goals for the institution's academic affairs for a second finite period, perhaps another four or five years. Since CAOs in their third or fourth years face a distinct set of challenges, some organizations have tried to help them focus specifically on those issues. The Council of Independent Colleges conducts a workshop for CAOs in their third or fourth year that takes up both the personal issues of whether one should consider another term and more general questions of what the appropriate goals and priorities will be for a second phase.

The particular concerns that a CAO may have at this stage in his career will vary according to whether one's professional life has been tied to a single institution, has moved every few years, or—in rare cases— has come to his or her current position from outside of higher education. These days, individuals in such fields as economics, food science, biomedical research, and nursing are in great demand in other sectors. Many CAOs continue to serve well beyond the fourth year, but eventually most CAOs decide they do want to make a change, whether it is to return to the faculty or to seek another type of position.

The Path to the Presidency: What CAOs Really Want

A significant number of those serving as college and university presidents are expected to retire by 2020. While individuals whose backgrounds are not in academic affairs can be superb presidents, it is our view that higher education should strive to maintain a leadership cohort that is experienced in the core functions of faculty member, head of department, and chief academic officer. The troubling fact, however, is that only a minority of chief academic officers—ranging from a high of 39 percent in community colleges to 23 percent in private doctoral institutions—wish to be college presidents.[9] It is somewhat surprising to see that the lowest percentages are in the private institutions, both large and small. Among small-college CAOs, only 24 percent intend to seek a presidency at some point in the future.

Several organizations have become concerned about the disinclination of CAOs to serve as presidents and have tried to address the issue in a variety of ways. The Council of Independent Colleges and the American Association of State Colleges and Universities, with the American Academic Leadership Institute, now run an Executive Leadership Academy (ELA), a year-long program consisting of two live seminars, several webinars, and an "experiential plan" that includes structured mentorships with exemplary leaders in other areas such as development and athletics. The ELA has attracted large and strong pools of nominations in its early years of operation—suggesting that the low number of CAOs who say they do not intend to seek a presidency is not the last word on this subject and that structured programs focused on providing skill development and career blueprints may be a path to success. In the three short years since the ELA began, the advancement rate to presidencies and executive vice presidencies has been extraordinary. For the 2010–11 and 2011–12 cohorts, almost half of the participants have already advanced.

The Lilly Endowment, working through the Council of Independent Colleges, operates a text-based program on presidential "vocation" and institutional "mission." The premise of the Lilly program is that many talented individuals do not have long-lasting or effective presidencies because there is a bad fit between the calling of the individual and the mission of the institution that has hired her or him. The Lilly program, which has been in operation since 2005, has led quite a few individuals to seek presidencies and helped about one-fourth of these to be selected to date. It has also helped some individuals come to recognize that they do not wish to pursue a presidency. In all cases, participants say that the readings and discussion, which are drawn from literature, history, philosophy, theology, and social science, have enriched their ability to serve in their current CAO roles. While it is limiting to view the CAO's role mainly as a stepping stone to the presidency, it is also one of the responsibilities of all CAOs to think about the future leadership of American higher education at both CAO and presidential levels and to consider their own roles in assuring the highest quality possible in both positions.

One of the most frequently cited reasons why CAOs do not wish to pursue a presidency is their discomfort with fundraising responsibilities. Until recently, one could blame ignorance of what fundraising is really like for the negative stereotypes that shape CAO's attitudes, but today almost all CAOs already bear some fundraising responsibility, and it is therefore somewhat surprising that so few CAOs see the positive aspects of the experience. In larger universities, CAOs often take the lead in fundraising for particular academic units, working with relevant departments. In smaller colleges and universities, the CAO typically works closely with the president in making the case in appeals for funds from alumni, parents, foundations, and other specific donors.

Although many individual institutions offer programs intended to develop future leaders on their campus, often very little attention is paid in these programs to fundraising. It is therefore incumbent on CAOs themselves to seek out opportunities to gain the perspective on the institution as outsiders see it. As a beginning, CAOs should ask their presidents to include them in some fundraising calls. CAOs of public institutions especially can gain experience in talking with local legislators. In response to calls for national programs in this area, the Council for Advancement and Support of Education (CASE) offers the Development for Deans and Academic Leaders program for academic officers, and in 2011 CIC and CASE devoted a multi-day institute entirely to joint meetings of senior academic officers and senior advancement officers, with plans to initiate a similar gathering in a few years.[10]

Eight Challenges for New CAOs

1. Managing the most complex aspects of the institutional budget
2. Defining the relationship between assessment and accountability
3. Following changing government regulations
4. Raising funds when donors say no
5. Understanding the changing identity and needs of the college library
6. Identifying what a peer institution is with facts instead of anecdotes
7. Dealing skillfully with representatives of the news media
8. Explaining what "government relations" really means

Building Programs and Partnerships beyond the Campus

Since so many choices need to be made in how CAOs spend their time in activities that go beyond the immediate needs of the campus, a word ought to be said about identifying and developing "peers." There is a tendency among some CAOs to regard only a very narrow group of colleges and universities as being peer institutions. Often these schools are not really true peers, but rather they are more selective and affluent institutions that the CAO hopes her or his own institution will emulate.

In fact, most CAOs can learn a great deal from acknowledging a wider array of colleague institutions. For the CAO of an institution that is neither affluent nor selective, it is important not to assume that the CAO of a very wealthy or selective institution has had experiences that are irrelevant to his or her own situation. Similarly, the CAO of a very strong institution should not assume that he or she has nothing to learn from an institution that may be far more market-sensitive. Other ways of identifying peers from whom one can learn require a certain amount of imagination. Dan Carey, the president of Edgewood College in Madison, Wisconsin, and Kevin Reilly, president of the University of Wisconsin system, forged a useful alliance that provides occasions for the presidents and CAOs of both institutions to get together across the public-private divide. Those in both sectors share a goal to increase the number of high school graduates who go to college. It will be interesting to see if their successors continue this effective public-private partnership.

Another area of professional development for which relatively few opportunities for CAOs currently exist is dealing effectively with the news media. Working with the college's own communications professionals to promote newsworthy achievements of the institution or its faculty and students requires a better sense of what is newsworthy than most CAOs possess. CAOs should therefore seek out opportunities to learn more, starting with their own institutions' communications professionals, then contact several local reporters, and ultimately build partnerships with representatives of the national media. This task is complicated by changes in journalism itself. Most newspapers and magazines are reducing their staffs and eliminating assignments that focus exclusively on higher education, leading to an increasing emphasis on sensationalist stories rather than the positive accomplishments of universities and colleges. The annual College Media Conference attracts mainly campus PR professionals but is also open to CAOs. Media organizations that focus exclusively on higher education, such as the *Chronicle of Higher Education, University Business,* and *Inside Higher Ed* seek connections with CAOs when there are developments on campus that are worth reporting. These journalists know what is truly newsworthy and can help the CAO to visualize the institution as the public sees it, a useful skill when building connections beyond the campus.

A final dimension of a CAO's responsibility for which there are not enough high-quality professional development opportunities is the area of government relations. Presidents and vice presidents for external relations are deeply involved in these matters, of course, but the growing tendency of both the state and federal governments to interfere with the academic operations of institutions suggests a need for much more deliberate preparation by CAOs to cope with these demands. In addition to the added requirements of accreditors, the U.S. Department of Education is now directly concerned with teacher preparation programs and with the definition of a credit hour. Furthermore, the governors of approximately forty-five states have already agreed upon a "common core" for the high school curriculum that has direct bearing on what college freshman programs can and should include.[11] Newsletters and publications from the National Association of Independent Colleges and Universities and the American Council on Education offer an efficient way for a CAO to remain informed about trends and developments in their area, and these organizations are willing to provide more detailed information to CAOs who request it.

It is my observation that too many new and inexperienced CAOs are hesitant to reach out for professional development opportunities, perhaps because of a pressing daily agenda, unawareness that a program exists, or fear of appearing vulnerable and inadequate to the job. This chapter has argued that most CAOs are not sufficiently trained, that they know it, and that expert help—in the form of multiple professional development programs—is easy to find and well worth the time and money that is invested.

NOTES

1. Harold V. Hartley III and Eric E. Godin, *A Study of Chief Academic Officers of Independent Colleges and Universities* (Washington, DC: Council of Independent Colleges, 2010).

2. Ibid., 19.

3. Ibid.

4. Hugh Heclo, *On Thinking Institutionally* (Boulder, CO: Paradigm Publishers, 2008).

5. Council of Independent Colleges, "Chief Academic Officers Institute." http://www.cic.edu/meetings-and-events/Annual- Conferences/CAO-Institute/Pages/default.aspx.

6. Hartley and Godin, *A Study of Chief Academic Officers*, 10; Wei Song and Harold V. Hartley III, *A Study of Presidents of Independent Colleges and Universities* (Washington, DC: Council of Independent Colleges, 2012): 8.

7. American Association of State Colleges and Universities, "Academic Affairs Summer Meeting 2012, July 26–28" (Washington, DC: American Association of State Colleges and Universities). http://aascu.org/meetings/aa_summer12/.

8. Council for Advancement and Support of Education, "Development for Deans and Academic Leaders" (Washington, DC: CASE). http://www.case.org/Conferences _and_Training/DALW12.html.

9. Hartley and Godin, *A Study of Chief Academic Officers*, 32.

10. Council of Independent Colleges, "2011 Institute for Chief Academic Officers and Chief Advancement Officers, November 5–8" (Washington, DC: CIC), http://www.cic.edu/meetings-and-events/Annual-Conferences/CAO-Institute/2011 -CAO-Institute/Pages/default.aspx.

11. Common Core State Standards Initiative, "Standards in Your State," by the National Governors Association Center for Best Practices and the Council of Chief State School Officers. http://www.corestandards.org/in-the-states.

CHAPTER FOUR

The Scope of Academic Leadership at the Top: CAOs, Presidents, and Trustees

R. Michael Tanner

In government and the business world, a leader who dodges responsibility for making a decision and taking action is accused of "passing the buck," and in contrast, the person eager to assert final authority declares boldly, "The buck stops here." Many wonder exactly where the buck does stop on a campus, since it surely has to stop with someone at the top of the institution. In fact, the legal answer depends on the domain of the decision, the lines of authority established within the college or university and those established for that institution by the larger society. Sometimes the buck really does stop with the chief academic officer—if that is what the president and the trustees want and the law supports.

In this chapter, we will discuss the relationships and interactions a CAO has at the top of the institution with those who are vested with the full authority of the organization. Budgeting for the campus and oversight of the deans will be two areas used as case studies in the practice of leadership. To set the stage, we briefly consider the formal constitutional underpinning for the authorities exercised by the college or university leadership. These formal authorities are the scaffolding from which the leadership derives its core strength. Habits and expectations are established and become accepted and entrenched over time, and these can shift the political power and the campus's sense of authority. Nonetheless, in times of stress or crisis, the legal authorities prescribe the rules of the game by which new initiatives are launched and tensions are ultimately resolved, and a well prepared CAO has to know the rules of that game.

It Starts with the Board

A private college or university typically is a corporation governed by the laws of the state in which it is incorporated. The authority to run

Three Necessary Roles for the CAO

1. Presidential partner
2. Trustee liaison
3. Budget leader

the institution is created by the articles of incorporation and is exercised and elaborated by the board of trustees of the corporation through formally adopted by-laws or statutes. For a public institution, the board of trustees is generally empowered by legislative acts of the state, and the trustees inherit their authority to run the organization from the state. The good governance of a given university is then entrusted to the trustees, and it is encoded in the procedures and statutes of the board and embodied in the trustees themselves. The board has policy and fiduciary responsibilities fundamental to the life of the university.[1] That being the case, a key provision of law or statute is the process of nomination of new trustees and their appointment to the board.

Who are the trustees, and how and why were they named to the board? In a private university, the board might be composed according to explicit intentions for representation of the constituencies who care about the university (alumni, business and civic leaders, for example), but the board is usually self-perpetuating; that is, the current trustees nominate and elect the new trustees. Naming future trustees is very much in the hands of the current trustees, and thus so is the future of the institution. Trustees of a public college or university, in contrast, are usually appointed by the governor of the state and confirmed by the legislature, though in a handful of states, they are publicly elected.[2] The process by which the trustees are chosen and installed, and how in a moment of crisis they might be removed from the board, says much about the nature of the board, their interests, motivations, aspirations, and allegiances.

The Context for Presidential Leadership

Appointing a university president is among the most important acts performed by a board. With carefully delimited delegation from the board, the president, or chancellor of a campus carries the highest level of authority for decision making in all domains, from student life to financial matters to academic judgments. The choice of "president" or "chancellor" sometimes depends on twists of institutional history, and we will use "president" as the generic term in this chapter. A stand-alone, financially self-sufficient campus in the United States will usually employ the title president for its chief executive officer. Large university systems can confound the language and confuse the layperson: a campus might be led by a president, who reports to the system chancellor; whereas in another system these titles can be reversed.

In simplest terms, the president as chief executive officer makes the decisions to conduct the business of the university, while the board sets the guiding policies and articulates principles that will shape the evolution of the university over the years and through changing times. When the board has great faith in the judgment of the president and appropriate safety checks are in place, the effective powers of the president tend to expand; the board accepts the president's recommendations without extensive independent confirmation and explicitly delegates more authority. Conversely, when the relationship between the president and the board becomes strained, the board might curtail the president's latitude by lowering threshold dollar amounts that trigger required board approval, asking for additional background or justification, becoming involved in screening candidates for high-level posts, and taking any number of extra precautions. Taken too far, this is a recipe for administrative paralysis: "A board that insists on micromanagement or recurrent interference dooms an effective presidency from the outset."[3]

Ideally, the president is in regular dialogue with the leadership of the board, alerting the key members to looming decisions, making sure that potential differences of views are ironed out early on, and developing refined judgment as to what the board wants to hear about and what the members would just as soon leave entirely on the shoulders of the president. Boards of public colleges and universities, in turn, will be in regular conversation with key figures in the state government and the legislature, probing the positions of state legislative leaders and of the governor and the governor's office with respect to finances, pending legislation, or major acquisitions, for example. The relationship between the president and the board is characterized by a constant flow of information, influence, and collective thinking. The relationships are filaments of different strengths and form a web among a larger cast of actors, which can include state government, alumni groups, and business leaders. Events and actions at one point can send ripples across the web for quite a distance, often invisibly to the outside world.

The CAO as Academic Leader and Presidential Partner

The chief academic officer, or provost, almost everywhere the second-in-command to the president, must work effectively within this complex web. The CAO reports directly to the president and usually carries the title of vice president. The title "provost" is another medieval term etymologically meaning the "official set over others."[4] In American universities, its use generally implies that the CAO also has primary responsibility for the institutional budget and may also be considered the chief operating officer for the campus. The provost serves as acting president or president *pro tem* whenever the president's authorities must be exercised and the president is unavailable. In some structures, vice presidents for other spheres, such as student affairs or administration, may have a formal reporting line to the provost. Whatever the case, a provost's comprehensive budgetary responsibility is the basis for substantive interactions with other vice presidents, whether or not there is a formal supervisorial relationship. While presidents have traditionally risen through the ranks of academe, increasingly they are being picked for their political skills and acumen and may come from outside higher education. The fraction of new presidents whose immediate prior position was outside higher education rose from 13.1 percent in 2006 to 20.3 percent in 2011, according to an American Council on Education survey.[5] Especially, then, the credentials of the CAO, as an academic who has experienced faculty life and performed faculty work in its many aspects, are a source of confidence and trust between the faculty and the college or university administration. The CAO often conveys a sense of the faculty perspective in speaking to the powers above, and the CAO is symbolically a public champion of academic causes and a defender of academic values.

The president and the provost are ideally partners in leadership. The president is the external voice of the campus and its public personification, whereas the provost is the one who runs the day-to-day

Best Practices between the Chief Academic Officer and the President

1. While you owe it to your institution to offer your best information and disinterested analysis during a decision-making process, defer to the president, who ultimately has final authority and responsibility for the decision.
2. Do not publicly take an entrenched position unless you know the president will back it.
3. Do not end run to the board unless you have another career in mind.
4. Understand the overall campus finances well, because if you do not drive the budget, the budget will drive you.
5. Have a plan for your career and where it can go if circumstances, conflicts, or ethical principles force you to put your job on the line.

and week-to-week operation of the academic institution. News reporters and those looking for statements or reactions from the campus will invariably want to hear from the president, not the provost. Even inside the campus, people looking to gain traction for their agendas will hope to bend the ear and gain the favor of the president. Only if the president has unequivocally delegated responsibility for the pertinent decisions to the provost will full attention focus on the provost. The two are the campus's principal guardians and authority figures, and a close, well-defined, congenial relationship is critical to the health and morale of the institution.

Agreeing on who speaks for the campus on which issues is the starting point. Every issue that can arise on a campus may ultimately come to either the provost or the president, and over time the division of responsibilities should be established and projected to the campus through words and actions. In theory, the campus organizational chart shows reporting relationships and establishes how decision making is structured and partitioned. In practice, life stretches the neat lines of organizational charts and causes jurisdictional boundaries to be crossed rather frequently. For example, the facilities and maintenance operations might report to the vice president for business affairs, who reports directly to the president. Thus, a water main break is handled by the facilities chief in consultation with the business vice president, and emergency response, intervention, and repairs are unambiguously the responsibility of that vice president. Yet if the damage from the flooding extends to student affairs spaces and the emergency maintenance fund held by the business vice president is inadequate for a repair project of this size, a common impulse is to turn to the provost to cover the secondary harm and the business vice president's budget shortfall. Before such an incident can be resolved, it may become an issue for the president and the whole leadership team. At such a moment, the president and provost need to have a common approach to finances and management.

Even without a crossing of lines, the exercise of authority in a hierarchy can test the partner relationship, since the president is the next higher authority to whom any decision of the provost can be appealed. With good communication, only rarely should a president feel compelled to overrule a provost's decision. A faculty member, for instance, might seek redress with the provost over a perceived injustice in an annual salary decision made by a dean. After considering the merits of the case in the context of other decisions made and examining the evidence of bias or unfairness supplied by the faculty member, the CAO may concur with an earlier decision of the dean. A concise statement of the evidence reviewed and the basis for reaffirming or modifying the dean's decision may satisfy the faculty member, but if not, the next appeal will be to the president. The president will, in turn, review all the evidence seen by the CAO and perhaps new arguments or evidence put forward by the faculty member. At that moment and unless there is genuinely new evidence introduced, it is institutionally very desirable for the CAO's review to be sustained by the president. In theory, moreover, the faculty member should have placed all pertinent evidence in front of the CAO, so there should not be much room for genuinely new evidence. If the president feels obliged to come to a sharply different decision, it could indicate that the institution's values and intentions in granting salary increases are not well understood or shared. It could imply that personal relationships or personalities are substantively influencing the decision process, and this implication could contradict academic personnel language describing the criteria for salary decisions. Of course, if the president does not initially see the case as the CAO did, the two can reconsider it and attempt to reconcile their points of view, but such conversations are not legally privileged. Thus, a very disgruntled and tenacious faculty member could file a lawsuit over the case, and the discussions between the president and CAO are fair game in legal discovery and could benefit the plaintiff's lawyer in advancing a discriminatory conspiracy theory.

It is far better if the general principles on which salary increases are awarded are well understood and shared in advance and possible interpretations are discussed and debated by the CAO and the president in the abstract, without a specific case on the table. The stronger the mutually agreed-upon value framework, the stronger the institutional position when the final decision is rendered.

This serves to illustrate a broader point about hierarchical decision making. A president has the formal authority to override the decisions of the CAO, but every override erodes the position of the CAO and invites further approaches to the president by anybody discontented with an opinion from the CAO. An unseasoned president may be tempted to give satisfaction and gain the gratitude of the discontented party as a warm and humane gesture, but succumbing to the temptation comes at the price of weakening the standing and authority of the CAO. If it happens regularly, the president will effectively end up doing the CAO's job, and neither the president nor the CAO will like or respect the result in the long run. A partnership built on trust, mutual respect, shared understandings, complementary strengths, and careful delineation of responsibilities and authorities is the foundation for success. At their best, the CAO is working to make the campus healthy and academically vibrant and thereby making the president look good, while the president is acknowledging the contributions of the CAO and is helping the CAO grow in the job and advance his or her own career.

The Provost and the President: When Things Go Well— Four Clues

BY LANE GLENN

1. *Respect Each Other's Specialized Roles.* While the president is the chief executive officer of the college and may have final decision-making authority, the relationship between the CAO and the CEO is much more effective when both have clearly defined roles and responsibilities and when they are thus accountable to each other and to those they lead and serve.

2. *Play to Your Strengths.* As the provost and the president arrive at an understanding of their specialized roles at the college or university, it will help also to learn each other's personal strengths and attributes. Put differently, do what you do well, and do not expect each other to do what he or she cannot do well.

3. *Practice Servant Leadership.* It is most important that as servant leaders provosts and presidents know each other's priorities and use their strengths to serve each other's priorities.

4. *Know the Fact— and the Data:* For well over a decade now, colleges and universities have been required by accrediting agencies or state departments of higher education to become more "data-driven" organizations. Whatever form this takes at a particular institution, provosts should be prepared to have firsthand knowledge of institutional "Key Performance Indicators," such as student retention and completion data, and transfer and employment data of graduates. They should understand the tools the college uses to gather and report this data and be able to use the data to help the college and the president meet goals and explain their challenges and successes to a public that is increasingly concerned with transparency and accountability.

Lane Glenn is the president of Northern Essex Community College in Massachusetts.

Despite the virtues and satisfactions of a good partnership, trust sometimes remains fragile, and there are natural reasons for wariness. A CAO may see his or her present job as a steppingstone in a career path leading next to a presidency. A presidential personality seeks out public visibility. The CAO may have that instinct for the limelight but not want to upstage the president. Indeed, in the event that a president runs into serious opposition, gets blindsided, or stumbles in some unexpected way,

The Provost and the President: When Things Don't Go Well—Four Clues

BY WILLIAM AUSTIN

1. *My president really believes in my leadership because I keep getting requests and suggestions to attend academic leadership conferences.* If your president asks you to attend one or two conferences and seminars, he or she believes in you. If you are continuously being pushed to attend, you are being nicely told that you are underperforming and need to work on your leadership practices.

2. *My president is meeting with the faculty leadership and discussing my performance. Is this a new performance evaluation system?* Your president continually evaluates your performance. Most chief executives do not decide without consultation to implement a 360-degree performance system. If this happens, stop and speak directly and privately with your president, realizing you may have to work to regain trust.

3. *My president really cares about academics and is so proud of the work I am doing that he just hired a consultant to sit in the office next to me to make a record of all our successes.* When the president hires a consultant to review your area, the intent is for a third party to come in and to do one of the following three things: (1) prepare a turnover file for your departure, (2) create an assessment of your ability and practices (first step toward your termination), or (3) if you are lucky, save you from your misplaced over-confidence.

4. *If things don't improve, what can I do?* Be smart. Your job, in order of priority, is to support and positively communicate the president's agenda, to keep the faculty developed and pleased with their work and their president, and to be the president's "go to" administrator for advice and support. An effective provost is the ultimate superhero sidekick; thus, remember your role, listen and learn, and save your personal agenda for your next promotion. If this all fails, start applying for college presidencies.

William Austin is the president of Warren County Community College in New Jersey.

the CAO is always standing in the wings as the heir apparent. This alone can make a president feel disquieted. If, in addition, the CAO has developed and exploited particularly strong relationships with some of the trustees, that can heighten the sense that the CAO is moving into the president's territory. Finally, the best partnerships are complementary—often as initiator president and executor provost. However, complementary skills can be accompanied by divergent styles, and a stylistic divergence that is too great can be strain on both parties. Even with the best intentions on both sides, some partnerships may never flow smoothly. One hopes that a fundamental incompatibility can be detected in the recruitment process before the campus's future and many careers are riding on the bond of the president/provost chemistry.

The CAO as Board Liaison

As CEO, the president presents the campus to the board of trustees and carries the voice of the board to the campus in public expression and in policy and practice. Structurally, the president may be one of a very small number of employees on the campus who report directly to the board, the others being people such as the general counsel and the ethics officer. The president is the nexus through which all items requiring board action flow to the board and interpretations of the board's positions flow back to the campus. Yet the notion that the president should be the unique connector and communicator between a college or university and its trustees is fundamentally flawed; a one-person single link between a large institution and those governing it is too thin and fragile. In reality, there are many other paths by which the trustees learn about the campus and form their views, and multiple ways that their views are made known to the campus. The level of interaction between the campus and the trustees depends on the scale of the institution, the proximity of the trustees to the campus, the trustees' backgrounds and interests, and relationships that they may have had prior to being named as trustees. After all, they were selected as trustees because of their interest in the institution, and that interest may well have arisen from a previous connection that is still active. Each trustee can bring a different perspective and a special acquaintance and wisdom with respect to the affairs of some branch of the campus. For example, an alumnus-trustee from the College of Business might have focused interests in that college and a special affinity for the dean, or a newscaster-trustee might lavish more attention on the College of Arts and Letters.

Such special lines of attachment can be helpful, but the board should not allow a series of special attachments to undermine the functioning of the board as a unified policy voice. If individual trustees begin to intrude on the operations of the campus in piecemeal fashion, that behavior has to be resisted at the campus level and reined in by the board before it spills into conflicts of interest and embarrassment. However, absent a known policy of the board, there are no grounds for a CAO's refusing to take a call or accept a visit from a person who has power over the university. However, there are grounds for declining to take actions requested that run contrary to the policies of the board or compromise the integrity of the institution. Similarly, it is acceptable for factual and educational material to be made available to a trustee, with the president fully apprised if not the conduit. It is a different matter if a CAO quietly presses a trustee to advocate for one of his or her idiosyncratic causes. At a certain point, such an independent approach can be construed as an end run around the president and the chair of the board, and such actions are perilous maneuvers.

Given the varied personalities, styles, and dispositions that may be involved, there is no universal prescription for how a CAO should best handle the multiple relationships. The CAO interacts with the president and trustees to promote the well-being of the academic enterprise while navigating carefully to avoid awkward entanglements. In this regard, there are several good practices to keep in mind. First, the president should be kept aware of approaches and visits by trustees and should be afforded the opportunity to be present and orchestrate any official visits. Second, any communications to a trustee from the CAO should occur with the knowledge of the president and the chair of the board; a significant matter should only go from the president to the board. Third, any actions a CAO might take as a result of a communication from a trustee, and the rationale for the action, should be documented in writing to avoid misunderstandings and later misinterpretations. Of course, a CAO at a public university should be mindful that written communications may at some point be disclosed in response to a Freedom of Information Act request and thereafter even appear on the pages of the local newspaper. Private institutions are not exposed to the same public scrutiny, but a CAO may still at some point find comfort in having an action, and the rationale for it, readily explained and not misremembered.

The CAO as Budget Manager

Needless to say, there are casual conversations in informal settings with exchanges that build institutional esprit de corps and collegiality, and the "good practices" described above would be stilted in that context. As the topics of conversation turn to serious campus business, it takes judgment to recognize when it is time for greater formality and to

Best Practices for System Provosts and Their Chancellors

BY NANCY ZIMPHER

The provost of a college or university is typically the second-ranking member of the administration, directly responsible for the oversight not just of the faculty body but also for academic affairs as a whole. In contrast, the work of a multi-campus system provost is broader and somewhat different—as are best practices in the role.

Systems can be massive in contrast to individual colleges or even large universities. The university system in Pennsylvania serves about 120,000 students on 14 campuses. In Maryland, the system enrolls close to 200,000 students at 12 colleges. The larger systems, in California and New York, for example, are more than twice this size. The State University of New York (SUNY), the largest comprehensive system of higher education in the country, comprises 64 campuses in five sectors of higher education, from community colleges to doctoral degree granting institutions. Its campuses enroll anywhere from 300 to 29,000 students and employ from 180 to 11,500 faculty and staff. In all, SUNY serves nearly half a million students and employs 88,000 faculty and staff.

A provost's portfolio on a single campus versus that of a system provost in its central office is proportionately more complex. As such, a system provost must possess all of the basic skills and knowledge of a campus provost but also a propensity to calibrate it on a wider scale. These examples illustrate some of the differences:

1. *Student Mobility.* A system provost must ensure that students have ample opportunity not only to transfer to and from one institution, but especially among the various institutions within the system. This perspective is also important when stimulating growth in research and entrepreneurship, delivering online education, and making data-driven decisions that determine college readiness, to name just a few.

2. *Collaboration with the System CFO.* There is also a closer relationship between program and budget to consider. While a provost strategically manages enrollment throughout the system to support state and local workforce demands, he or she must work hand-in-glove with the system's chief financial officer to ensure that state funds are distributed among the campuses in a manner that supports the program needs at each campus while also serving the larger system's mission and goals.

3. *Shared Services.* The identification of opportunities to share services among campuses within the system, be they administrative positions, procurement contracts, or grant applications, can go a long way toward creating a smarter,

more efficient university system that is able to allocate its resources to the greatest benefit of the students it serves.

4. *Campus President Performance*. In their oversight of the system's faculty, a provost also works closely with the system chancellor to review the performance of individual campus presidents. This typically also involves leadership development and assisting the chancellor in presidential searches and the evaluation of candidates.

In New York, we term this approach "systemness." Through it, we exercise the power of SUNY to unite our 64 campuses, exploiting their individual strengths and leveraging our collective impact on the state.

Nancy Zimpher has served as the first female chancellor of the State University of New York (SUNY) since 2009. Prior to this, she served as the first female president of the University of Cincinnati and, before that, as the first female chancellor of the University of Wisconsin–Milwaukee.

move graciously in that direction. As one example, setting and managing the budget for the campus is one of the undertakings that flexes all joints in the relationships among the board, the president, and the CAO. Popular surveys have repeatedly found that money is the topic most often provoking quarrels between married couples, so it is no surprise that presidents and provosts might find that budgets and financial management test and fray their own relationship and those with the trustees.

The allocation of financial resources is one of the most powerful articulations of institutional values by the leadership. Ideally, the leaders are spending the money available to advance the highest institutional priorities and are in full awareness of the competing options both now and in the future. In practice, however, every constituency within the university or college can have a different view on what is most important. The president and trustees are ultimately entrusted with defining the institution's vision. The vision is well rooted if the campus has articulated and embraced a strategic plan in which competing visions have been put on the table and major contradictions and tensions resolved. Every resource allocation can then be considered an expression or interpretation of such a strategic plan.

At a small independent college, the CAO may not have a formal authority over the entire budget. The main outlines of the budget allocations may be the purview of the president working with the CFO. Nevertheless, the CAO should not let that lull him or her into thinking that engagement with the budget begins after allocations to academic areas are already made. To the contrary, if decisions about investments in new facilities are made without CAO opinions, debt payments on a new sports complex, for example, can render it practically impossible to pursue an academic initiative that requires major capital investment. There are "opportunity costs" to be weighed in every decision, and the academic opportunities should not be forgotten. CAOs at all institutions, no matter what their size, should expect to be full participants in major discussions of the financial position of the campus, including projections and plans for the annual operating budget, comprehensive accounting of expenditures, and capital planning.

A provost is charged with managing the budget for the campus and working with the CFO and must, in dialogue with the president, grasp the liabilities, the revenue potential, the cost drivers, the academic inspirations, the investment opportunities, and the risks taken by all those with some authority for the central budget. For a large campus, this is an annual challenge that can only be undertaken with help from many operational leaders. There will always be more demands intelligently pressed than there will be funds to meet them in both good times and bad. In times of plenty, a provost is expected to be caring and generous to everyone with a good idea; in times of austerity, a provost is called on to make the tough decisions no matter how strong-willed the many petitioners prove to be. The surest way to handle the competing requests is to have articulated thoughtful, tested principles that will advance the campus's goals and then show them to be the basis for wise budgetary decisions. In these instances, alignment and cooperation between provost and president are critical. While the president ultimately has the final say, the provost has to be confident that taking the heat for a tough decision will not be wasted. The trustees set the context through their policies for tuition and fees, endowment pay-out, and investment choices. Yet the president and the provost have to educate and persuade the trustees as they set policy and then talk through and agree on the broad outlines of implementation.

What sometimes can be revealed in financial decision making are very different personality traits and attitudes that are deeply ingrained and emotionally potent. No matter what the nature and domain of the decision to be made, it is important for leaders to recognize their own emotional make-up, to be self-aware and self-managing, so that conflicting immediate emotional responses can be held in check and not allowed to escalate to needlessly damaging confrontation.[6] In the press of business, however, a calm and thorough examination of every decision may be an

The Thing I Very Much Wish I Had Known on My First Day as CAO
■ Never underestimate the resilience and power of long-standing cultures.

unattainable luxury. The president, the provost, and the CFO have to know each other well enough to allow a range of options, perspectives, and analyses to be put on the table for discussion. While the president has to take responsibility for the final choices made, all have to take responsibility for the process and defend the rationales behind them.

Direct Reports: The CAO and the Academic Deans

Another illustration of the CAO's role in a hierarchy of authority is working with the deans, typically all of whom report to the senior academic officer. Just as a provost serves as the communicator and interpreter of the policies and intentions of the president and trustees to the deans, so too are the deans the communicators and interpreters of the provost to the department heads and the faculty. Not all deans will be effective in this role, however, and with some the CAO may find frequently that much is lost in translation. If so, it will be prudent to put much more in writing to a specific dean and to copy more people. In some cases, a dean may cultivate a special relationship with the president, and the CAO and the president will also have to agree on how any attempts to rise above the CAO's authority can be addressed most efficiently.

The CAO should expect and promote the success of all deans at the college, since the aspirations for each one will be embedded within the vision for the campus. As such, the definitions of success for each dean and the methods by which they will be assessed should be made clear as quickly as possible. The accountability of the deans to achieve the goals of the college should be accompanied by a commensurate commitment from the CAO and as much personal support as possible. A dean may have areas of leadership that need further development, and the CAO can help connect him or her to people within the organization who have the complementary skills or occasionally bring in outside advisors who can help address an area of weakness. The CAO is the most appropriate person to put in place the framework of incentives to assure that the dean's authority and responsibilities are aligned with the vision of the college or university.

Although an effective CAO should always be ready to offer thoughtful advice and reliable information, some circumstances will call for restraint and a shift in approach. In the hierarchical exercise of authority, certain actions expect independent judgment to be exercised at each successive step up the hierarchy. For example, we described above the handling of an appeal of a dean's decision on a faculty member's annual salary adjustment. Suppose the dean is perplexed as to the appropriateness of a request for an increase and asks the CAO for advice. If the CAO goes through the file and studies the merits of the case in detail and then gives the dean unequivocal advice on the amount of the increase, the dean will feel compelled to follow the CAO's advice. Thereafter the CAO has lost the presumption of independence in reviewing the dean's judgment. When pressed, the dean might reasonably say, "The CAO made me do it." In a variety of personnel actions and grievances, the review or appeal process assumes independence at the next level. A CAO is not prohibited from informing a dean about policies, procedures, and institutional norms. However, the further the CAO gets into the specific substance of a particular case, the more his or her independence will be suspect and susceptible to challenge in the future.

Another example of a shift in relationship occurs when the CAO discovers that a dean has violated the trust placed in him or her in some way. Sometimes a small matter, such as an inappropriate use of a flexible account, might be handled by questioning the dean, clarifying the proper use of the account, and correcting what may have been an inadvertent error or simple misunderstanding. In a more serious situation, the CAO's first responsibility is to protect the institution and its people from possible harm and then to follow the steps of a tested administrative or judicial process in deciding what is to be done with the transgressing dean. The CAO should access the human resources office and the campus's legal representation in such cases, and the president needs to be informed of the facts. If the case could result in disciplinary action or even criminal charges, the CAO will benefit from professional procedural and legal guidance.

A more common challenge in the CAO-dean relationship occurs when the CAO discovers that a dean has, often with the best of intentions, greatly overspent her or his accounts. One hopes that strong financial systems and fiscal controls will raise an alarm before the dean has gone very far down the deficit path. Whatever the original reason, however, an experienced CAO also learns that when a dean with a string of debt-financed accomplishments leaves for another job, the CAO and the president are left to pay the bills and to recruit a new dean.

Lessons Learned: The CAO and the President

BY ALICE BOURKE HAYES

1. *When Your President Leaves.* Do all you can to share your institutional knowledge and make a smooth transition for the new chief executive officer. However, also recognize that a new president may want to assemble a new leadership team, and if that appears to be the case, be prepared to explore career alternatives.

2. *When There Is Tension Between You and the President.* You owe the president the best advice you can give even when it is not welcome and challenges her or his position. You also owe the president loyalty and public support. If you cannot give this, be prepared to explore career alternatives.

3. *How Involved Should Trustees Be in the Academic Life of the College or University?* Many of the trustees come from a corporate or public service sector, and the demands of scholarly research and communication are unfamiliar to them. Invite trustees to campus for public events and introduce them to faculty members and students. The better they know the working reality of the institution, the better they can support you. Also, do not fear sharing difficult information with the board. While it is natural to want to avoid looking weak or indecisive, you will look even worse if a concealed problem comes to light.

4. *Working with the President on Development.* Work with the president to identify a manageable number of trustees and alumni with academic interests and make a point of establishing regular personal contact with each of them. Send a report or a press clipping regularly, and invite them for lunch at least once annually. They will enjoy being informed insiders and will be better able to support you when a medium or major "ask" is strategically scheduled.

Alice Bourke Hayes wrote the chapter on effective relationships between the CAO and the president in First Among Equals: The Role of the Chief Academic Officer *(1997). Now retired, Hayes served as the CAO of both Loyola University (Chicago) and St. Louis University. She then served as president of the University of San Diego.*

Future Challenges Loom Large

Presidents and CAOs must establish their own style of harmony. While the president's voice will capture more public attention, the provost's voice will often carry greater credibility with the academic enterprise because the CAO has come from the faculty and his or her statements can

The Single Most Important Piece of Advice for a New Provost on the First Day in the Position

- To effect change, first change the systemic underpinnings of the present practices while explaining the reasons for change, then educate everyone to the ways of the new world and their place in it, and then patiently and firmly stay the course.

be correlated directly with educational decisions. In times of rapid transformation, the campus community's trust and faith in the leadership to guide the institution wisely is a precious resource. Continuing consonance between values chosen for rhetorical emphasis by the president and those manifest in the CAO's programmatic and personnel decisions can ensure that trust.

Despite the long history of recognized excellence in the U.S. system of higher education and the reassuring continuity of European universities over the centuries, an increasing number of observers are predicting a fundamental restructuring of the entire higher education landscape by 2020. As Christensen and colleagues put it, "What the theory of disruptive innovation suggests is that the business model of many traditional colleges and universities is broken. Their collapse is so fundamental that it cannot be stanched by improving the financial performance of endowment investments, tapping wealthy alumni donors more effectively, or collecting more tax dollars from the public. There needs to be a new model."[7]

In their analysis, the disruptive technology driving the transformation is the Internet and online education. Evidence that the conventional business model is broken can be seen most starkly in the escalating price of attending college when compared to the median income of the American household. For public higher education, the cost to the student has been rising more rapidly than inflation largely because net student tuition revenue has been used to offset the loss of state funding. At the same time, an increasing number of young Americans have accepted the lifetime importance of obtaining at least a baccalaureate degree and plan to attend a college or university.

Whether or not the dynamics of transformation of higher education will follow the examples of other disrupted industries, there is little question that its institutions now need to redesign their instructional systems and strategies to navigate through the challenges emerging. It will be as complex for CAOs and presidents as were the war protests and transformative social movements for previous generations of academic leaders. Private soul-searching, hard analyses, and direct confrontations with different value systems will need to occur before final decisions can be made. Whatever the circumstances, it will be a time for both creativity and excellence from CAOs and their colleagues at the top.

NOTES

1. Association of Governing Boards of Universities and Colleges, *Effective Governing Boards: A Guide for Members of Governing Boards of Public Colleges, Universities, and Systems* (Washington, DC: AGB Press, 2010), 7.

2. Ibid., 3.

3. Ibid., 9.

4. In its colorful history, "provost" was at one time used to designate the warden for a prison, so today's provosts are comparatively beloved. *Oxford Dictionary of English Etymology,* ed. C.T. Onions (Oxford: Oxford at the Clarendon Press, 1966), s.v. "provost," 719.

5. Bryan Cook and Young Kim, *The American College President—2012* (Washington, DC: American Council on Education, 2012), *Errata,* Table 20, 10.

6. Daniel Goleman, Richard Boyatzis, and Annie McKee, *Primal Leadership* (Boston: Harvard Business School Press, 2002), 40–48.

7. Clayton M. Christensen, Michael B. Horn, Louis Caldera, and Louis Soares, "Disrupting College," Executive Summary (Washington, DC: Center of American Progress, Innosight Institute, February 2011), http://cdn.americanprogress .org/wp-content/uploads/issues/2011/02/pdf/disrupting_college_execsumm.pdf.

CHAPTER FIVE

Ground Level: How to Lead the Faculty as the First among Equals

Linda A. McMillin

"Whose side are you on, anyway, the administration's or the faculty's?"

"Whose side are you on?" During my years as CAO, I have often measured my success by the frequency with which I hear this question and from whom. Eventually, I have come to believe that the more I am asked about which side I am on, the more likely it is that I am making appropriate decisions. Faculty expectations, in particular, run high for chief academic officers. Professors hope that these leaders who are culled from among colleagues will remember their former lives and still feel loyalty to their peers even as they "cross over" into that alien world of administration.[1] In many ways, this question of sides defines the position—CAOs sit at the crossroads between faculty and other institutional constituencies, and their chief occupations are translation, interpretation, and negotiation across what faculty perceive as a great divide. One learns that the CAO needs to be on both sides, and neither side, at the same time.

My standard answer to this question of sides is to claim no single allegiance and to move beyond the false dichotomy the question implies. Instead, I try to articulate a higher, more important side—that of the academic program—and invite the faculty to find common cause with me. What is the academic program? It is that mixture of majors and minors, graduate programs, knowledge creation and research application, general education, community service, noncredit and co-curricular activities, athletics, and major intellectual, civic, and fine arts events that colleges and universities offer to their students, their communities, and their societies. It is the educational and intellectual output that we provide to the world. Who would not want to support the academic program? It is what we do.

The academic program in the abstract is an easy enough ideal for all to champion. In my case, I need to champion the academic program embodied at Susquehanna University. This program has a variety of boundaries and limitations, some determined by mission: undergraduate, selective, liberal arts, traditional age population, residential; and some determined by pragmatic realities: rural, tuition-driven, eastern Atlantic region, modestly endowed, small alumni base. While both mission and pragmatics can change over time, CAOs need to keep everyone, and especially faculty, focused on an institution's particular mission and fiscal realities.

Staying focused on mission is difficult. We all know what the pecking order is in higher education—from community colleges at the base to "Research I (RI)"[2] institutions at the apex. For faculty members who receive their PhDs in the rarified air of RI institutions, such aspirations seem natural even though a large majority will fashion careers in much less lofty places—and some will find no academic position at all. So the challenge is not only to help colleagues stay focused on, but also be committed to—even excited about—the mission of their particular institution. CAOs must meet this challenge early and often—in recruitment and mentoring of new professors; in decisions about tenure, promotion, and other faculty rewards; and in the allocation of every professional development resource. Provosts and deans can also help hold the faculty, other administrators, and themselves accountable to institutional mission through meaningful and effective assessment of student learning and institutional effectiveness activities. All of these various processes need to align with institutional mission and reflect a level of integrity and consistency that faculty members can recognize. Exploring ways to do this will make up the first section of this chapter.

If staying focused on mission is a challenge, helping the faculty understand and operate effectively within the limits of institutional resources can be an even greater test for the CAO. Indeed, college administrators

The Thing I Very Much Wish I Had Known on My First Day as CAO

- Do not take things personally. When a faculty member is angry or unreasonable, it is rarely about you. Focus instead on what is needed, then be clear about what you can, and cannot, do for her or him.

rarely get to choose between funding a good versus a bad idea. Rather, they are usually forced to prioritize from among a lengthy list of outstanding programs and initiatives. Faculty members never like to have a project turned down for funding. However, a "no" becomes more palatable if they are fully informed as to what resources are available, how they will be deployed, and the process through which funding is accessed. For long-serving deans, transparency is key; secret side deals—real or imagined—are a bane to faculty confidence and morale.

Keeping Mission at the Center

When I became provost, some of my faculty colleagues took to calling me "boss." Of course, the biggest change when one crosses from faculty to full-time administration is that one enters a hierarchy in which one clearly answers to a superior and is responsible for the management of subordinates. However, faculty members are not a part of that hierarchy. Without question, CAOs wield influence, moral suasion, and, almost always, the power of the purse over faculty colleagues, but faculty members remain colleagues with whom one collaborates within larger collegial structures. This is particularly true in those areas where the faculty holds primary responsibility: curriculum, professional standards, and peer evaluation. Here, CAOs can influence how policy is developed and even weigh in at the appropriate moment, but nothing is advanced by fiat.

A CAO's first responsibility to the faculty is to know the academic policies of the institution and to make sure they are executed fairly and consistently. In all personnel procedures—recruitment, evaluation, tenure and promotion, and disciplinary actions—the CAO is the administrator professors depend on to guarantee the integrity of the system. Indeed, one of the fastest ways into a lawsuit is not to follow institutional procedures as derived from faculty handbooks or collective bargaining agreements. Within these procedures, CAOs are responsible for ensuring that faculty voices are heard and respected at every level. At times, this means making

The CAO and Institutional Mission: Four Imperatives

1. Make mission central in recruiting new faculty members, both adjunct and full-time
2. Connect mission to early-career mentoring among the faculty
3. Align faculty reward structures with institutional mission
4. Link mission to institutional assessment goals

sure that faculty members hear each other and that opportunities for collective conversation and deliberation are both free from intimidation and open to multiple perspectives. Following this, as processes wind their way through administrative layers, CAOs become the chief translators and representatives of faculty values and judgments.

Guaranteeing the integrity of institutional processes is at the foundation of the CAO's work with faculty members. Policy and process are also places where CAOs have everyday opportunities to engage professors in conversation about mission, especially in areas such as recruiting, mentoring, assessment, and rewarding excellence.

1. Make mission central in recruiting new faculty

Recruiting faculty members provides multiple moments for a CAO to put mission at the center of the campus conversation. Departments and faculty peers have a primary role in defining positions and determining professional qualifications. However, they should regularly be asked to outline how exactly this particular position, defined in this or that way, will advance the mission of the institution and its current strategic priorities. Of course, CAOs need to follow through by prioritizing requests accordingly. In addition, senior academic administrators are usually a stop on the circuit in the on-campus interview process. The questions CAOs ask of job candidates and the way they characterize institutional policies and culture are also opportunities to emphasize the particular mission of the institution.

One area of recruitment—diversifying the professoriate—has been an important part of institutional missions across every sector of higher education for four decades or more. However, even with our collective good intentions, recent studies document that "faculty of color remain significantly underrepresented in higher education. Nationally, faculty of color, including Black/African Americans (6 percent), Latina/os (4 percent), Asian Americans (6 percent), and American Indians (0.5 percent), make up only 16 percent of the full-time professoriate. Furthermore, only 5.3 percent of the full professors in the United States are African American, Hispanic, or Native American."[3] The most common explanation for higher education's lack of success has been "a shortage of [minority] doctoral graduate students and institutional racism."[4] Provosts have continuing roles to play in addressing both of these issues and advancing their campuses' missions.

Exemplary "pipeline" programs to increase the number of minority PhDs span institutional types. For instance, undergraduate institutions can identify promising minority students and mentor them toward graduate school through participation in the Mellon Mays University

The Three Biggest Challenges Facing CAOs with Regard to Faculty Relations

1. Recruiting and retaining the next generation of diverse faculty
2. Rewarding faculty work in ways that are equitable and consistent with institutional mission
3. Hiring non-tenured faculty in ways that are equitable, inclusive, and consistent with institutional mission

Fellowships program. Many graduate programs have their own recruitment and support structures for graduate students of color or participate in consortia such as the Compact for Faculty Diversity. The Ford Foundation Fellowship Program has been a longstanding leader in supporting graduate school participation, and the National Science Foundation has been focused on minority recruitment into STEM fields. These are just a few examples that CAOs can consider in determining the best fit for their institutional mission. Whatever the case, CAOs play a central role in initiating grant applications, prioritizing funding, and supporting faculty and others so as to sustain and build viable programs that endure.

More difficult to address, and more insidious, are issues of campus climate that undermine the stated mission at most colleges and universities and complicate minority faculty recruitment. CAOs must have an understanding of the ongoing ways racism and sexism, for example, are shaping their campus culture. They also need to take a clear-eyed look at their own power and privilege within these structures before they can begin to comment on that of others. Forming strategic partnerships with Chief Diversity Officers can be especially useful to both offices. Together, holders of these two positions can lead ongoing efforts to assess campus climate and use this data to open meaningful conversations with the faculty about structures of bias within local institutional culture. One important place to start such a conversation is within search committees, where unconscious cultural bias often keeps faculties replicating the status quo.[5]

Finally, deans and provosts should not underestimate the power of making personal commitments. Senior academic officers need to operationalize their institution's policies and statements on affirmative action, on diversity and inclusiveness, on anti-discrimination, and on harassment in everything they do. The best time to make institutional progress on campus climate is when there is no immediate crisis. Academic vice presidents should routinely engage in informal conversations with faculty members about their campus experiences. It is particularly important to know professors of color, to listen to their stories and build on their insights. "Supportive administrative leadership" was cited by faculty members of color as an important reason why they stay in the academy, and senior minority faculty mentors are key in recruiting the next generation.[6]

2. Connect mission to early-career mentoring

New faculty orientation is another moment in which institutional mission can emerge front and center. All the processes and rituals associated with welcoming new teachers and beginning the academic year—meetings, workshops, receptions, convocations—are richly symbolic moments and clearly illustrate an institution's values and priorities for those watching closely. CAOs want to make sure that the symbols under their purview purposely communicate what is most important, be that student-centeredness, academic challenge, new research, community service, institutional citizenship, or some combination of these and other priorities. Getting the symbolism right is only the beginning, however. The best new faculty programs are rarely one-shot gatherings; rather, they continue episodically, and in high profile ways, throughout the first year and even into the second. Mentoring—both formal and informal—is expected by new faculty members, who feel it is an important component of their success.[7] CAOs need to make sure that new faculty members emerge with a solid understanding of where they have landed and of how to be successful in this place.

Of course the dominant question for many new professors is, "What must I do to earn tenure?" Rumors abound at every institution about the "right" number of publications, the minimum average student evaluation, or the key committee membership that will make tenure a guarantee. At the same time, we all know that tenure is never assured. Multiple factors concerning institutional need and fiscal constraints are outside the influence of individual performance and the CAO's influence. Additionally, the anxiety of pre-tenure professors will rarely be completely ameliorated, no matter how clearly expectations are articulated.

Nevertheless, it is the provost's responsibility to make sure that expectations are laid out clearly and consistently with new faculty members and that they are given regular, frank feedback on how their individual performance is being measured against these criteria. Here the challenge is making sure that policy formulated at the college or university level articulates with practices at the departmental level. At times, a dean's or chair's desire to "protect" new faculty members may lead to overemphasizing, or undervaluing, some aspect of faculty work in unbalanced or even unrealistic ways. In other instances, a department head who sees his or her role as mainly that of faculty advocate may be hesitant or uncomfortable giving critical formative feedback. In the end, one of the most important ways that CAOs can create consistency is to make sure that deans and department chairs are given ample opportunities to develop their skills in personnel management. The American Council on Education (ACE) and the Council of Independent Colleges (CIC), for example, offer excellent workshops in this area.

In addition, CAOs need to bring together department chairs and deans across disciplines to talk together about how they can make policies and practices more consistent. Ironically, one of the most important outcomes of such a conversation can be a greater appreciation of disciplinary differences within the institution. While tenure portfolios are first evaluated within a department, most institutions include reviews at school and college-wide levels. Faculty members who evaluate the work of those who labor in significantly different ways than they do sometimes need to appreciate that a great variety of faculty work can be excellent and to recognize and value as "faculty work" those activities that make up the standards of excellence in each discipline present at their institutions. Professors in areas where performance outweighs prose or in professional disciplines like nursing or business can feel that their work may be undervalued or even dismissed by peers in college-wide review processes. Again, it is most important for a CAO to advertise and then uphold fair and inclusive evaluation practices, understanding that *all* disciplines present at their institution represent aspects of a shared mission and need to be valued as such.

In the end, tenure should only be given "in the selfish best interests of the institution."[8] The most effective way for a CAO to guarantee this outcome is to make sure that these "interests," as defined by institutional mission, are at the heart of standards, policy, and practice in tenure review. That a CAO would come down on the opposite side of a collective faculty judgment should happen rarely, and if it becomes routine, faculty voice in peer review is undermined and the integrity of the process breaks down. Consequently, ongoing conversations with faculty members that cultivate shared values are essential and should result in departmental and committee decisions that are easily endorsed as the faculty becomes the embodiment of those values. Indeed, the key ingredient of tenure—often overlooked at present—is not that an institution makes a lifetime commitment to employ a faculty member, but that a faculty member commits his or her life's work to the ongoing mission and prosperity of the institution.

The Chief Academic Officer and Institutional Rankings: Recommendations and Responsibilities

BASED ON AN INTERVIEW WITH ROB FRANEK

- *Rankings have been redefined.* The *Princeton Review's* ranking system has been redefined over the past five years. The new system incorporates several faculty-focused items that CAOs should be aware of, including faculty accessibility to students, i.e., actual office hours; faculty qualifications and expertise; and the development of new academic disciplines.

- *Current college "experts" are students.* Interviewers from the *Princeton Review* realize that current students are the best persons to talk to about the factors shaping rankings because students are the clients for these services. CAOs are advised to go directly to their own students to hear how successful their new programs and faculty are performing.

- *Ranking factors are student driven.* The *Princeton Review* incorporates more than sixty lists in its "top twenty" rankings, and almost all are student driven, including factors such as financial aid availability and the quality of campus culture.

- *Partnering with ranking agencies and publications is encouraged.* CAOs are challenged to think about rankings in a fresh way by partnering with a publication like the *Princeton Review* and inviting its representatives to campus to view new infrastructure and experience new programs. Rankings are not "gotcha" exercises to be feared or avoided.

- *All ranking surveys and publications do not hold the same priorities.* While the *Princeton Review* invites partners and places a high value on student engagement and satisfaction, other publications may not do so to the same degree. Thus, it is critical for the provost to learn and manage what each ranking service views as most important.

- *Two institutions worthy of ranking recognition.* The C. T. Bauer College of Business at the University of Houston has created a culture of success reflected in the number one ranking of its entrepreneurship program by both the *Princeton Review* and *Business Week*. On a larger scale, the SUNY system deserves recognition for its guiding vision under the leadership of Chancellor Nancy Zimpher (see sidebar on page 44 on best practices for provosts of larger systems). Zimpher is viewed by those at *Princeton Review* as a leader who grasps that institutional improvements on a major scale can take five to ten years to implement and filter down, and yet the immediate, in-the-moment student experience today also plays a role in rankings improvement.

(cont'd)

3. Align faculty reward structures with institutional mission

In the late 1990s, I was part of a project sponsored by the Associated New American Colleges that sought to examine if and how institutional mission aligned with faculty work habits and faculty reward systems. One key finding was that while mission often did shape faculty work, it rarely was perceived by faculty to shape rewards.[9] While faculty members understood and valued the missions of their institutions and attempted to prioritize their work accordingly, rewards—tenure, promotion, merit pay, even non-monetary recognition—were more likely associated with the publication of traditional forms of scholarship. Indeed, James Fairweather's work from the same decade found that "regardless of institution type or mission and irrespective of program area, faculty who spend more time on research and who publish the most are paid more."[10] Fairweather more recently confirmed this finding in a study published in 2005.[11]

That professional research continues as "coin of the realm" at research-centric institutions is no surprise for even an inexperienced dean, but that it should be the most valued currency across the entire higher education landscape raises some challenges and contradictions. Many institutions have policies that rank teaching as at least as important, if not more important, than research for the accomplishing of their mission. While I have often argued that professors who are passionate about their research bring that passion to the classroom, conscientious teaching still requires significant time and attention and, where teaching loads are high, can compete directly with time for research. In addition, as the proportion of tenure-track faculty shrinks in comparison with part-time and contingent colleagues, service expectations for those in tenurable lines has also grown. The result is a ratcheting up of faculty work on all sides, as professors attend to the needs of their students, keep institutional processes on track, and try to find time to do the scholarly work necessary to be rewarded. As teachers across all ranks and disciplines reflected in the recent survey from the Collaborative on Academic Careers in Higher Education (COACHE), "The expectations for excellence in all areas are higher than ever before."[12]

Faculty members have responded to these pressures by working more, as Schuster and Finkelstein report in *The American Faculty:* "Since 1984 the weekly work effort of faculty has increased in almost linear fashion from about 40 hours per week to nearly 49 (48.6)—about 20 percent."[13] Such a system does not seem sustainable. This has prompted higher educational leaders who study faculty work to worry about the future. As R. Eugene Rice observes, "The faculty career is becoming less attractive and increasingly regarded as hardly tenable, certainly not the kind of career that could attract the best of a new generation."[14]

Aligning mission with faculty work and rewards is one of the biggest challenges facing current CAOs. It is a conundrum that higher education leaders have been trying to crack starting with Ernest Boyer's *Scholarship Reconsidered* in 1990. Boyer's attempt to expand definitions of research beyond the discovery of new knowledge, to raise in stature the "scholarship of teaching and learning," and to increase flexibility in and across faculty careers created much excitement and hope for transforming faculty work. Indeed, it generated numerous projects and studies sponsored by nearly every higher education organization and spanning all institution types, not to mention thousands of campus-based faculty workshops and retreats. The more recent *The Scholarship of Teaching and Learning Reconsidered* highlights the many positive outcomes for teaching and learning resulting from the numerous projects sponsored by the Carnegie Academy for the Scholarship of Teaching and Learning (CASTL). Additionally, *Faculty Priorities Reconsidered* reports on a single multiyear project involving nine diverse institutions (public, private, liberal arts, large research, for profit, a school of medicine) supported by AAHE. Both of these volumes offer much pragmatic advice from many different types of colleges and universities for CAOs to consider. However, it is clear that no one has found *the* answer and that significant change remains elusive. I was struck in particular by Rice's pessimistic conclusions: that expanding notions of scholarship has only expanded faculty work— "more responsibilities added to a full plate"— and that "pressures to return to the scholarship of discovery, as the only form of scholarly work to be recognized and counted, are almost insurmountable."[15]

CAOs continually need to assess the current state of faculty expectations and rewards at their own institutions, and this assessment needs to take place on two levels. First, the question of what policies are in place to create space to recognize and reward multiple forms of excellence in faculty work consistent with the mission of the institution needs to be answered. For example, are their multiple ways of balancing a tenure portfolio? Can professors meet average teaching load requirements across more than one year? Are there named professorships and university awards for excellence in all areas of faculty work? Yet finding ways to introduce more flexible policies where needed can be difficult. In describing such efforts at Indiana University, Mary Burgan writes, "The task force's proposal . . . seemed sensible and modest to me, but I was struck by the institutional anxieties that it inspired."[16] Judith Gappa, Ann E. Austin, and Andrea Trice's *Rethinking Faculty Work* makes a thoughtful case for how to create change processes in a variety of institutional contexts that respect and build on faculty values.[17]

Second, even with appropriate policies in place, CAOs must also assess how they work in practice. Flexible faculty work policies and expectations can be very attractive to new professors. Gen X faculty members, in particular, have been "vocal about wanting increased flexibility [and] greater integration of their work and home lives."[18] However, the fear that taking advantage of flexibility may have negative career implications—placing someone in the second tier—often remains. For example, Princeton has had a tenure extension policy in place for new parents since the 1970s. However, it was not until 2005, when President Shirley Tilghman made it an "opt out" rather than "opt in" system—that is, new parents were automatically given an additional year rather than having to make a request—that assistant professors made significant use of the policy.[19]

Finally, CAOs still need to "follow the money." They need to monitor who gets rewarded and for what. A key place to begin is by examining the status of mid-career associate professors. This is the cohort that often takes on the largest service role in the institution. Thus, it is wise to ask, How do those who step into leadership as department heads or key committee chairs fare in terms of salary and progress toward promotion to full professor as compared to their colleagues who decline such roles to focus exclusively on research? Even at research-intensive institutions, this career phase is receiving scrutiny. For example, "Ohio State University is creating alternative paths for associate professors to be promoted to full professor, giving scholars credit for directing research centers that get grants, for example, rather than strictly for landing individual research grants and producing publications."[20] CAOs need to make sure that those who do work that aligns with mission and keeps the institution moving forward are at the very least not disadvantaged financially for their efforts.

Raising Your Ranking: How the Bauer College of Business Did It

At the C.T. Bauer College of Business at the University of Houston, everything starts and ends with student success. Our mission is focused on the creation of knowledge that will address new business realities so that our students are prepared for effective and responsible business leadership worldwide. We design student-centric programs and we focus on three things:

1. *Academic rigor complements industry experience.* We listen to the needs of business by bringing academicians (research professors) and industry professionals (professors of practice) together to create models of best practice. This is the DNA of our curriculum. This process facilitates continuous conversations between industry and higher education so that our students are better prepared to lead their organizations. An exhaustive inventory of elective courses speaks to the emphasis we place on keeping coursework both relevant and rigorous.

2. *Life is not confined to problems from a text book.* We complement the traditional classroom experience for students with active mentoring programs and lunch-and-learn sessions that bring successful industry leaders into the classroom, consulting projects that become integrated into their coursework, and roundtable sessions with successful alumni. Students are expected to take what they learn to work the next day.

3. *Make a difference in the communities we serve.* We actively partner with multiple community organizations and engage our students in outreach activities that benefit our community. Our students often hear the phrase, "Of those to whom much is given, much shall be required."

On a personal level, I teach every semester. Too often, I find administrators who are removed from the student experience and who have forgotten what keeps academic life dynamic. I think that academic deans must teach and stay committed to the classroom experience.

Latha Ramchand is Dean and Professor of Finance at the C.T. Bauer College of Business at the University of Houston. Bauer is considered among the top 60 business schools worldwide and has been ranked as the number one entrepreneurship program in the United States by both the Princeton Review *and* BusinessWeek. *Rob Franek, senior vice president at the* Princeton Review, *mentions Bauer's rise in national rankings as a model to be studied.*

4. Link mission with institutional assessment goals

Rather than debate whether assessment is an unmitigated evil foisted on faculty by the new corporate university or the answer to revolutionizing student learning and thus justifying our existence to external audiences, I will begin with the assumption that, for better or for worse, it is an activity that has become a regular part of faculty work—perhaps for the main reason that our accrediting bodies require it. So if we are going to do assessment, let us do it in ways that build on institutional mission. As Stanley Katz has observed, "It is hard to imagine a principled objection to careful evaluation of learning outcomes or to thoughtful suggestions for improvement in pedagogical strategies."[21] To be done well, the faculty needs to design the processes, analyze the results, and implement improvements going forward.

Pat Hutching's *Opening Doors to Faculty Involvement in Assessment* is a good place to start for advice on how to engage the faculty in this important activity. At the top of her list of recommendations is: "Build assessment around the regular, ongoing work of teaching and learning." Such an approach begins in the classroom and can lead to departmental conversations focused on "what most members of the professoriate know and care most about: their discipline or field."[22] This is where assessment can be the most meaningful for faculty and can lead to thoughtful improvements. However, provosts need to respect the idiosyncrasies of the disciplines and not look for a single universal approach. Hold all departments accountable for the documentation in annual reports while remembering that the ten-year accreditation cycle is the right time frame to think about comprehensive assessments, not a single year. It is only in these larger periods that trend lines can be established and change seen. However, thinking in ten-year chunks makes it even more imperative that CAOs keep a constant flame under the institutional assessment process—not allowing it to die out, only to be desperately rekindled the year before an accreditation visit.

Finally, it is important for provosts to find ways to model the culture of assessment within their own work activities. How is the work of the provost's own office assessed on a regular basis? Asking for regular faculty feedback on one's own work and the processes one directs and using that feedback to make improvements can be a powerful way to affirm the value of assessment.

Managing in a New Fiscal Reality

While many of us across higher education may feel that we have spent our entire careers in a time of limited resources, the years since the

Top Ten Ways to Earn (or at Least Not Waste) Social Capital with the Faculty. Provosts should never spend social capital on "mini-crises" of their own creation or that can be avoided. To that end:

1. *Keep the trains running on time, i.e., know what you are responsible for and make sure those things happen in a smooth and timely fashion.* Attention to detail is a major part of the job. The faculty will not embark on a new initiative with someone who has not proven capable of processing check requests or signing appointment letters in a timely fashion.

2. *Pay attention to process.* CAOs need to know the traditions of their institutions and the "way it has always been done." Process is more than simply following the rules. CAOs need to make sure that the faculty has been given meaningful ways to be engaged.

3. *Make decisions.* After attending to process and considering all appropriate information, make timely decisions. A hard decision does not get easier with delay.

4. *Remember that nobody really cares how it was done at your previous institution.* This does not mean that CAOs should not introduce new ideas and best practices, but avoid long anecdotes of how something did or did not work in your previous life. "We" should only refer to current colleagues.

5. *Know how to run a meeting.* This includes setting a realistic agenda that goes out ahead of time, staying focused on that agenda, making sure people leave with a clear sense of what is expected of them before a next meeting, and keeping a record of decisions made.

6. *Answer email, but know when to pick up the telephone.* Emails can be overwhelming, but they need to be answered in a timely fashion: 48 hours if possible. Also, remember that every email you write is public and can be subpoenaed.

7. *Listen.* Listen not only to the words but also to body language, tone, and context. Listen after you speak to make sure you have been heard, and listen last, i.e., do not insist on having the last word.

8. *Take responsibility, even when it is not your fault.* In Trumanesque fashion, let the buck stop with you. Apologize without excuses and fix the problem. Move on.

9. *Do not take yourself too seriously.* Be known for humility and laughter.

10. *Hire and manage competent administrative and support staff.* Set clear expectations, give specific and useful feedback, hold people accountable, and, if necessary, let someone go.

financial crisis of 2009 have reinforced this reality for everyone. And while the popular press often presents our institutions as spendthrift organizations that reflexively raise tuition to build climbing walls, the view from the professoriate is of a constant struggle to prioritize, cut, and reprioritize in order to meet educational mission and balance budgets. What follows are three final ideas to support faculty colleagues as we work together to overcome these national concerns.

1. Aim for transparency, transparency, transparency

Faculties need to understand the financial realities of their institutions—they need to know what resources are available and how they are spent in enough detail to ask questions, offer opinions, and make judgments about institutional priorities. For most state institutions, some level of budgetary transparency is a requirement of law; for private institutions, it is a choice that requires the cooperation of the president and CFO. However, simply making information available in a library archive, an annual report, or a 990 form on the IRS website is not enough. Spreadsheet is a foreign language and GAAP accounting an exotic culture for many classroom teachers. Thus, the first obligation for CAOs is to advocate that this information be readily available on campus, and the second is to make sure that they are fluent in the language of budgets. It is only by having a developed set of skills themselves that CAOs can effectively translate and invite faculty into worthwhile conversations about resources.

Faculty members sometimes complain that administrators purposely complicate and obfuscate in order to preempt substantive questions and preclude meaningful input into financial matters. CAOs need to counter any such impulses forcefully—both in themselves and among their administrative peers, particularly university budget managers. At the same time, faculty members often significantly underestimate the time and skills needed to keep the fiscal and physical infrastructures of our institutions whole and functioning. They can cast administrative work as trivial or superfluous. CAOs need to counter this as well. Mutual respect for professional competency needs to flow in both directions between faculty and administrators—especially in difficult ongoing discussions about resources. CAOs are the linchpin in facilitating these dialogues.

When dealing with resources, transparency about information needs to be matched by transparency about process. The perception of secret "side deals" can significantly undermine faculty morale. When resources are limited to support certain activities such as travel, supplies, and research assistance, all faculty members should know the procedure for being considered. The actual process can vary considerably based on institutional mission and priorities, but everyone should have an equal opportunity to make a case. At the same time, resources are not always equally available to everyone. Some disciplines have much greater access to grant funding, and donors often restrict their contributions in unpredictable ways. The result, often, is that well-funded programs attract even more largesse and the underfunded remain so. While acknowledging this reality, CAOs can offer some counterweights by encouraging grant activity in new areas, by connecting professors with development officers who are seeking faculty partners to cultivate alumni donors, and by using discretionary dollars to bridge some of the gaps. The result will not be equality, since some programs will thrive and others will not regardless of funding, but CAOs can make sure that faculty with energy and ideas can find access to potential resources.

Routine budgetary processes benefit from transparency as well. My first introduction to a somewhat radical ideal of transparency came when I was a young department head and a change in endowment spending brought some new resources to support departmental budgets. Led by the then-CAO, department heads collectively reviewed departmental budgets together, came to understand each other's requirements, and ultimately made a recommendation to cut up the new pie, not evenly or even proportionately, but in ways that addressed critical needs. As CAO myself, I adopted this approach to annual budget making in both academic and administrative units regardless of whether the pot was growing, shrinking, or remaining the same size. The conversations are sometimes difficult, but they lead both to a shared understanding of why some budgets—science and music in our case—needed to be proportionately larger, and to an *esprit de corps* that fosters creative solutions and collaborations. I realize that CAOs at some larger universities might not find this approach scalable, but the key is finding ways to move faculty beyond departmental silos and to ask them to understand and share responsibility for the whole of the college or university.

A third area of transparency is in decision making. Once, when interviewing for an administrative position, I asked both administrators and faculty, "How do decisions get made here?" The almost universal response was: "Wow, what a good question!" followed by some tentative speculation and ending with an admission that it was not always clear. Such confusion is not surprising. Decision making, even at small colleges, can be very complex and subject to misunderstanding, unclear and dated spheres of responsibility, and needlessly complicated systems of governance. Nonetheless, CAOs should do what they can to bring greater clarity to decision making so that faculty time can be well spent, and so that resources move quickly and efficiently to where they are needed.

First, everyone needs to know at the start who makes which deci-sions. Ideally, CAOs should strive to move decision-making authority as close to those affected by it as possible. CAOs most often are responsi-ble for the delicate negotiations between faculty and business offices that keep resources flowing responsibly and appropriately. Second, the spe-cific parameters of a given decision need to be well defined. CAOs need to specify what they are asking for from the faculty: general advice, a recommendation, or a formal vote. While expectations are often clearer for routine decisions that are defined in shared governance policies, groups coming together around ad hoc issues benefit from written charges that define the constraints and outcomes. CAOs also need to be clear about which resources are on the table and which are not. Finally, CAOs should be able to tell faculty the timetable for a decision. Leaving faculty in limbo about resources they hope to have in order to perform at a high level is unfair. If there is a delay, this should be communicated in a timely fash-ion along with the new deadline.

Clearly transparency, process, and timely decisions need to go together. However, there are moments when they can work at cross purposes—when some information must remain confidential, when crisis or oppor-tunity requires bypassing existing processes, when a decision must be made or delayed with little time for explanation. Such moments, even when resulting in greater resources or positive outcomes, can be deeply disturbing to the faculty. Collegial culture depends on the integ-rity of both process and players. So violating these norms costs admin-istrators the most important social capital—trust—and reinforces the ste-reotypical capriciousness of administrators in general. However, in the end, these same individuals do have to act in the best interests of the institution even when that may not completely align with faculty proto-cols, but beware of how habit-forming it can be to have a convenient crisis to move a process along. Long-term institutional goals will be much better served when process and transparency are respected.

2. Convene candid conversations about salaries

Even inexperienced deans come to know that altruism alone is not enough to recruit and retain a high quality faculty. Rather, they need to assure that compensation at their college is competitive as well as equi-table. Indeed, it is better to have direct conversations about compensa-tion than to let it simmer for any length of time below the surface be-cause, as "numerous surveys of faculty have demonstrated over the years, compensation is closely interwoven with faculty morale."[23] While con-versations about individual compensation can be tied up in larger issues of performance, the provost or dean should be able to speak clearly and

Faculty Members Behaving Badly: Three Strategies

BY JEANINE SILVEIRA STEWART

Managing an academic program and members of the faculty within a tenure system requires Zen-like patience at times. It also requires the discipline to abide some benign quirkiness while aspiring to foster a healthy community. The admonition to "pick your battles" is apt, but it is too vague to serve as practical guidance for the CAO who must respond on the institution's behalf to faculty conduct issues ranging from misguided actions to serious misconduct. Patterns of bad behavior require fair and consistent management to permit the institution and its workforce to achieve their highest goals.

Three elements can aid in establishing a readiness tool-kit for managing misconduct consistently and effectively:

1. *Prepare to Engage Conflict.*

Regularly review both legal and institutional (policy-level) categories and definitions of misconduct and commit to consistency in engaging offenses. There are three broad categories of misconduct that may apply to faculty members:

- Sexual (acts committed without mutual consent or where consent cannot be freely given, as in the case of relationships with significant differences in maturity or social status/power)
- Academic (fraudulent or deceptive acts; sabotaging the professional work of others; acting to limit the freedom of others such as when placing individual ahead of community interests)
- Employee (violation of laws, institutional policies, or norms such as appropriate subordination within the leadership hierarchy)

Many behaviors that trigger the provost's involvement qualify as mildly offensive transgressions. Some common examples are as follows:

- Undermining and Power Plays
- Being Easily Offended—Portraying the Victim
- Elevating Self by Diminishing Others
- Berating—Intimidating—Defaming—Criticizing—Violating Policies (e.g., discrimination) or Social Norms (e.g., breach of confidentiality)
- Anger, Rage, Superiority
- Disregarding Professional Boundaries

Paradoxically, it is usually easier to confront egregious misconduct that rises to the level of a clear statutory breach. The lawyer is called, a team of internal talent is composed (e.g., HR, deans, general counsel, and safety officers), and the matter is resolved in accordance with relevant laws and institutional

(cont'd)

policy. These matters may be stressful and trying, but the college or university's standards are clear. The resolution of less egregious, grayer matters ("bad behavior") can be far more complex. These can require more nuanced judgment and are often accompanied by political risk since the provost must simultaneously serve the community's interests and hold in confidence the details of any personnel action. A critical challenge will be the development of a stable internal standard that can encourage consistent practice over time.

2. *Clearly Correlate to Mission.*

In responding to bad behavior, institutional mission and culture can guide the establishment of both the criteria for action and the method of intervention. It is both easy and tempting to avoid confrontations over conduct that has not yet violated the law or that may not have become disruptive to the entire college community. Yet an institutional community that must endure frequent episodes of bad behavior by professionals risks a threat to morale. In such scenarios, mission-focused employees feel helpless and self-serving employees feel empowered when institutional leaders fail to manage bad behavior in a timely and consistent way.

Published mission statements from a variety of higher educational institutions tend to share common themes such as quality and affordability, diversity and social justice, developing and applying ideas, and operating with integrity while supporting free inquiry. These themes set clear community standards for behavior, especially among the faculty and others who are fully vested in the governance function and overall longevity of the institution.

For example, a pattern of incivility in a department limits the productivity of co-workers and can ultimately increase the cost of operating and compromise efforts to achieve quality and affordability. For institutions where residence life is an important part of the educational program, building community is an implicit component of the mission and all must be held accountable for fostering the common good. In addition, linking conduct to mission will promote the perception that responses to bad behavior are seeded in the fundamental objectives and cultural values of the college or university.

3. *Lead Proactively.*

A proactive approach crucially depends upon expanding awareness of the types of bad behavior that can poison an academic community and, in turn, limit the success or freedom of its members over time. It is critical to expand community awareness of bad behavior by framing misconduct in terms of the harmful impact such behaviors have on all members of the community, such as isolation or intimidation or the loss of trust and community that results when others violate societal norms as evidenced in the chart below. It is also crucial that the actor in a bad behavior scenario understand the impact on his or her career and status.

Impact of Bad Behaviors

Isolating	Intimidating	Violating Norms
■ Rigid intolerance of difference	■ Cultural insensitivity	■ Lying
■ Scapegoating	■ Criticizing	■ Manipulating
■ Shunning	■ Anger & volatility	■ Breaching confidentiality
■ Excluding from governance roles	■ Threatening	■ Aggressively self-promoting
	■ Continually interrupting	■ Passive-aggression

When a faculty member's bad behavior is addressed successfully, two things should change: the behavior and the person exhibiting it. Opportunities for professional growth are lost entirely when bad behavior is ignored until it becomes egregious. Late-stage interventions are often dictated by legal language. The best chance to support the community and potentially to salvage an employee's career is by addressing negative conduct as soon as a pattern becomes evident.

Just as it can be challenging for any highly educated professional to accept critical feedback, it can also be difficult for any provost to learn that his or her initial assumptions about a pattern of bad behavior may have been flawed. Hold meetings with alleged bad actors as two-way conversations and be prepared to listen, to re-frame issues for enhanced mutual understanding, to discuss, and to follow up in writing as well as in person. Clear connections to institutional mission will facilitate these conversations.

Jeanine Stewart serves as provost and dean of faculty at McDaniel College in Maryland. She earned her Ph.D. in psychobiology at the University of Virginia. Stewart's expertise in positive organizational scholarship has been shared in numerous workshops and conference presentations addressing difficult campus workplace issues for the Council of Independent Colleges and other associations.

openly about where overall salaries at their institutions stand vis-à-vis an appropriate set of peers. In *The American Faculty*, Schuster and Finkelstein have observed that faculty salaries "vary systematically by institution type."[24] Higher to lower salary averages follow the prestige hierarchy, with faculty at doctoral-granting institutions earning the most and those at community colleges the least. This is not surprising to those who have worked in higher education for some years, but it can be remarkably shocking to new faculty emerging from doctoral programs and heading down the prestige ladder to their first job. While CAOs cannot single-handedly counter this market reality, they are responsible for helping faculty understand who their institutional peers are from the start of their employment.

University conversations to determine peer groups can be fraught, and a process that is data driven is preferable to one that relies on anecdote. The state of Virginia, as one example, has been using a system of applying cluster analysis to IPEDS data to determine national peer groups for faculty salary comparisons for all of its state institutions, from UVA to community colleges, for over thirty years: "The peer group process is composed of three phases: (1) data identification and collection, (2) statistical modeling, and (3) institutional meetings. The first two phases are quantitative in nature. The third phase is to select peers and allow institutions to present their particular interest and focus, something that the statistical modeling is not able to adequately address."[25] Susquehanna University employs a variation on this methodology, using an approach that shifts the conversation from a debate about the merits of other institutions toward a discussion more appropriately focused on Susquehanna's own institutional characteristics and priorities. Once agreement is reached on variables and weights to be used in the cluster analysis, the list that emerges is not easily "cherry-picked" by either faculty or administrators. While institutions may use a variety of approaches for determining a peer group for benchmarking faculty salaries, the academic vice president needs to be able to stand behind the validity and integrity of the benchmark group and be able to articulate this to faculty colleagues.

In addition to external benchmarking, issues of internal salary equity need to be of concern to CAOs. As Schuster and Finkelstein note: "Women faculty continue to earn lower salaries than male faculty"—a situation that has improved little over the last thirty years.[26] Academe's gender gap (female $.80/male $1) is somewhat less than that of society at large ($.77) and is complicated by rank, length of service, and field of specialization.[27] Nonetheless, deans need to understand when and where such inequities exist in their own institutions and work toward resolving them.

Another source of internal inequity arises from the growing differentials in salary by academic discipline. Again, Schuster and Finkelstein comment: "A large and accelerating divergence among disciplines has emerged that, in the main, places primarily academic-based fields (most notably in the humanities) at a disadvantage relative to some fields that are primarily anchored in the broader economy."[28] A more recent study found that 75 percent of elite liberal arts colleges that traditionally have had equal pay policies have begun to differentiate pay by discipline at the entry level.[29] The market reality is now such that if a college or university

---

The Single Most Important Piece of Advice for a New Provost on the First Day in the Position

---

■ Pace yourself. Your job will be a marathon, not a sprint. Slow changes that stick are better than fast ones that do not.

---

maintains an accredited business school, engineering program, nursing degree, or education certification, it will need to offer higher compensation to attract faculty in those fields. Neither CAOs nor CFOs can change this reality nor should they obfuscate about it, but they can address some of the consequences in ways that promote equity and collegiality.

The need for a market differential is greatest at the entry level, and entry-level salary has a significant impact on lifetime earnings. Thus, CAOs should find ways to ameliorate this difference over time, possibly via promotion adjustments that bring all members of a particular rank to a minimum level, for example. In benchmarking faculty salaries, it may be appropriate to conduct occasional checks by discipline to make sure that higher salaries in some areas are not skewing the overall average in ways that hide disciplinary pockets that may be lagging behind.[30]

3. Address the part-time faculty conundrum

The authors of *The American Faculty* dedicate an entire chapter to what they call "the sweeping reconfiguration of academic appointments."[31] This includes both expansion in the use of part-time faculty and the significant increase in full-time appointments off the tenure track. While actual deployment varies considerably from institution to institution, this phenomenon challenges institutions in all categories. As of this writing, non-tenurable positions outnumber the tenured/tenurable by some estimates as much as three to one, and the majority of new full-time faculty appointments are made off the tenure track.[32]

The use of adjunct faculty continues to be a subject of great concern for academic administrators. Low pay, insecurity, and a poor work environment is the norm for this group, according to recent studies that also document a large number of part-time faculty harboring frustrated aspirations for full-time academic employment.[33] Other studies, however, complicate this picture by demonstrating that a majority of part-time faculty prefer part-time appointments, opting for flexibility and limited responsibility because they have other employment outside the academy, are retired, or are balancing other familial/non-employment obligations.[34]

This contrast is indicative, perhaps, of the distinction between a more traditional use of part-timers in professional fields such as the arts in which practitioners offer courses providing students a "real world" perspective, and the more troubling practice of outsourcing lower division core courses in the humanities to otherwise unemployed PhDs.

The growth in full-time appointments off the tenure track has led researchers such as Schuster and Finkelstein to view this as the new and growing practice most likely to transform the academy—if it has not already done so.[35] The concerns raised here include the creation of a lower tier, nonprofessional class of academic workers with significantly less security and little to no assurance of academic freedom. Adrianna Kezar and Cecile Sam provide a comprehensive overview of the situation in "Understanding the New Majority of Non-Tenure-Track Faculty in Higher Education: Demographics, Experiences, and Plans of Action." This ASHE report summarizes existing research, highlights the complexity of institutional realities, and offers practical advice for academic administrators and non-tenure-track faculty themselves to move toward better, more equitable practices. One of their most salient observations regards the lack of intentionality that has brought us to the current situation: "Instead of incorporating non-tenure-track faculty in thoughtful, meaningful ways that look toward the institutions' long-term goals, colleges and universities seem to take a reactive approach to non-tenure-track faculty—responding to immediate demands and fluctuations."[36] Provosts may not be able to reverse the trend of employing greater numbers of faculty members off the tenure track (and in some cases, may not want to); however, at the very least, they should guarantee that part-time and non-tenure-track professors are deployed at their institutions in ways that are intentional and mission driven and that these employees are supported, compensated, and integrated into the faculty appropriately.

A first step would be for CAOs to assess the status of non-tenure-track appointments on their own campuses. When, where, how, and to what extent are such appointments being made? Kezar and Sam recommend developing an academic staffing plan that includes a determination of "what the appropriate ratio is of tenure-track to non-tenure-track faculty, full time and part time, and in what areas these faculty should be deployed."[37] The "right" mix will likely vary considerably by institution, but it should be able to be articulated in ways that are consistent with mission and current priorities. Intentionality should also mark the terms of employment for all faculty members, with careful thought given to hiring processes, renewal cycles, and annual evaluation. For example, one institution without a tenure system, Antioch University, recently worked through a comprehensive articulation of common faculty em-

Lessons Learned: The CAO and the Faculty

BY ROY AUSTENSEN

1. *The Pace of Technological Change.* The pace at which new devices such as smart phones and iPads as well as social media have developed has gotten well ahead of the ability of most faculty members to make effective use of them. Thus, there is often now a disjuncture between the actual availability of information technology at many institutions and the need for it in academic planning. Curriculum development can sometimes get way ahead of the availability of the information resources to support it.

2. *The Erosion of Traditional Faculty.* Some of the fundamental tasks of the CAO such as hiring for mission, faculty development, new faculty orientation, and faculty engagement in strategic planning and budgeting are made far more difficult, if not impossible, because of a growing dependence on adjunct faculty positions. The "faculty career" as we have known it is in danger of disappearing.

3. *Increased Globalization.* The increasing globalization of college classrooms in the United States has created pedagogical challenges for professors not accustomed to different learning styles and insufficient mastery of English in an internationally diverse student body.

4. *Expanding Anti-Intellectualism.* The anti-intellectual bias of our time has become so strong that many politicians find it useful for securing votes and achieving other agendas at the expense of higher education. Sometimes provosts do not realize that they can do more to encourage and enable members of the faculty to communicate with general audiences and especially with opinion leaders in the community.

5. *Lack of Affordability.* This may be the biggest challenge of all. Too many chief academic officers have failed to realize that they need to play a more forceful role in transforming higher education into a more financially sustainable enterprise. Perhaps because of this, fear persists about a growing adoption of the for-profit model, i.e., the development of a standardized curriculum that can be delivered with no variation to large numbers of students via the Internet.

Roy Austensen wrote the chapter on effective relationships between the CAO and the faculty in First Among Equals: The Role of the Chief Academic Officer *(1997). After serving as provost and vice president for academic affairs at Valparaiso University from 1992–2009, Austensen continues to teach there as professor of history.*

ployment policies across a multi-campus institution in ways that endeavored to balance both shared traditions and regional variations.[38]

The American Association of University Professors has also offered a variety of provocative proposals for the integration of non-tenure-track faculty into the academy with the recommendation in 2010 "that all long-term college teachers be granted tenure at the percentage appointments they currently have"[39] and the proposition currently released for comment that all faculty members be given a vote in institutional governance regardless of employment status.[40] It seems unlikely that either idea will become the norm, but both are useful in defining one end of a spectrum of possibility. CAOs need to take the lead in determining how non-tenured colleagues can be effectively included in campus life and in making sure that all teachers, regardless of employment status, are accorded professional respect. Kezar and Sam have observed that "campuses that institutionalize better policies and practices for non-tenure-track faculty started by communicating the message that non-tenure-track faculty are valued and respected."[41] Toward this end, the dean or provost needs to function as the chief academic officer not just of tenured and tenure-track faculty, but of *all* faculty.

Conclusion: Deeply Trust the Best Intentions of Faculty

I began this essay with the question, "Whose side are you on?" to illustrate the position of the CAO at the juncture of the faculty and administration, and I hope I have demonstrated that in the end the question of "sides" is ultimately unproductive. CAOs need to help their campuses move beyond reflexive divisions and toward more effective cooperation based on mutual trust and professional respect. Clearly, this is easier said than done. Faculty members consistently cite experiences in which they feel their trust in one another was misplaced. This is why, as Dave Porter argues, trust needs to be both extended and modeled from the top down:

> "Integrity first" requires that what is proclaimed publicly be consistent with what is whispered privately in the multitude of micro-meetings that characterize academic administration. Even impeccable integrity and complete trustworthiness, however, are not enough. . . . Those in positions of leadership must be willing to convey trust in others. Micromanagement and manipulation are simply not effective long-term strategies for influencing faculty members. Faculty . . . know when they are trusted and respected and when they are not. The failure to convey trust in others will impede the development of trust in the organization regardless of the integrity or good intentions of those in charge.[42]

"Deeply trust the best intentions of faculty," says Lourien Alexandre, Vice Chancellor of Academic Affairs at Antioch University.[43] Trust is built in the day-to-day interactions between the faculty and their senior academic officer as well as in the processes that surround personnel management and resource allocation. It is also built in those conversations in which faculty professionalism is recognized, faculty concern for students is assumed, and faculty commitment to the institution is unquestioned. Trust is earned through transparency, and it is repaired when CAOs take responsibility for what goes wrong—even if it is not their fault—by apologizing, fixing the problem, and moving on.

"Faculty are production; we're overhead," a CFO colleague once told me. It is important for all administrators, and especially CAOs, to remember this. Administrators create the infrastructure that supports and enables the essential work of the faculty in the academy. Without the faculty, this infrastructure has no purpose or meaning. As useful proof of this, CAOs should teach a course every year or two. This keeps us in touch with "production" and reminds us why we entered higher education in the first place: our passion for a discipline and the joy and challenges of trying to share that passion with students in effective ways.

NOTES

1. I have argued elsewhere that faculty and administrators do live in very distinct and separate worlds. See Linda McMillin, "Through the Looking Glass: Faculty to Administration," *Chronicle of Higher Education,* 21 October 2011, A104.

2. This refers to a Carnegie classification that no longer exists and yet continues to have valence within the academy. For more on the ways classification and rankings shape institutional ambitions, see Alexander McCormick, "The Complex Interplay between Classification and Ranking of Colleges and Universities: Should the Berlin Principles Apply Equally to Classification?" *Higher Education in Europe* 33, no. 2/3 (2008): 209–18, esp. 209–14.

3. Uma M. Jayakumar, Tyrone C. Howard, and Walter R. Allen, "Racial Privilege in the Professoriate: An Exploration of Campus Climate, Retention, and Satisfaction," *Journal of Higher Education* 80, no. 5 (2009): 538.

4. Ibid., 541.

5. See Pauline E. Keynes, "New Paradigms for Diversifying Faculty and Staff in Higher Education: Uncovering Cultural Biases in the Search and Hiring Process," *Multicultural Education* 14, no. 2 (2006): 65–69.

6. Caroline Turner, Viernes Sotello, Samuel L. Myers Jr., and John W. Creswell, "Exploring Underrepresentation: The Case of Faculty of Color in the Midwest," *Journal of Higher Education* 70, no. 1 (1999): 56.

7. Cathy Trower, "A New Generation of Faculty: Similar Core Values in a Different World," *Peer Review,* Summer 2010, 28. See also Tracy Collins, Scott Slough, and Hersch Waxman, "Lessons Learned about Mentoring Junior Faculty in Higher Education," *Academic Leadership* 7, no. 2 (2009): 1.

8. Joel Cunningham, then president of Susquehanna University, said this to me in my first tenure evaluation discussion as a new department head circa 1995, and it has stuck with me ever since.

9. For more on the project, see Linda McMillin and William G. Berberet, *A New Academic Compact* (Boston: Stylus Press, 2002).

10. James Fairweather, *Faculty Work and the Public Trust: Restoring the Value of Teaching and Public Service in American Academic Life* (Boston: Allyn and Bacon, 1996), 67.

11. James S. Fairweather, "Beyond the Rhetoric: Trends in the Relative Value of Teaching and Research in Faculty Salaries," *Journal of Higher Education* 76, no. 4 (2005): 401–22.

12. Trower, "New Generation," 28.

13. Jack Schuster and Martin Finkelstein, *The American Faculty* (Baltimore: Johns Hopkins University Press, 2006), 79.

14. R. Eugene Rice, "Future of the Scholarly Work of Faculty," in *Faculty Priorities Reconsidered,* ed. KerryAnn O'Meara and R. Eugene Rice (San Francisco: Jossey-Bass, 2005), 310.

15. Ibid., 308.

16. Mary Burgan, *What Ever Happened to the Faculty?* (Baltimore: Johns Hopkins University Press, 2006), xiv.

17. Judith M. Gappa, Ann E. Austin, and Andrea G. Trice, *Rethinking Faculty Work* (San Francisco: Jossey-Bass, 2007).

18. Trower, "New Generation," 27.

19. Anne-Marie Slaughter, "Why Women Still Can't Have it All," *Atlantic Monthly* (July/August 2012): 98.

20. Robin Wilson, "Why Are Associate Professors So Unhappy?" *Chronicle of Higher Education,* 3 June 2012, http://chronicle.com/article/Why-Are-Associate-Professors/132071/?sid=at&utm_source=at&utm_medium=en.

21. Stanley Katz, "Beyond Crude Measurement and Consumerism," *Academe* 96, no. 5 (2010): http://www.aaup.org/AAUP/pubsres/academe/2010/SO/feat/katz.htm.

22. Pat Hutchings, *Opening Doors to Faculty Involvement in Assessment* (National Institute for Learning Outcomes Assessment, 2010), 13.

23. Schuster and Finkelstein, *American Faculty,* 234.

24. Ibid., 249.

25. State Council of Higher Education for Virginia, "Council Agenda Item 10," *Agenda Book,* 10 July 2007, C24, http://www.schev.edu/SCHEV/AgendaBooks/AgendaBookJuly07/AgendaBookJuly07.pdf.

26. Schuster and Finkelstein, *American Faculty,* 283.

27. Ibid., 255.

28. Ibid., 283.

29. Paul Marthers and Jeff Parker, "Small Colleges and New Faculty Pay," *Academe* 94, no. 4 (2008): 45–49.

30. The College and University Professional Association for Human Resources (CUPA-HR), which collects institutional data by department, can be useful here. See "Who We Are," *The College and University Professional Association for Human Resources,* 2013, http://www.cupahr.org/about/index.aspx.

31. Schuster and Finkelstein, *American Faculty,* 191–92.

32. Ibid., 195.

33. Coalition on the Academic Workforce, *A Portrait of Part-time Faculty Members,* June 2012, http://www.academicworkforce.org/CAW_portrait_2012.pdf.

34. James Monk, "Who Are the Part-time Faculty?" *Academe* 95, no. 4 (2007): 33–37.

35. Schuster and Finkelstein, *American Faculty,* 195.

36. Adrianna Kazar and Cecile Sam, "Understanding the New Majority of Non-Tenure-Track Faculty in Higher Education: Demographics, Experiences, and Plans of Action," *ASHE Higher Education Report* 36, no. 4 (2010): 78.

37. Ibid., 100.

38. Antioch University, "Faculty Employment at the University," Antioch University Repository and Archive, http://aura.antioch.edu/policies_500_3x/.

39. Cary Nelson, "Reforming Faculty Identity," *Academe* 97, no. 4 (2011): 56.

40. American Association of University Professors, "New Report on Contingent Faculty and Governance," 2013, http://www.aaup.org/AAUP/newsroom/2012web highlight/congovreport.htm.

41. Kazar and Sam, "Understanding the New Majority," 86.

42. Dave Porter, "Assessment as a Subversive Activity," *AAUP Journal of Academic Freedom* 3 (2012), 15.

43. Lourien Alexandre, Vice Chancellor of Academic Affairs, Antioch University, phone conversation, May 10, 2012.

CHAPTER SIX

The CAO as Planner: Strategic Planning and the Office of Institutional Research

John D. Simon

One of the most important roles for the CAO is leading the academic community in envisioning what it needs to be, in shepherding the energy and ideas generated into a meaningful strategic plan, and then in implementing the strategies. But how is this accomplished? Colleges and universities include many constituencies that want, if not demand, to contribute to academic plans, including faculty, students, alumni, governing boards, granting agencies, and state legislatures. Often each group has its own priorities, and it is the job of the CAO to bring together these sometimes disparate visions into a coherent and focused strategy to advance the quality of academic activities. Success requires understanding and envisioning what the institution needs to be in the future and then leading a robust and engaging process that generates sufficient buy-in from these various communities so that the objectives of the strategic plan can be achieved. Unfortunately, a strategic plan can consume up to two years to complete, involving endless hours of meetings, assessments of current programs, SWOT (strengths, weaknesses, opportunities, and threats) analyses, spreadsheets of potential funding scenarios, and Power-Point presentations for faculty, alumni, and governing boards. Then, following affirmative votes of faculty committees and boards, the ultimate outcome is simply a large binder that sits on various office shelves, is rarely consulted, and does not serve as the roadmap for the future that it was intended to be.

In designing a strategic plan, we often focus on the following objectives:

- Identify core areas critical to the academic strength and reputation of your university.

- Identify opportunities for developing a comparative advantage.

- Identify resources—existing and new—to realize a compelling vision.

- Identify opportunities to make the institution more than the sum of its parts.

- Identify the right time frame(s) for implementing strategies—long enough to allow for success through sustained investment, but short enough so that there is accountability.

These are broad objectives that must, in the end, arrive at an institutional vision for the future incorporating a set of more focused strategies to start moving the institution in desired directions. Yet the devil is in the details. Let us consider some of the reasons why strategic plans fail. An understanding of some of the forces in play will help the CAO understand why the tools presented later in this chapter can help avoid common pitfalls and lead to the identification and implementation of successful strategies.

First, because of the large time commitment necessary for creating institutional strategic plans, there is a strong desire to get it right the first time. I would argue that we actually have a fear of getting it wrong, of failing in the job, of looking stupid—or even worse, of wasting faculty time. Second, CAOs find themselves caught in the middle of an often political struggle between defending the values and programs at the institution today and the expectation that strategic plans will demonstrate innovative thinking and big aspirations that propose significant institutional change. This tension can lead to unintended outcomes of seeking and proposing strategies that are the "least bad" options rather than taking the time and the risk to work toward the best possible solution. Third, the forces outlined above often combine in a way that if we are not careful can focus on seeking answers to the wrong questions and diverting our attention from the real issues we need to be discussing.

Finally, in trying to balance the demands from various constituencies and still appear as thoughtful and decisive leaders, provosts affirm some of the behaviors that inhibit real change in academic institutions: impatience for results, discomfort with ambiguity, and fear of taking on questions in areas that are largely unknown. It is simply human nature to seek to focus on well-defined and answerable questions, to gravitate to certainty, to feel comfortable with repeatable and reliable data that the office of institutional research can provide, but this will not lead to the best strategic plan and can hinder colleges and universities from innovating. The remainder of this chapter is not a specific "how to" manual, since strategic planning at any institution must be done respecting the culture of that institution. Instead, four major guideposts are offered to help CAOs avoid the common traps that lead to planning failures and binders that become dust collectors.

Guidepost #1: Take the Time to Understand

A provost should begin this process by posing two questions:

- How well do you know your institution?

- How well do you understand your peer institutions and the external environmental factors that affect planning?

The answers to these question depend on how long you have been at this institution, how well you understand the landscape of higher education, and what experiences you have had prior to becoming CAO. A large number of deans and provosts have served as a department chair and held positions of responsibility within a single school. These narrower administrative experiences may not afford the opportunity to understand the wide range of activities occurring at a university and the external factors that can and will impact the institution. CAOs promoted from within often have an advantage because they understand the culture of the institution. Conversely, a desire for institutional change can lead to an external hire who brings new ideas and experiences to the institution—and a steep learning curve for the CAO.

Successful strategic planning requires a deep understanding of one's institution and a strong, trusting relationship between the CAO and the Office of Institutional Research. Here self-analysis occurs and one needs to choose carefully what data is followed and how it is used. Whether by our own devices or by the requirements of accreditation agencies, magazine rankings, and governance boards, most institutions compile a large array of numerical information. Recent tensions over faculty productivity have given rise to new businesses designed to aggregate information about academic institutions and provide new methodologies for thinking about how we evaluate institutional effectiveness. While accurate data is important, it is also important to remember that any calculation is true only to the extent to which its assumptions actually mirror reality. The CAO, in partnership with the Office of Institutional Research, must be committed to conducting meaningful assessments rather than just running analyses using historical data.

The job of the CAO early in a strategic planning process also includes creating the time for candid campus conversations, framing key questions for the community, and probing for unarticulated needs so that implementation plans are well informed. Furthermore, the CAO should constantly ask whether the efforts being undertaken are aimed at solving the right problems. This is an excellent setting to introduce the concepts behind design thinking. In her book, *Solving Problems with Design Thinking,* Jeanne Liedtke describes this approach: "It (design thinking) emphasizes the importance of discovery in advance of solution generation, using market research approaches that are empathetic and user-driven. It expands the boundaries of both our problem definitions and our solutions. It is enthusiastic about engaging partners in co-creation. It is committed to conducting real-world experiments rather than just running analyses using historical data."[1] These guidelines are an ideal backdrop for the brainstorming phase of strategic planning, and by allowing sufficient time for conversations, the CAO will raise the odds that the right questions are asked and the best set of strategies identified. A caution: The view from the top of the central administration is often obstructed. Well-intentioned ideas based on superficial knowledge of what goes on in schools and departments can produce unintended consequences that create more problems. This is why it is so important to engage constituencies across the institution in the co-creation of early roadmaps and later implementation plans.

Guidepost #2: Think Opposable not Oppositional

CAOs should frame this segment with the following questions:

- Do your stakeholders envision new possibilities together, or are they wedded to their individual viewpoints?

- Do you build teams of like-minded people, or do you embrace diversity of thought?

Now that it is clear that the CAO needs to take the time to encourage campus conversations, such conversations need to be productive and forward-looking. Yet, sometimes when institutional stakeholders listen to each other, they do not try to understand each other's perspectives and build on them. Instead, they listen for weaknesses in the arguments and use those to bolster their own points of view. F. Scott Fitzgerald said, "The test of a first-rate intelligence is the ability to hold two opposed ideas in the mind at the same time and still retain the ability to function." This ability enables one to think of new solutions and new ways of thinking that integrate the best from opposing points of view. In his book, *The Opposable Mind: Winning Through Integrative Thinking,* Roger Martin explains that the ultimate goal is not to compromise but to use tension to spur creativity.[2] Not only will this lead to better solutions, but it can also serve as a check on whether the right questions are being raised. The best outcome of integrative thinking is that people's perceptions, conversations, and even ways of thinking, can be changed.

As an example of integrative thinking, consider the University of Virginia's new degree program MS in Data Science. This program engages faculty from computer science, system engineering, and statistics in creation of a core curriculum that is integrated across courses, with several large, complex data sets woven across courses to increase program cohesion. The challenge was to identify the home unit of the degree program that could foster the partnership and support the innovative structure of the curriculum. The partnering departments are located in the College of Arts & Science and Engineering, and each school operates its own administrative infrastructure for professional degree programs. While the CAO could place the degree program within either school, a single association would not support the innovative nature of the program offering. After much consultation with faculty groups, the decision was made to create the university's first school-wide data science institute and offer the degree through that institute. This broke new ground at the University of Virginia and is the first degree program to be offered outside of an individual school. The new structure enables the interdisciplinary nature of the program to thrive and supports the necessary partnerships between schools required for the program to be a success.

Guidepost #3: Making Small Bets and Learning Fast Is a Great Strategy for Innovation

CAOs should address these two questions:

- Should your strategic plan be built upon bold, innovative initiatives?

- Are you able to revisit or revise strategies once a plan is approved?

Most CAOs are aware of the increasing questioning by the public about the value of a college or university education. This has resulted in both unstable support and greater efforts to establish mechanisms of accountability. CAOs must now undertake complex and human resource-costly planning processes against a backdrop of these challenges:

- Concerns over tuition and student debt

- Changing patterns in federal research funding

- Keener competition for faculty, students, and financial resources

- Changing definitions and methods of teaching and learning

- Rapidly evolving means of information access and learning spaces

- Heightened expectations by undergraduates and their families for personal services and co-curricular programs

- The competitive, adaptable world of on-line education

- The rise of global institutions

These forces have caused a growing demand to develop strategic plans that present bold, innovative approaches to change colleges and universities in ways that address these major issues. Still, provosts learn that while bold aspirations and broad predictions often sound visionary, they generally do not materialize. In fact, they can hinder innovation in higher education because the roadmaps for implementing such changes are often difficult to establish and act upon.

Strategic plans sometimes fail because they over-focus on where the university is at one point in time rather than articulating a living strategy to guide forward movement. Cynthia Montgomery, in her book *The Strategist*, explains, "Strategy—the system of value creation that underlies an 'organization's' competitive position and uniqueness—has to be embraced as something open, not something closed. It is a system that evolves, moves, and changes."[3] It is this construct—the development of a living strategic plan—that must sit at the core of how a provost or dean conceptualizes and operationalizes moving forward as a strategic thinker. The best discussion of how to do this that I have seen is presented in a book entitled *Little Bets* by Peter Sims. The basic premise is learning by doing and, if one does fail in implementing a strategy or choosing the wrong strategy, failing quickly so you can learn fast. Sims conceptualizes the process of "strategy" in four words: *immerse, define, reorient, iterate. Immerse* is defined as taking the time to understand your institution and gather fresh ideas and insights; only through this process can one understand deeper human motivations and desires and absorb how things work from the ground up. The *define* step calls a planner to use insights gathered to formulate specific problems and needs before solving them. As the process continues in complexity, it is important to be flexible in pursuit of larger goals and aspirations—to have an ability to *reorient*. Making use of small "wins" to make necessary pivots and chart a changing course to completion can be more productive for the institution than the more familiar technique of focusing on the end stage at the outset. As the institution moves forward, the external context will change, and the planning team needs to be able to *iterate*, that is, to refine and test aspirations equipped with better insights and information.

Guidepost #4: Change Management Is Not Change Leadership

In the fourth phase, two final questions are necessary:

- Can you envision the end state that you want to achieve through strategic planning?

- Do you elicit support for initiatives at all levels of the institution or only by your direct reports?

Planners who have taken the time to develop an understanding of their institution should now be ready to visualize the end state they want to achieve. Most importantly, they are now in a position to articulate the goals and aspirations that will serve as the foundation of a successful strategic plan. Quite often these goals and aspirations necessitate change. It is then the job of CAO to help the college or university's constituencies envision how they can realize these goals and aspirations, to co-develop with those constituencies the roadmap(s) for implementation, and to own the responsibility for making it happen. Often, this is called an exercise in change management, but actually the role of the CAO is one of change leadership. The difference is a critical distinction.

In carrying out aspects of the strategic planning process, the CAO and the various groups engaged in planning draw on a set of tools to help structure the planning process itself. These tools are intended to keep the change effort under control, and they include a schedule of regular meetings and charts to depict visually the timing of strategies and their anticipated implementation schedule, and lists of metrics and associated responsibilities for data collection. At this juncture, an effective relationship with, and timely responses from, the Office of Institutional Research can make a significant difference in the quality of strategic decision making. Perhaps a "change management office" or a "strategic implementation officer" will be appointed to coordinate these activities, but it should be noted that these tools are the management of the desired changes, not the leadership of change.

Change leadership, which is the job of the CAO, focuses on the vision and processes that enable an institution to change its mission and methods of operation. There are several ingredients in change leadership, and the CAO should use these to frame the management process:

- Develop proponents throughout the organization and make sure there is buy-in from key members of each stakeholder group, including faculty, students, alumni, and board members

- Realize that change needs to cascade throughout the organization

- Take the time to make the case; in the words of John Morley, "You have not converted a man because you have silenced him."[4]

- Create ownership—the CAO cannot possibly do it all

- Develop a communication strategy that motivates the desired change and stay on message

- Assess the cultural landscape and the institution's capacity for change.

In an article entitled, "Lesson on Leadership: It's Not about You. (It's about Them)," a professor of public leadership at Harvard's Kennedy School of Government observed, "The dominant view of leadership is that the leader has the vision and the rest is a sales problem. . . . I think that notion of leadership is bankrupt. That approach only works for technical problems where there's a right answer and an expert knows what it is."[5] In academic institutions, strategic planning is not a technical problem, and the CAO is not the expert with the wisdom and knowledge to make all decisions for the community. Rather, the challenge for a provost is to engage the institution's constituencies with the core issues and problems they face and help them develop their own solutions.

To put a sharper focus on this approach, I draw upon two goals that are currently central to achieving the strategic plan at the University of Virginia: changing the budgetary system from central control to responsibility-centered management, and engaging medical school faculty in undergraduate teaching. While the institutional advantages of both

The Ingredients in Change Leadership

- Develop proponents throughout the organization, making sure there is buy-in from key members of each stakeholder group—faculty, students, alumni, board members.
- Realize that change needs to cascade throughout the organization.
- Take the time to make the case; in the words of John Morley, "You have not converted a man because you have silenced him" (*On Compromise*, 1874).
- Create ownership—the CAO cannot possibly do it all.
- Develop a communication strategy that motivates the desired change and stay on message.
- Assess the cultural landscape and the institution's capacity for change.

are easy to articulate, their implementation exemplifies the need for change leadership and not simply change management. It is not appropriate for the president, provost, and CAO to decide that the institution will have a new budgetary model. For this to work, the reasons for the change must be embraced deep within the university's structure so that those who gather and prepare budgetary information in various schools, programs, and support services all understand why the university has implemented such a change and so they can embrace the incentives the new structure has to offer. For this to occur, a clear explanation of what the new budget model enables and how it increases support for strategic priorities and competitiveness must be consistently articulated by those in leadership positions. It is not enough for the provost and deans in the College and School of Medicine to advocate that scientists in medicine teach undergraduate courses and incorporate their research knowledge into the undergraduate experience. The departments that this will affect, including biology, chemistry, and statistics, must also see value in this partnership and not view it as threatening their hiring plans or as a takeover of college science teaching by medical faculty. Finally, it is the job of the CAO to lead others to understand why it is in a university's or college's best interest to accomplish these changes with them as participants in helping the institution achieve its strategic aspirations.

Conclusion: Plans Are Choices

In higher education, strategic planning cannot occur or be sustained without support and trust between the various constituency groups, most importantly, the faculty, administration, and governance bodies. Also, as we have noted previously, if the provost does not oversee a responsive and innovative Office of Institutional Research, a price will paid in developing the right metrics for evaluating meaningful success. Yet beyond metrics and data analysis, success will be based in how well the CAO achieves engagement, alignment, and commitment among stakeholders while setting boundaries and focus. The CAO has the responsibility to set and articulate the standard of excellence, even though a clear definition of excellence as well as an effective plan to sustain it seem elusive on some campuses. Recently, at the University of Virginia, I asked all eleven deans to prepare a short definition of excellence. While many responses were thoughtful, one stood out: "I would say excellence is enabling young men and women to realize their full potential as human beings, possessed of the knowledge, skills, and qualities of mind that have long characterized the educated person. In a university with graduate schools, as distinct from a college, it also means excellence in preparing students for the professions, including the academy itself. For UVA, it means becoming engaged and responsible citizens or civic leaders." I liked this definition because it affirms our focus and calls for strategies aimed at the people we educate and the programs they are enrolled in. The role of the CAO in setting aspirations for excellence and the institutional strategies to attain it must maintain a balance between change leadership in response to external forces and the advocacy of core institutional values. Aristotle said, "Excellence is never an accident. It is always the result of high intention, sincere effort, and intelligent execution; it represents the wise choice of many alternatives. Choice, not chance, determines your destiny." This rings true for colleges and universities as well as for their CAOs. Excellence in planning must entail high intention, sincere effort, intelligent execution, and wise choices.

NOTES

1. Jeanne Liedtke, Andrew King, and Kevin Bennett, *Solving Problems with Design Thinking* (New York: Columbia Business School Press, 2013), 2.

2. Roger Martin, *The Opposable Mind: Winning Through Integrative Thinking* (Cambridge: Harvard Business School Press, 2007).

3. Cynthia Montgomery, *The Strategist* (New York: Harper Collins, 2012), 4.

4. John Morley, *On Compromise* (1874), Project Gutenberg, March 2004, http://www.gutenberg.org/ebooks/11557.

5. Shankar Vedantam, "Lessons in Leadership: It's Not about You. (It's about Them)," *NPR* (11 November 2013): http://www.npr.org/2013/11/11/230841224 /lessons-in-leadership-its-not-about-you-its-about-them.

CHAPTER SEVEN

Difficult Change in the Provost's Domain in Curriculum, Faculty Appointments, and Teaching Strategies

Robert M. Groves

The job of a provost or chief academic officer requires listening and reflection in all its aspects. The shared governance among faculty and administrators of universities makes many of the business books on organizational leadership and strategic planning from the private sector seem somewhat naïve. Many of the lessons of large, well-established organizations do apply, however, when discussions of interdisciplinary and multidisciplinary initiatives arise. Just as automobile manufacturers struggled with the integration of design and engineering in earlier decades, almost every provost sees opportunities untaken in potential collaboration across schools, departments, and disciplines. Furthermore, the increasing value of interdisciplinary work is becoming obvious at the same time that other forces on higher education and new tools of pedagogy demand attention to new ways of doing things.

This discussion is a collection of thoughts on interdisciplinarity and the importation of new teaching techniques.

Between the Disciplines

Within a university, disciplines like mathematics, sociology, physics, and computer science are organizations of concepts, frameworks or theories, methods, and members. The disciplines are generally organized around a set of key questions or issues large enough in scope that they can never be fully explored. "How did the universe begin?" ask some physicists. How groups of people shape the nature of societies is the meat of sociology and anthropology. "How does an author use words to convey his/her intended meaning; what properties of text lead to multiple possible meanings?" asks the literary critic. And on and on . . .

90

The value of a discipline is that it maintains the focus of attention of its scholars; it tracks progress and change in the set of answers to key questions and approaches to addressing them. It creates evaluative processes of what is admired in the discipline through rankings of journals, awards for scholarship, and professional reviews. It coordinates the curriculum of educational activities to transmit knowledge of the field from one generation to the next.

As disciplines evolve, they sometimes spawn new fields, as in physics and mathematics offering key components of engineering. In some sense, new fields arise from fissures between two separate fields as they "rub up against one another." When the knowledge of one field confronts the knowledge of another, explosions of human creativity sometimes result.

This is especially obvious now in a simple scan of problems and progress in the world. For example, the impact of urbanization and population growth on nonhuman species is well documented from a biological and environmental science perspective but has not motivated strong collective action. Why? Genes have importance to human outcomes, but the environment appears to impact genes in complicated ways. How does that happen exactly? The process that moves human thoughts to behavioral intentions to action seems to be a complex mix of brain science and psychology. How does that work?

Many of these unanswered questions are not legitimized as central to the core of any one field in a traditional university. Their import for the world's future, however, looms large.

So one of the jobs of a modern university is to give permission for scholars to investigate issues on the edges of fields. This type of work is organized precisely opposite from the way that universities are organized. Instead of questions being legitimized by an existing unit, the questions often arise from unasked questions in a field. Instead of the discipline guiding a scholar to a body of knowledge on which to base his or her original research, the researcher must ferret out research on his/her own, searching literature that is foreign to his/her home field.

Single disciplines build great assurance of the continued relevance and importance of the key questions facing the field; they have a history of meaningful answers. In contrast, the "hit rate" of new interdisciplinary fields is lower; hence, while universities must encourage the combinations of fields, they must also know that some combinations will not be sustainable as offering broad and deep new knowledge to society. Interdisciplinary fields need questions of quasi-permanent status to justify their ongoing relevance.

What's a provost to do? Encourage cross-disciplinary fertilization. I've offered to help sponsor and support a brown-bag seminar series of interdisciplinary groups and thereby let multiple faculty assess on their own whether disparate fields' approaches can be combined for novel answers to old questions. When multiple faculty members attract students to these interchanges who want to learn these new approaches, we should support new courses to convey them, hopefully team-taught.

But more needs to be done. The university should foster an environment in which the faculty can easily collaborate on new scholarship and research. The university should support promotion review processes that fairly judge the scholarly contributions of those working in multiple fields simultaneously. When an interdisciplinary field has assembled a set of long-run accomplishments, theories, methods, and occupations, then the university should mount educational programs for the next generation in that field.

Through these actions, the university can support faculty on the cutting edge of knowledge and educate the next generation of leaders.[1]

Joint, Inter-Disciplinary, Multi-Disciplinary, Trans-Disciplinary

One problem is that disciplines tend to be internally focused. This is a strength, but it also makes it difficult for them to learn of external needs and opportunities for knowledge advancement. When the needed new knowledge comes from two disciplines or fields, it is helpful to have university appointments that span the two fields.

Not all minds fit the joint appointment mold. Not all problems can be solved by joint appointments. On the other hand, scholars working in multiple fields simultaneously are doing some of the most important knowledge expansion now being experienced. Some research universities have strong supports for joint appointments. On those campuses there are scholar/teachers who make significant contributions to two or more units routinely and are treasured by their colleagues in each unit as bringing important perspectives to their fields.

Joint appointments work when three features exist: (1) making workloads proportionate to appointment fraction, (2) implementing a system of merit review that consistently values the joint contributions, and (3) having a fair system of tenure review that rewards the joint contributions.

How to do this? Let's use a simple example of a professor who has a 50 percent appointment in department A, and a 50 percent in department B. A sustainable relationship would have a 50 percent workload in each of the departments, including research, teaching, and service. Half of the committee service, half the number of classes. Hopefully, the research activity would be of benefit to both units, and the units should proportionately enjoy any financial benefits of the research.

At merit review time, those with joint appointments should be reviewed with criteria that reflect the same aspirations as with other faculty but reduced expectations, given the 50 percent appointment. On some campuses, the next higher level reviews the ratings to make sure the joint appointments are treated fairly (e.g., a dean-level review of all joint appointments between departments within a school).

If a non-tenured faculty member is given a joint appointment of the nature described above, at time of tenure review a review committee with members from both departments is formed. Each department votes on the tenure, using the joint committee report. If both departments agree, that is the outcome forwarded. If one department votes for tenure and the other declines, then another feature must be in place. If the university-level review step recommends tenure, the department voting for tenure absorbs 100 percent of the time of the candidate and the joint appointment is appropriately adjusted.

The impediments to successful joint appointments are generally administrative, not intellectual. They can be removed through administrative actions. We need more minds who can think across disciplines. Great universities have created administrative systems that nurture such minds.[2]

An Evolution of Joint Appointments

There is important value in a university environment that nurtures combining knowledge across traditional boundaries. Such campuses tend to be more nimble at exploiting new opportunities to solve important problems. They are also more resilient to changes in the external world, ones that demonstrate that traditional approaches need renewal. For universities that have missions to improve the world, it is logical that such atmospheres permit the problem to define the needed knowledge sets instead of the knowledge sets solely defining what is a legitimate problem.

Common structures and appointment processes are not serving well these interdisciplinary thinkers. Some universities are mounting new joint appointment procedures in order to:

- Reflect different levels of intensity and length of time of such joint appointments

- Make explicit what are the rights and responsibilities of the departments/units, the jointly appointed faculty, deans, and provost in the appointment

- Set up procedures to manage any cross-unit issues that arise during the appointment.

One structure to address these problems offers alternative levels of commitment. It has three types of joint appointments, varying in intensity of citizenship:

1. "Affiliate faculty" is the shallowest of the shared citizenship models, well suited to a faculty member who wishes to teach or do research in another unit for a specific term or whose classes in their primary unit attract many students from the other unit but who do not wish to be active members of the other unit.

2. Courtesy joint appointments would tend to last longer, with specific and agreed-upon duties, with salary obligations in the primary unit but with specific duties in the secondary unit documented and supported.

3. Shared joint appointments convey full rights, but fractional citizenship and funding in multiple units, with the permanency of the status appropriate to rank.

In all of these, the next higher level of administrative authority has the responsibility of making the "jointness" work (e.g., the provost would be responsible for joint appointments involving two schools). In all such appointments there would be written, explicit agreements on the duties of the appointees in the units, with assurance that their service, teaching, and research are proportional to the salary support provided by the unit (never exceeding 100% in total). The new proposed policy specifies merit review procedures that fairly combine the reviews from the multiple units. It specifies joint tenure and promotion review procedures that range from the primary unit merely seeking input for affiliate faculty under review to, for a shared joint appointment, a joint promotion review panel, separate votes of the two units, and explicit protections to the shared joint appointment candidate under the circumstance of split votes between units.

The goals of such appointments are clear. Provosts want to make the institution even more inviting as a place to do original scholarship that spans fields. They want departments and programs to be able to take advantage of faculty that offer alternative insights to students in those fields even if they have part of their teaching and research life in another unit. They want students to be exposed to the latest combinations of approaches toward the big issues facing this world.

While joint appointments can effectively spawn interdisciplinary advances in a university, they often have much more diverse academic staff. Joint appointments work for some issues but not for others.[3]

Diversity of Another Sort

Modern universities are complex beasts. They have evolved many steps away from their original form, where there were basically two sets of staff—faculty and staff administrators. In those days, teaching dominated the focus of faculty. The staff supported the facilities and services necessary to the teaching mission. The two groups were quite different. The faculty had advanced degrees and often privileged socioeconomic backgrounds; they lived the life of the mind. The staff were more practically oriented, often with less formal education.

On the faculty side, the past saw most faculty members doing the same thing: teaching the same number of courses, each lasting 12–15 weeks, and having the summers to sharpen their knowledge in their field.

Modern universities have many more than the two groups above. Further, the differences among the various groups are more and more difficult to articulate. Over the past decades, the typical American university took on many of the duties of advanced research units as well as higher education institutions.

At many universities, faculty members vary in what portion of their time they spend in the formal classroom, in mentoring students in research settings, and in conducting their own research. Some are full-time teachers; some are full-time researchers. As some research enterprises become team-oriented, the teams often contain post-PhD researchers who do no classroom teaching. (Often, however, this staff has rich and ongoing relationships with apprentice undergraduate and graduate assistants in their scholarship and research.) Some may have joint appointments with outside collaborating universities or research institutes. Great universities assure that the balance among teaching, research, and service is achieved at the level of the whole university, even though it may not be achieved for each faculty member.

Students in these environments benefit from engagement in scholarship/research as well as classroom education. They are able to learn by doing original scholarship. They then exit with the skills that will prepare them for a world demanding continuous self-directed learning.

In contrast to yesteryear, staff in today's universities must have the education and skills to navigate the complex regulatory environment affecting financial aid, research using human subjects, contracts with partner organizations, relationships with institutions in other countries, and a host of issues that earlier editions of universities never encountered.

The challenge of this new world to universities is to foster cultures where these diverse faculty and staff excel in their individual contributions, are rewarded commensurate to these contributions, and are respected for the unique blend of activities they perform in service of the university's mission. The diversity of staff talents strengthens the university. University cultures where each group honors the contributions of the other to the larger institution tend to be better places to work.

The final focus of new diversity within the institution that provosts need to understand is the role of new learning technologies. On-line software platforms offer new tools to instructors in higher education. The tools, however, require some changes in the pedagogical approach. We live in a period of intense experimentation, with new techniques arising continuously. One of the great challenges to provosts is how to help their institution navigate these changes, avoiding the latest ill-conceived fad but actively assuring that new approaches of lasting value are adopted by their universities.[4]

The Instructor as Director of a Play

Throughout my teaching career, my preparation for a course and my delivery of a course changed little. I typically selected a set of readings from the best published literature that I could find; they were often assembled into a "coursepack" of duplicated articles. Each week several articles would be assigned for reading. I prepared lectures relevant to the readings, emphasizing what I believed were the key points in the readings and providing what I believed was a conceptual structure of the ideas to frame the various readings. I assigned exercises of various types—most often requiring the students to go beyond just regurgitating the learned material and instead requiring them to combine the concepts to make new observations or use the concepts to solve a completely new problem not yet introduced in the lectures or readings. Both comprehension and expression of the information were the goal.

While I didn't give much thought to this aspect of my class preparation, I was really not the only instructor in the class. The scholars whose work I assigned for reading were helping me (admittedly without their knowledge). I assigned what I believed were seminal contributions to the field for the students to read. I often assigned work from those using different approaches or coming to different conclusions, merely to force students to grapple with the disagreements that all fields possess. Many times, I judged that the articles were better than what I could produce myself for the given issue. I thought that what I was doing was "my" course, but I wasn't teaching "me"; I was teaching a field.

A different paradigm seems to be emerging, however. Courses using online technologies tend to be shorter than the traditional 15-week course. Indeed, some MOOCs are using building-block modules that are designed to be useful in other courses. One can easily imagine that this might gradually affect how the products of scholars are presented in courses throughout the world. In addition to articles and books, we can all imagine small software modules associated with their contributions. These can be simulations of findings of research or visualizations of results. We can imagine a 10–15 minute lecture from the author of the seminal work, summarizing the chapter or article assigned. We can imagine a debate between two authors in video form on the details of the controversy. Thus, I'll be helped in teaching from these "colleagues" in the field in some new ways. The coursepack of the future may be a multimedia mix of modules.

As I reflect on this, the value of the instructor in this new world is the same as that in the past. The instructor will assemble the pieces of a course based on his or her expert judgment of the key concepts, techniques, and findings of the field, with special knowledge of the student audience. The best judgments will be made by faculty members themselves working on the cutting edge of their fields, permitting them to update their courses continuously as the field evolves. In that sense, nothing has changed. The instructor is the still the director of the "play," determining each scene, but the actors may be others acting in new ways. What's new is that the other actors will bring new tools to help the play.

This development, in my opinion, is quite different from what is happening on some campuses—the replacement of entire courses taught by local instructors by an imported online course. Indeed, we've read about faculties on such campuses rejecting such moves. The importation of whole online courses from other campuses, with no local faculty input or active involvement, asserts that an area doesn't need local expertise (beyond the selection of the course). Furthermore, without continuous updating of the online course, it asserts that the knowledge represented in the imported course is forevermore static.

I know of few fields of human knowledge that are completely static. The future needs cutting-edge scholars as Georgetown faculty, as did the past; it needs courses that are continually updated. What's new is that these faculty members will have exciting new ways to present the work of others in their fields, to the benefit of all students.[5]

Learning Adaptive Learning

Talented instructors know their material so well that they also know all the different ways the material can be misunderstood. To them, every possible question, every exercise in a course has wrong answers that help diagnose the nature of the misunderstanding. These are the matters that are hopefully discussed in one-on-one sessions between a struggling student and an instructor. The discussions apply remedial instruction about the concepts or techniques that the student doesn't grasp to achieve a complete understanding.

For some years, such deep subject knowledge has guided the development of "adaptive testing," used in the Graduate Record Examination and other computer-assisted tests. In these tests, students answer different questions depending on their performance. If the student answers the first question in a knowledge domain incorrectly, an easier question is administered next. This continues until a correct answer is given. If the student answers the first question correctly, a more difficult question is presented. This variability, tailored to the individual student, permits much shorter tests for some students, as their answers quickly identify their level of comprehension of the material.

As courses go online, the same computer-assisted structure can be helpful. Each module of course material is initially presented in the manner proven to be useful for the *majority* of students, and then short exercises/questions about the material are presented. If a student answers the questions correctly, he or she proceeds to the next phase of the presentation. In contrast, every type of wrong answer can generate a different remedial experience, one customized to the type of misunderstanding the error usually implies. (This is like the help session in the instructor's office after class.) Following that experience, a similar exercise is presented to allow the student to demonstrate his or her newfound knowledge. Then the student moves to the next module.

What is exciting about this opportunity is that it can offer much more personalized learning experiences, when the adaptive learning application is designed by a master in the field. One can see how this would be especially useful for struggling students who, for whatever reason, don't take advantage of office hours in traditional courses. Even more attractive is the fact that the repair of misunderstandings is accomplished quite quickly, before bad logic is applied repeatedly. Quick repairs of knowledge are easier to make; cognitive errors made repeatedly are harder to "unlearn."

Finally, another attraction of adaptive learning applications is that they allow some self-pacing. Indeed, it resembles common pedagogical techniques of tutors of individual students, letting the student set the pace of the course. Every instructor knows students in his/her class who master the material faster than the course design can present it. Adaptive learning applications allow the talented students to move through the course much more quickly, at a pace that suits them. Such self-paced learning, however, will cause some complications for current 15-week structure of many universities.

Another aspect of designing adaptive learning courses is that much work is required at the front end of the process. A detailed cognitive map of the material is useful. For each node in the map, all the possible misunderstandings should be identified. For each misunderstanding, a repair strategy must be proposed and developed. For each repair, an exercise should be designed to verify that the repair was successful. For errors made late in the course, the repair may involve returning to much earlier material, but the designer must decide whether that material should be presented in some new way, given the error made by the student.

Talented instructors in face-to-face settings invent the diagnostic questions and remediation "on the fly" when a student presents with a given confusion. With adaptive learning applications, they design from the beginning such repairs. Once designed, however, both the students and the instructors enjoy its benefits. With good adaptive design, all students learn faster. With good adaptive design, the student-instructor interaction can focus on more higher-level discussions of the material. This can enrich the on-campus experience for students.[6]

But What Does the Faculty Think about It?

All of the ideas reviewed above are new to some campuses. They challenge the status quo. The job of a provost involves assessment of many new ideas. We in the academy live in interesting times, with external challenges to long-held assumptions about how to produce quality education. This moment is spawning a variety of innovations and changes.

At the provosts' offices, in kicking around a new idea, the question often arises, "Does anyone have a sense of what the average faculty member would think about this?"

Most provost offices have advisory groups involving deans, faculty, staff administrators, students, and others. They are helpful to us; however, the provosts can never learn enough about how faculty might view a given issue. It is central to increase trust and collaboration between the faculty and the administration. To achieve this, we need honest communication. More importantly, we need to find out what faculty view as their challenges and day-to-day problems and what they view as the strengths of institution.

No provost today can effectively exert power without first giving it up. Faculty governance demands allowing large numbers of others to comment on the way forward. It requires listening. It requires attempting always to find a way forward among the diverse opposing viewpoints. Few issues affecting the faculty generate 100 percent agreement. Hence, effective leadership requires the wisdom of knowing when there is sufficient density of opinion that action can safely be taken.

One tool for such communication is a survey of the faculty, asking them their reactions/attitudes/feelings about a range of components of their work life on campus. For this to work, faculty must feel free to express their real opinions. The areas covered by the survey might include research environment and institutional support; teaching load and student quality; nature and distribution of service responsibilities; facilities and work resources; personal and family policies; health and retirement benefits; interdisciplinary work and collaboration; mentoring; tenure and promotion opportunities, clarity, and reasonableness; recruitment and retention; and institutional governance and leadership. Following the release of the report, the Provost's Office can organize a main-campus-wide discussion of results.

The value of a survey lies in its repetition, making possible comparisons over time for the same faculty. Are key indicators getting better or worse? Is there evidence that interventions mounted since the last survey achieved their purpose?

None of the ideas above—from joint appointments and adaptation to learning technologies—can be adopted smoothly without ongoing consultation with and listening to the faculty.[7]

Conclusion

The turnover rate of provosts and presidents attests to the fact that these jobs are difficult. This may be especially true at this time. Higher education institutions must change at a rate that is uncomfortable to most in the academy. For some institutions their very existence depends on their ability to rethink traditional boundaries, to bring into the educational programming new techniques, and to reward faculty activities that are not protected by centuries of history of disciplinary thought.

Given the shared governance structures of most universities, such change can go forward only with unusually frequent, honest, and multidirectional communication. Talk may be cheap; not talking is so costly that the institution may lose its future.

NOTES

1. Robert Groves, "The Land Between the Disciplines," *The Provost's Blog*, 16 July 2014. https://blog.provost.georgetown.edu/the-land-between-disciplines/. (The following references all refer to this blog.)

2. "Joint, Inter-Disciplinary, Multi-Disciplinary, Trans-Disciplinary," 3 April 2013. https://blog.provost.georgetown.edu/joint-inter-disciplinary-multi-disciplinary -trans-disciplinary/.

3. "An Evolution of Joint Appointments," 25 September 2013. https://blog .provost.georgetown.edu/an-evolution-of-joint-appointments/.

4. "Diversity of Another Sort," 9 January 2013. https://blog.provost.georgetown .edu/diversity-of-another-sort/.

5. "The Instructor as Director of a Play." 11 December 2013. https://blog
.provost.georgetown.edu/the-instructor-as-director-of-a-play/.

6. "Learning Adaptive Learning." 31 July 2013. https://blog.provost.georgetown
.edu/learning-adaptive-learning/.

7. "But What Do the Faculty Think about It?" 9 October 2013. https://blog
.provost.georgetown.edu/but-what-do-the-faculty-think-about-it/.

CHAPTER EIGHT

The CAO and the Curriculum: Developing and Implementing Effective Programs for a Contemporary Student Population

Lon S. Kaufman and Saul J. Weiner

Curriculum Development—a Free Ride for the Provost?

Curriculum development is one of very few activities in higher education where true shared governance exists on a campus. Disciplinary curricular content is defined by the appropriate faculty and vetted at every level of the college or university by committees generally made up solely of faculty members. The final approval for the institution is then typically granted by a board of trustees (or equivalent) with its approval followed by that of the state board of education.

Throughout this process, the role for the chief academic officer can be minimal if the system is working effectively. Various administrative functions can and will exert control over teaching load, space, and budget, but the purely disciplinary academic content is the privilege and responsibility of the faculty. The CAO can helpfully provide a scaffolding to assure that the process is carried out in accordance with institutional statutes and policies. When handled appropriately, intrusions on academic content should be rare. Thus, it would seem on the surface, aside from perhaps asserting the need for testimony regarding the budgetary impact of the curriculum in terms of real costs, or the prescribed space needs for a new course or program, that curriculum development would be a simple matter for the CAO's office. However, as we will see in what follows, challenges can emerge quickly and need to be addressed carefully and thoroughly. The provost's leadership can make a significant difference.

First Priority: Learning Outcomes Assessment and Periodic Review of Curricular Content

Little seems to make many professors and their department heads more anxious than the need to define learning outcomes and, in tandem, to develop and employ a set of rubrics to assess the level to which the students have achieved those outcomes. The goal of the exercise is, of course, to constantly improve the efficiency through which the information deemed important by the faculty—be it factual, intellectual, or skill-based—is learned by the students. It is not a referendum on the quality of the faculty, or for that matter of the student, although it is sometimes assumed to be such and used as a blaming tool. At the University of Illinois at Chicago (UIC), constantly informing ourselves of better ways to teach and interact in the classroom to ensure that a diverse population of learners achieves the desired or prescribed learning outcomes is a constant challenge and, as a research university, a constant opportunity. If as a nation we are to increase the number of students who go to college and to help those coming from underserved backgrounds achieve success, it is critical that we understand how to define meaningful learning outcomes and how to use a full cycle of assessment activities to best achieve those outcomes in diverse classrooms.

For academic leaders, assessing professional programs in which there are prescribed learning outcomes and means of assessment, the ease with which they can be moved from traditional face-to-face delivery to a fully asynchronous on-line mode presents one set of challenges. Similarly, the daunting task of defining a coherent set of learning outcomes for doctoral degrees that are essentially independent research-based apprenticeships presents another. Finally, even building learning outcomes and assessments in undergraduate liberal arts and humanities programs can be challenging in working with faculty members who sometimes view any assessment as an attack on academic freedom.

As a result of the above factors, it often becomes the role of the provost to champion the value of full cycle assessment by supporting an office where expertise and software to support and train faculty and staff are available. The challenge is to change the campus culture to one embracing continuous assessment. This becomes an exercise in communication, patience, and trust, and it will eventually test the strength of the relationships among the CAO, the deans, department heads, directors of graduate and undergraduate studies, and the faculty.

This role of the CAO has been supported in recent years by the adoption of full cycle assessment by the Council for Higher Education Accreditation and all of the regional accrediting bodies. Prior to this, a lack

Key Roles for the CAO in Curriculum Development

- Establishing and maintaining an effective learning outcome assessment model
- Conducting periodic reviews of curricular content
- Balancing program closures and cost savings
- Matching types of degrees with modes of delivery
- Resourcing interdisciplinary programs and courses
- Guiding the creation of a common curriculum

of learning outcomes and full cycle endorsement had resulted in delays in accreditation and follow-up visits to campuses. Going forward, chief academic officers can call on these new policies as they mobilize their communities. Tying full cycle assessment to the regular review of the college or university's academic programs, often mandated by the state board of education, is also very helpful. Unfortunately, such boards are sometimes more concerned with performance measures such as grades, graduation rates, and budgetary success than with quality of learning, appropriateness of delivery, and the ability to use information in a manner that achieves learning objectives. The press to adopt a national standard for critical thinking skills, as measured by pre- (first-year) and post- (senior) assessments, while neither defining what part of the skill set is missing nor how to change the learning outcome, is in essence grading, not assessing.

Most states, if not individual institutions, will require by statute or policy a periodic review of each academic program on a campus. These generally take the form of a self study and subsequent review by internal and external review teams. In these instances, a helpful focus in solving issues that arise is to identify other colleges that have solved these issues and invite consultants from those institutions to help address remaining challenges. It is often the case that the review comes back to the provost's office. If such reviews are to improve the curricular content, including the delivery of that content, the CAO has an excellent opportunity to engage the faculty and its senate to assure that the curricular content has not become diluted, lowered in quality, or otherwise compromised.

Closing Academic Programs: Small Savings from Large Actions

In some regions, there appears to be an increasing push on the part of boards of trustees, presidents, and state education committees to close academic programs. This can cause CAOs to feel pressure on a regular basis to take the lead on this issue. In reality, academic administrators—and faculty—often discover that there are little to no savings in such closures, since most of the budget is contained in the salaries of tenured faculty, none of whom will be released as a consequence of such closures. Because most programs being closed are already anemic with respect to student enrollments, the savings in terms of classroom usage, staff time, and facilities can also be minimal.

Closing even a single academic program can become one of the more contentious activities on a campus and one where there may be little guidance by way of policy or handbook. Is closure an academic function, and as such the right and responsibility of the faculty? Or is closure an administrative function for which the provost holds the responsibility? And whatever the case, how should it be handled procedurally? It becomes imperative that the CAO explore carefully and collaboratively the consequences of program closure, since there can be an inverse correlation between the political support for a program and the number of students enrolled in it.

Matching Types of Degree with Modes of Delivery: Proactive Opportunities

For those developing new academic programs, there are two curricular questions to address initially: type of program or degree (major, minor, concentration, certificate, professional, or graduate); and mode of delivery (face-to-face, blended, fully online, synchronous, etc.). While in the past some on-line programs required special accreditation, this is no longer the case; in general, faculty now define the mode of delivery as a tool by which to achieve a specific curricular intent. As such, mode of delivery has become an integrated part of curriculum development. The same is essentially true for the range of program type and degree granted. Being able to address these two elements simultaneously has allowed provosts and the faculty to move more efficiently through a curriculum development process by encouraging coincident planning of appropriate academic advising and student support. Curriculum development thus becomes a more holistic event, starting with academic content, learning outcomes, and intended learners, and accompanied by delivery mode, type of program, and assessment model as tools to achieve these goals.

Pressure will sometimes be brought by a variety of institutional or external constituents to increase access via on-line programming and to use this programming as an entrepreneurial strategy to attract out-of-state and international students to boost institutional income streams.

In this context, the role of the CAO should be to promote the institution's desire to provide access, to increase the number of persons who receive an education, and to increase revenue when appropriate. At the same time, the senior academic officer needs to assure that all of the educational products that bear the institution's name and logo and reflect on the reputation of its faculty do so with educational quality as their trademark and highest priority.

The Long-term Benefits of Interdisciplinary Curricula

On any campus there will be curricula that are not strictly confined to or owned by a single discipline or academic unit, and it is often in these broader areas that the leadership of the CAO becomes instrumental in coordinating the institution's academic, intellectual, bureaucratic, and even financial interests. As warranted, town hall meetings, visits to university educational policy committees, faculty task forces, and individual conversations with the deans and their associate deans of instruction, are all in play. At the same time, CAOs learn that moving this type of agenda forward from the center of the institution requires its own set of skills. We illustrate with a case study on an issue of basic importance to many colleges and universities: creating a common curriculum though the development and implementation of a single general education program for all undergraduate students.

Creating a Common Curriculum: The CAO at the Center

The University of Illinois at Chicago has spent many years discussing how to reform its curriculum. Beginning in 1985, the institution began a twenty-year debate, including faculty groups and task forces that met in 1985, 1987, 1997, and 1998, to vet and discuss general education. Those conversations were meaningful, engaged, often contradictory, and lacked a strong impetus to change an entire system. That conversation would undoubtedly have continued for many more years had it not been for the coincidence of two events: new leadership in the provost's office and the mounting pressure of its North Central Association (NCA) reaccreditation scheduled for 2007. Even earlier, in 1997, the NCA found fault with our general education system, required a follow-up report on our progress toward developing a set of learning outcomes, and requested a full cycle assessment program in 2001, with expected changes to be implemented by its scheduled visit in 2007. In general, the NCA was critical of our "cafeteria style" (i.e., long, unstructured lists of courses under the three divisional headings of Natural Sciences, Social Sciences, and Humanities) and recommended that we create a new model that would be more coherent and circumscribed.

The UIC is a diverse, urban-focused, research-intensive university. The graduate student population is among the top three nationally for diversity. The university, with 17,000 undergraduates and 9,000 graduate students, operates a suite of health science colleges, community clinics, and a hospital. UIC was ranked eleventh in the world and third in the United States among universities less than fifty years old by *Times Higher Education* of London. The university brings in more revenue from tuition than from its annual allocation from the state of Illinois and operates under a modified Responsibility Center Management (RCM) budget.

In the fall of 2003, the provost's office hosted a series of facilitated open meetings focused on the basic underpinnings of a UIC education. In the spring of 2003, based on the information gathered from these meetings and the realization of the importance of our general education program to the impending NCA reaccreditation, the provost's office and the Senate Committee on Educational Policy (SCEP) charged the College of Liberal Arts and Sciences' (LAS) Educational Policy Committee (EPC) with developing a new general education curriculum for the campus. The EPC submitted its curriculum in 2005, and it was instituted for freshman in 2007 and transfer students in 2009. The campus went from a system that required a single cultural diversity course and a set number of courses in the general fields of humanities, social sciences, and natural sciences to one in which students had to select at least one course from each of six themes:

- Analyzing the Natural World

- Understanding the Individual and Society

- Understanding the Past

- Understanding the Creative Arts

- Exploring World Cultures

- Understanding U.S. Society

In developing the new model, the EPC attempted to provide enough structure to guarantee a certain level of intellectual breadth, while at the same time allowing students the opportunity to select courses or clusters of courses around areas of their own interests. However artificially imposed the structural threat of an external review may have been, it truly served to focus the faculty members on what was important and gave a time frame by which the conversation would have to end. That everyone knew we had to have a new system in place by a certain date helped focus the discussions on the most central elements: What do we want the students to know? What skills should they develop? What is a liberal education, and how can curriculum support this notion? While the external deadline served as an incentive for forward movement, the reform would never have been approved by the necessary faculty bodies had not faculty input been gathered at every stage of the process: the provost's office sponsored open comment sessions and structured cross-college meetings and working groups. Every college had the opportunity to provide feedback on the model developed by the EPC. The proposal was modified at several points because of the feedback received by the committee.

The early stages of the committee's discussions were heady and exciting: faculty members were actively engaged and quickly came up with lists of thematic areas that they thought ought to be part of a general education curriculum. The initial list was quite long and in many ways optimistically and operationally naïve. At one time, the committee toyed with nine categories, where government, the environment, and technology, for example, had their own categories. Taking that long list and creating a curriculum that students could readily understand and various faculty bodies would ultimately approve—since any curricular reform would require the vote of the various colleges as well as of the faculty senate—was a process that was premised on realpolitik and compromise. But here again, the necessity of creating a system that would be thematic and broad without being too cumbersome allowed the committee to focus its work.

It was extremely important to the EPC that students themselves were aware of the intellectual rationale behind the general education curriculum and each of its six categories. Similarly, the committee was faced with the necessity of creating assessment tools for the courses within the curriculum based upon those rationales. The faculty committee spent considerable time creating learning outcomes for the general education program as a whole and for each category. The language for the overall program is as follows:

> The General Education Program at UIC is designed to serve as a foundation for lifelong learning. It will help prepare students for the world beyond the college experience, a world in which one needs to be able to:
> - Think independently
> - Understand and critically evaluate information
> - Analyze and evaluate arguments
> - Develop and present cogent written and oral arguments
> - Explore one's own culture and history as well as those of others
> - Understand, interpret, and evaluate the arts
> - Think critically about how individuals influence and are influenced by political, economic, cultural, and family institutions[1]

Of course, the outcomes here are by necessity very general, but they do serve to give students an overview of what a liberal education ought to provide. The goals for the individual categories are more specific and hence provide justifications that are meaningful to students as well as helpful to faculty who teach these courses. As an example, in the discussions about the Natural World goals, the committee asked itself: Why do we want all students, no matter what their major, to take science courses? The learning outcomes for the Natural World category zero in on the most central intellectual aspects of these courses:

> Courses in this category should introduce students to scientific and mathematical concepts and methods. They should be designed to facilitate the students' ability to do one or more of the following:
> 1. Understand and critically evaluate information and concepts in the natural and mathematical sciences
> 2. Use and understand scientific method to analyze ideas and obtain knowledge
> 3. Appreciate the value of and difference between scientific laws, theories, hypotheses, and speculation
> 4. Use scientific and mathematical reasoning to make relevant distinctions among ideas
> 5. Think critically about contemporary issues in science and technology
> 6. Logically and clearly communicate experimental results and observations to others
> 7. Analyze quantitative information and draw conclusions from these analyses[2]

Once the committee had created these outcomes, it also helped to create the assessment mechanisms for each. At the time of the general education discussions, the campus was also seeking to create new assessment models for its courses. The general education courses became the pilot for creating our campus course assessment model, and here too, because faculty were intimately involved in creating the system from the beginning, the process went more smoothly than had been expected.

One of the most interesting aspects of the discussions during this period was that the faculty was highly cognizant not only of what a general education curriculum should be in the abstract but also what such a curriculum should be for our particular kind of students—a largely urban, highly diverse student body. For example, in discussing the old system's cultural diversity requirement, the committee criticized the requirement because it was so generic and because it did not necessarily serve to broaden a student's horizons: a student had to register for a course that in some way explored a culture other than the mainstream American one. Since 60 percent of our students have a parent at home whose native language is not English, taking a course on American society and culture might actually serve to broaden their perspective more than taking a course that focused on a non-American culture, especially since nonnative students often registered for courses that focused on their own cultural backgrounds. As a result, the EPC ultimately recommended both a World Cultures category as well as an American category to make sure that our diverse students had experience in both. Although this general education system has been in place now for more than five years, it is a program that has continued to evolve: courses are added and taken away, categories tweaked, and general changes are still being considered.

Overall, this process and experience have demonstrated to the institutional community that success in curriculum development, no matter what the size or history of a college or university, depends on successfully maintaining a balance between faculty initiative and CAO support with leadership and engagement from both sides critical to student success.

NOTES

1. General Education Program, "Purpose of the General Education Program," University of Illinois at Chicago, 2011. http://www.uic.edu/depts/oaa/gened/purpose .html.

2. General Education Program, "Setting the Foundations for University Study," University of Illinois at Chicago, 2011. http://www.uic.edu/ucat/catalog /GE.shtml#e.

CHAPTER NINE

Technology and the Changing Classroom Experience: Best Practices for Curriculum, Resources, and Personnel

John G. Flores

For several decades, new classroom technologies—and the faculty implementing them—have struggled for respect among an institution's more traditionally based professors. Over this period, typically young, entrepreneurial teachers were compelled to provide statistics and additional reports to illustrate that technology-driven instruction was an enhancement over earlier models. All that has changed. No longer are numbers or prior justifications required as technology-based teaching, often via distance learning, has moved from the edge to the center of many college and university curricula. New classroom technologies have become as common as email, Twitter, and Facebook accounts, and as one key result, higher education is now able to provide access to a vastly larger percentage of students and to help them succeed once they enroll.

Certainly the early adapters welcome this growth, if not vindication. At the same time, these visionaries also recognize that real growth is not simply measured in raised enrollments but also in becoming better, more focused, and more effective in critical teaching and learning activities.

The Technology Challenge for Chief Academic Officers and Their Faculties

Change is inevitable when a program or an entire college is bound to a technical platform, but provosts need to be aware that some technology changes will be effective and some will merely mask endemic flaws in that institution's course sequences and content. Hence, CAOs need to develop a *systematic* approach to new classroom technology planning, implementation, and evaluation. Perhaps the strongest impetus for this has become the increased need nationally for accountability in higher education as parents, alumni, and state legislators have joined the call for proof of value in baccalaureates and graduate degrees.

In response, provosts and deans need to demonstrate an understanding of both technology and learning processes and of how the two can combine to produce student achievement. Across the spectrum of member institutions in the United States Distance Learning Association (USDLA), we have found no single formula to be universally successful. Different majors, different institutional missions, and different student expectations produce a variety of results. Yet with all of these differences, our continuing research and interviews with CAOs do confirm that certain broad principles apply, and it is those solutions and strategies that academic managers should employ when implementing and assessing new instructional technologies.

The USDLA, founded in 1987, was the first nonprofit association in the United States to support research, development, and praxis across the entire span of instructional technology and distance education. Presently, the globalization of online programs and technology-based teaching underscores the need for easily adopted and assessed standards of quality at all levels of higher education. Just as many observed several decades ago in the United States a natural expansion of colleges and universities across state lines, many are now also noting a similar dynamic with programs extending across national borders.

Educational technology continues to proliferate on campuses of every size and type, and the greatest challenge for future CAOs will not be in deciding between online and blended models or between MOOCs and mobile apps. In fact, it will be a more traditional and simple kind of assignment: to develop flexible, sustainable practices that ensure quality

Ten Best Practices for CAOs in Educational Technology

1. Institutional Mission
2. Academic Standards
3. Program Integrity
4. Student Admission and Enrollment
5. Faculty Resources
6. Teaching and Learning Expectations
7. Student Learning Environment
8. Access to Student Support
9. Program Evaluation Responsibility
10. Third-Party Accountability

in delivery and application. To accomplish this, provosts should consider incorporating the following principles in all new technology-based programs.

Ten Best Practices for CAOs in Educational Technology

1. *Institutional Mission.* New technology-driven courses and programs must be guided by goals and objectives that fit appropriately within the university or college's mission and identity. Provosts, faculty, staff, and students all need a clear understanding of their role in the implementation and delivery of these curricula.

2. *Academic Standards.* The pertinent department or program must articulate a standard for educational quality and consistently apply that criterion throughout the institution, independent of geographic location or means of delivery.

3. *Program Integrity.* Educational expectations must be disclosed to students from the outset in catalogues and program literature. Any pertinent technology provider's operations must be characterized by integrity and be consistent with the laws, regulations, and policies of the locales in which it operates.

4. *Student Admission and Enrollment.* Participants in technology-based programs must be treated ethically, with all information about costs, enrollment, cancellation, grades, transcripts, and educational resources furnished prior to the start of the degree.

5. *Faculty Resources.* Faculty staffing will vary with the college or university, but there will always need to be a core of experienced teaching specialists and practitioners. These teachers will need to be supervised and evaluated as a regular activity of both the CAO's office and the resident technology provider.

6. *Teaching and Learning Expectations.* New courses and programs must be mission-sensitive, pedagogically sound, and compatible with the technologies provided or required.

7. *Student Learning Environment.* While good technology is the necessary first step, successful programs will also provide a broader infrastructure, including resources such as library holdings and personnel, and dedicated academic advising comparable to that made available to students in other programs. These resources need to remain available throughout the student's full enrollment.

8. *Access to Student Support.* The student support described above needs to be disclosed in advance of registration and needs to remain available throughout the student's full enrollment providing maximum benefit for learning.

9. *Program Evaluation Responsibility.* New and ongoing instructional technologies must be routinely evaluated, and all individuals with an involvement in the program should be included in the evaluation process. Evaluation responses will then need to be integrated into a continuous improvement cycle.

10. *Third-Party Accountability.* The vital role of any third parties in delivering the educational experience must be confirmed and evaluated through written agreements detailing roles, expectations, and obligations.[1]

CAOs learn over time that any technology-driven program must reflect the academic, technical, and professional quality expected in any face-to-face program offered by the institution.

Social Media and the Coming Transformation of Higher Education

BY JOHN HALL

American higher education was an early incubator for social media. Now technology is returning the favor, becoming the most disruptive and revolutionary phenomenon in higher education. Just as the telephone made the telegraph obsolete, and the word processor, the typewriter, social media technologies will upend post-secondary education as we know it. Higher education administrators and academics who fail to understand and embrace the enormous power of social media do so at their own peril.

What Is Social Media?

Social media can broadly be defined as applications that enable a community of users to develop, experience, and share content via web-based and mobile applications.* Content can be traditional, such as news or radio, or user-generated, such as Wikipedia articles. When most people think of social media, Facebook often comes to mind. It is difficult to fathom how these social networks represent such a monumental shift for higher education—at least outside of a residence hall or admissions office. Social networks, however, are simply an element of what social media is and a miniscule part what it is transitioning into. Social media encompasses podcasts, wikis, blogs, microblogs, virtual worlds, Internet forums, media sharing, and bookmarking sites.[†] The real power of social media emanates from its unparalleled ability to replicate a sense of community and connection amongst its participants in virtual contexts. Social media allows participants to exchange ideas, content, and experiences and to feel a sense of belonging in ways that arguably can simulate traditional face-to-face social groupings.

Social Media, Higher Education, and the Role of the Chief Academic Officer

What does all this mean for higher education and its leaders? Social media alone will not revolutionize higher education. Social media coupled with mobile devices, including smartphones and tablets, however, create a perfect storm for radical change. As social media chips away at the traditional structures of education, "boundless" learning is freeing students from the confines of a campus, set hours during which they can receive instruction, and even the computer. The impetus for traditional online learning, the computer, will gradually be considered as restrictive as the classroom. Additionally, the core structures of education will change in ways that were unimaginable just a few years ago. No longer will education "end" for students upon the completion of a degree program. Some of the effects on education in the future will be:

1. *Anytime, anywhere learning.* Social media and mobile devices allow for anytime, anywhere learning. As a result, it is probable that within the next five to ten years, an 18-year-old will be able to go to work full-time, earn a living, and access instruction via social media technologies while on breaks at work and during free time. Such an opportunity would significantly reduce instructional costs; the high costs that families now pay for room, board, and textbooks; and the high opportunity cost of attending college.

2. *Lowered costs.* Costs will further be lowered by artificial intelligence, voice recognition, and advanced game theory that will be effectively delivered via social media platforms. Fortune 500 companies and the U.S. military already employ these technologies. Their efficacy in effectively "automating" significant portions of instruction, enhancing student outcomes, and reducing human instructional costs has been well established.

3. *A social media-based instructional model.* Platforms such as TED-Ed, Khan Academy, Coursera, and edX demonstrate that quality higher education instruction can be delivered to mass audiences at little to no cost to the educational consumer via social media technologies. We are essentially witnessing the early foundations of a social media-based instructional

(cont'd)

model that could present a tremendous opportunity for early adopter universities and cause many of today's colleges that do not act to become obsolete.

4. *Increased customization.* Last but not least, social media technologies are allowing for the customization of instruction while altering traditional student-professor roles and the way students master curriculum. As students gain much more control over their learning experience than ever before, the same social media technologies that are the backbone of popular virtual gaming worlds are being utilized in instructional programs that can intelligently adapt to each learner's needs while focusing on student mastery.

Social media promises to create "boundless" learning, to substantially change the higher education business model, and to alter the ways instruction is delivered radically. Colleges and universities that understand how social media will transform higher education as we know it and embrace the promise of these technologies will be best equipped to take advantage of the many opportunities afforded by this revolution.

John Hall is president of Greenwood & Hall, a customer relationship management and marketing firm that provides contact center services for higher education institutions, Fortune 500 corporations, and government agencies (www.greenwoodhall.com).

* Cecilia Rios-Aguilar, Manuel Sacramento González Canché, Regina Deil-Amen, and Charles H. F. Davis III, "The Role of Social Media in Community Colleges" (Tucson: Center for the Study of Higher Education at the University of Arizona and Claremont Graduate University, 2012).
† Andreas M. Kaplan and Michael Haenlein, "Users of the World, Unite! The Challenges and Opportunities of Social Media," *Business Horizons* 53, no.1 (Jan.–Feb. 2010): 59–68.

Conclusion: New Technologies, Traditional Responsibilities

Today's university classrooms reflect the broad range of program models from traditional face-to-face, to blended, to completely online and available at any time. The same can be said of learners, whether one is a baby boomer, generation X, millennial, or a member of the current net generation.[2] All students now demand the same or higher quality in online programs as they do in a face-to-face classroom. As we move from the traditional setting of face-to-face to more distance learning–based, online opportunities, professors must also be ready to accept new expectations and challenges. Millennials and digital natives are now the majority in higher education; they are tech savvy, and they expect to learn via the Internet. In turn, their teachers need to be skilled in the use of electronic resources and social media in order to reach beyond traditional classroom boundaries when necessary. Beyond this, it is the provost's responsibility to provide the level of telecommunication resources and choices that students expect. Course design, content delivery, and teacher expertise—whether through a traditional face-to-face classroom or virtually, using a new learning management system—are three basic areas that the CAO will need to understand and manage along with the members of the university's technical team.[3]

Not too many years ago, students could ask which colleges offered full online degree programs. A better question today is which ones do not. However, there are also many cautions that CAOs should observe in trying to make their degree programs available anywhere and anytime. Massive Open Online Courses (MOOCs) are an excellent object lesson in this regard. The MOOC was initially viewed as a means for universities to offer courses on a global scale, free of charge, initiating a kind of new educational democracy. However, participating institutions as well as private MOOC companies are now experiencing serious drawbacks, low completion rates, Return on Investment (ROI) issues, and a growing list of related concerns. In response to this phenomenon, instructional systems are now being designed that speak to adaptive technologies and allow course material to be delivered in multiple learning strategies rather than via a one-size-fits-all model. Adaptive technologies have become the new educational technology frontier, and CAOs need to grasp that being able to deliver coursework at their institutions through multiple learning strategies can move online classes to new levels of success. Lifelong learning access, educational quality, and valuing personal experience are common core elements for future growth in any technology-based degree program. Without geographical boundaries, new instructional technology models have leveled the higher education playing field through increased access and a quality guarantee.[4]

Educational technology in support of online education is now the mainstream. With over 7 million students having taken an online course, providing opportunities for colleges and universities to excel in this equalizing of educational opportunities has become a primary responsibility of the CAO. While the institutional technology puzzle can be a challenge for even veteran academic leaders, with several million student consumers in the balance, it is still most often the provost who must ensure academic excellence, rigor, and accountability.[5]

NOTES

1. George Collins and John G. Flores, USDLA Research: Distance Learning Accreditation, 2011, www.usdla.org.

2. Daryl Diamond, Mary T. Kolesinki, and Evelyn Nelson-Weaver, *Digital Solidarity in Education: Promoting Equity, Diversity, and Academic Excellence through Innovative Instructional Programs* (New York: Routledge, 2014).

3. The Sloan Consortium, "Changing Course—10 Years of Tracking Online Education in the U.S.," Babson Survey Research Group and Quahog Research Group, LLC, 2013, http://www.onlinelearningsurvey.com/reports/changingcourse .pdf; "Going the Distance: Online Education in the United States," 2011, http://www .onlinelearningsurvey.com/reports/goingthedistance.pdf; and "Class Differences: Online Education in the United States," 2010, http://sloanconsortium.org/sites/default /files/class_differences.pdf.

4. J. Flores, "White Paper: Enabled by Broadband, Education Enters a New Frontier," United States Distance Learning Association, November 2010, http:// heartland.org/policy-documents/enabled-broadband-education-enters-new-frontier.

5. J. Flores, "White Paper: Expanding the Classroom: Mobile Distance Learning across America," United States Distance Learning Association, August 2011, http://www.usdla.org/assets/pdf_files/USDLAWhitePaper.English.FINAL .9.15.pdf.

CHAPTER TEN

Academic Governance: The Art of Working with People

James R. Stellar and Michael A. Baer

Younger deans learn from older deans and other mentors that effective governance operates on a deeper level than simply that of a productive faculty senate. Adopting a more encompassing definition of governance—and the CAO's best roles within it—will help academic leaders succeed over a longer term. As our chapter title states, governance is viewed as broader than campus "legislation." Rather, it is seen as the process of working effectively and consistently with all of the people who constitute the institutional community. We believe this less narrow approach is healthy, and we find that shared academic governance works best when there is an open distribution of information, regular discussions of key directions and outcomes, and collaborative considerations of policies and procedures.

The Structure of Academic Governance and the Role of the CAO

If there ever is a position defined as "in between," it is the position of chief academic officer in higher education. The person in this role is central to almost all of the college or university's defining operations, from entering students to retiring trustees. As such, the CAO's office embodies an ongoing melding of ideas, power, and mission, but as Robert Birnbaum has written: "Administration is frustrating. Closure is elusive, systems come undone, solutions create new problems, no group is ever satisfied without another being dissatisfied, and criticism about process can overwhelm substance."[1] The office of the provost is often at the confluence of this frustration. One has to maintain a very long view in the role, since many of the initiatives will take years to bear fruit, yet still remain highly attentive to details. In short, the provost must be optimistic

The Thing I Very Much Wish I Had Known on My First Day as CAO

- What was just a personal opinion yesterday is now a potential institutional policy.

and yet the hardest of realists. He or she must faithfully serve the president while faithfully representing the faculty.

In this context, academic governance depends on a deep understanding of faculty process from the department level to larger groupings of colleges and divisions, including the independent, sometimes willful bodies of professors called the academic senate. In fact, it is very helpful if the provost has served as a chair or a dean along the way so that he or she has first-hand knowledge of how this process works. A clear understanding of how faculty members think and the history of one's own institutional culture helps significantly when attempting to meld the top-down and bottom-up forces described above.

When one moves to a new institution to become a provost, as both of this chapter's authors did, it becomes critical to learn and keep learning about local systems and local culture, since general administrative training only covers part of the story. A provost must know the players at an individual level, must understand the groups and coalitions that exist both hidden and seen, and must learn the major moments of institutional history that continue to affect faculty opinion. Typically, a grace period of a semester is given, but the work outlined above begins on the first day. While a CAO must always be learning, the steepest portion of the learning curve is at its beginning, and the best chance to win faculty appreciation as well as loyalty is in the first semester of service. That said, provosts beware, because consistency is also extremely important, and hard-won faculty loyalty can be lost in a single incident on a single day without warning.

Learn the Power of the Faculty First

Through thousands of hours of work before most provosts met them, faculty members developed the skills to deliver the courses that support the two fundamental missions of any college: knowledge generation and knowledge dissemination. Even veteran provosts, however, will only have a professorial-level depth of knowledge in one or two focused areas of their institution. Yet research universities and many comprehensive colleges have accepted as part of their missions to prepare graduate students to replace professors in all institutions of higher learning. This defines their inherently closed, even conservative structure and is the basis for having developed a system of shared governance. Who else other than those with disciplinary expertise understand in necessary depth what a department needs when they set out to hire new faculty? Departments rely on search committees composed largely of faculty members from related areas of knowledge to identify the best intellectual leaders in the field. CAOs sit at a distance from this detailed interaction between faculty members and their field. The same is true for course design and approval. For example, how can a provost from the biology department fully understand the significance of a theater department or a fine arts department course proposal? He or she cannot.

Thus, provosts rely on a general knowledge of and experience with their own institution and its broader goals and then on the faculty to set disciplinary goals and evaluate the work of their colleagues at the time of hiring, reappointment, and tenure decisions. During these decisions, the CAO must operate through several levels of the academic hierarchy to understand and facilitate key actions that begin in departments. This is where it is useful for the dean or academic vice president to have come up through that system as a professional. There is no better knowledge than "felt knowledge" when it comes to questions of academic quality, and doubly so when the CAO is operating outside of his or her discipline.

So how does the chief academic officer accomplish all of these priorities? How does a new academic dean maintain a careful balance between individual faculty wants and those of the institution as a whole? Seven suggestions follow:

1. Get out of the office

We have come to believe that it is very important to get out of the provost's office physically and engage with campus community members on a weekly basis. Typically, such advice is couched in terms of what the provost will learn from talking to faculty or students across the campus. However, each interaction is also an opportunity to bring what the provost might know about a situation to the individual and to complete a useful, professional exchange. Beyond this, when the CAO arrives at a faculty member's office, there is an opportunity to show respect and build a useful bond for future reference.

In his 2012 book, *The Righteous Mind: Why Good People Are Divided by Politics and Religion,* Jonathan Haidt argues that the conscious mind is really like the rider on an elephant in which the elephant makes most of the decisions.[2] At a gut-level, this is not very different from the relationships that occur in academic governance. The CAO is nominally

Seven Aspects of Effective Academic Governance

1. Getting out of your office
2. Doing small things before big things
3. Taking necessary time for decision making
4. Relying on the strategic plan
5. Developing (big) data
6. Learning governance from students
7. Trusting the faculty senate

in charge, but faulty members know and understand the route and the dangers of the path. The CAO and the faculty work together as the decisions are made about support for an idea, a program, or a budget request. Thus, when the CAO shows up in a professor's office for a chat, there is the chance to communicate privately and honestly as well as to exchange facts and theories that can contribute to the eventual decision. Effective CAOs stop often to listen, since it is important for the senior academic officer and the faculty to have as many points of communication as possible. This is a core element of productive governance.

2. Do the small things before the big things

If a junior member of the faculty approaches the provost with a complaint about a cold or dark classroom, it is an opportunity to do something small that reinforces something big—the importance of good teaching. When responding to the concern, one must not only be in touch with the Facilities Office but also with others in the chain such as department chair and division dean to demonstrate that the CAO respects the academic hierarchy. In some cases, like a small facility renovation, the chair and dean will generally not mind your involvement in the problem and may, in fact, appreciate it. However, if there is any controversy at all, the CAO must take the time to consult with the dean and the chair to resolve it. Even in simple cases, a consultation is necessary to address the potential concern that the good small outcome was based on privileged access and not the merits of the case. Any and all consultative activities such as this are elements of shared governance, that is, a demonstration of respect for decision making at all levels of the college or university regarding support for good teaching and open communication.

The classroom situation is a small one, but there are many others just as important and just as telling. Answering emails and texts rapidly

Three Emerging Trends

1. Provosts are seeking advice from other provosts and CAOs when facing a major institutional policy decision.
2. Online Education: too many provosts still have not thought it through. Develop a clear professional position concerning online courses and programs at your institution.
3. If your college or university is typical and the percentage of tenure-track faculty has decreased over the past two decades (and the academic administration has grown), do not deny it. Offer faculty colleagues accurate statistics, clear reasons why, and a plan for professional development going forward.

is an excellent example. It says that the CAO is involved and paying attention, particularly to direct reports from those who may be under pressure from circumstances and need a senior officer to make a decision or move the issue up to the presidential level. Arriving on time for meetings is another statement made by the CAO that is watched closely. Even though most academics learn that some committee meetings will regularly start five, ten, or even fifteen minutes late, it should not be because the provost is late. Fortunately, with the availability of mobile devices, any downtime before a meeting becomes a chance to get a few e-mails answered, text messages sent, or accomplish something else online that will lessen the need for time and focus later. Better yet, these moments allow time to interact informally with faculty colleagues already present. There are numerous weekly instances like these that can shape shared decision making and effective academic governance.

Why is this important? At the level of the individual faculty member, it is about respect. If that associate professor feels respected, he or she is more likely to be reasonable in academic deliberations at a later point. Conversely, think about what will happen if the CAO's behavior is insensitive and uninformed. Who among faculty will want to cooperate? They might do it because it is required, but the moment for progress will have passed, and the provost or vice president of academic affairs will be viewed differently, and negatively, from a single interchange.

3. Take necessary time with decision making

On many busy campuses, the need to make a key decision in the moment does occur; however, when possible, it is wise for the provost to take as much time as necessary to consider, to discuss with staff, and to research a problem. The discussion with staff and further research are obvious, since one learns more from each extended process. Yet sometimes simply taking extra moments alone to weigh a set of complex options can result in a clearer, firmer decision. One feature of being a CAO is that the responsibilities of the position continue to grow over time, and the role becomes physically exhausting no matter how efficiently one's schedule is managed. The faster the pace, the larger the challenge for the provost to find adequate time to think, particularly about big picture issues, rather than simply reacting to day-to-day needs for immediate decisions.

Some deans have noted the wear and tear that becomes apparent in the second and third years of service. We recommend, before this develops, scheduling time off campus for personal and professional activities in order to provide a fresh perspective. Allow for time on your calendar to get away now and then, even taking business trips and sometimes extending them by a day just to shift perspective. This is healthy and works to counter exhaustion or frustration with difficult issues. Annual retreats for staff and faculty can provide physical and intellectual breakthroughs and remind tired deans that taking a bit of extra time on a difficult decision can also strengthen relationships with those who will be affected by its outcomes.

4. Rely on the strategic plan

CAOs learn that strong strategic plans demand effective academic governance. Such plans are time consuming, require engagement of large numbers of individuals on and off the campus, and are difficult finally to complete. Still, they are also an excellent way to engage all institutional constituencies in shared decision making and clarifying major steps forward. Once developed, approved by the academic governance structure, endorsed by the provost and president, and reviewed by the board, the plan should be widely disseminated inside and outside the institution. By setting priorities in this manner, it is clear that decisions have been made through a shared governance structure that included all major constituents.

For the community, the plan gives voice to what the institution is, and its governance can then be re-shaped to support any new and emerging initiatives. The plan also creates the framework for academic decision making. In this process, it will help prioritize which individual and departmental efforts contribute to the whole institution more strongly and which initiatives are not synergistic. Synergy is critical because many colleges no longer can dedicate the resources necessary to provide high quality programs across as wide a span as they once did, and it should not be overlooked as a component of effective governance.

Sustainability and the Provost: Not Just Another Mandate

BY WILLIAM THROOP

Provosts already have too much to worry about, including shrinking budgets, affordability challenges, retention and graduation rates, student engagement, diversity, and deferred maintenance, to name a few. On top of this, a group of vocal students, or perhaps a president who has signed the president's climate commitment, says that the college must begin to address sustainability more seriously. As one more campus initiative, this demand is easily marginalized. If, however, sustainability serves as a framework to address multiple institutional challenges simultaneously, it can become an organizing principle that maximizes the effectiveness of the provost's actions.

To serve as a strategic framework, sustainability must be interpreted broadly. It is not just environmentalism dressed up in new clothes or a technical approach to increasing energy and resource efficiency. The Association for the Advancement of Sustainability in Higher Education (AASHE) characterizes sustainability "in an inclusive way, encompassing human and ecological health, social justice, secure livelihoods, and a better world for all generations." A sustainability framework thus approaches institutions as interrelated economic, social, and ecological systems.

These few examples illustrate several options provosts and academic deans might consider:

1. Sustainability pedagogy emphasizes students completing projects on campus, service learning in the community, working in teams, and integrating lived experience into classroom discussion. These practices tend to increase student motivation and learning, which is correlated with increased retention rates.*

2. Economic sustainability and affordability are tightly linked. After five years, the actions spurred by American College and University Presidents Climate Commitment have saved reporting institutions over $100 million.† At Green Mountain College, we addressed some early faculty resistance to the development of online programs by documenting ways they can diversify revenue, increase access, provide a low carbon footprint education, and enable faculty to have greater flexibility in their course scheduling.

3. The social dimensions of sustainability encompass initiatives on diversity, effective governance, and town-gown relations. Reframing these as elements of sustainability can enlarge the constituency invested in their success and break down some of the silos that impede progress.‡ To use sustainability as a strategic framework, the provost must view facilities, operations, and educational programs as interlocking systems characterized by multiple

(cont'd)

feedback loops. Institutional change then comes from finding leverage points that alter system structures and by harnessing student and faculty creativity going forward. For this framework to be effective, sustainability must be seen as a strategic approach not a doctrine, and its social and economic dimensions need to receive as much attention as its environmental one.

William Throop has served as provost and vice president for academic affairs at Green Mountain College since 2002. In 2012–13, Throop served as chair of the board of directors of AASHE.

* G. D. Kuh, J. Kinzie, J. H. Schuh, E. J. Whitt, & Associates, *Student Success in College: Creating Conditions that Matter* (San Francisco: Jossey-Bass, 2005).
† Presidents' Climate Commitment, "Celebrating Five Years of Climate Leadership," American College & University Presidents' Climate Commitment, http://www.presidentsclimatecommitment. org/reporting/annual-report/five-year -report.
‡ J. Dillard, V. Dujon, & M. C. King, *Understanding the Social Dimension of Sustainability* (New York: Routledge, 2009).

5. Develop (big) data

Behind the academic processes of curriculum development, registration, grading, and outcomes assessment lies a technical resource that is just now beginning to be extensively tapped: data. Effective institutional governance depends on accurate data, and deans and academic vice presidents should not hesitate to seek, gather, and analyze data in as large amounts as possible. Gone are the days of a dean's informal cracker barrel wisdom when it comes to considering a tenure decision or eliminating a dated program. In fact, many CAOs are building models through which they share large amounts of key data with faculty decisions makers to create an atmosphere of trust, understanding, and joint direction setting.

While one would rarely make faculty hiring decisions solely on the basis of enrollments, it is easier for a provost to explain to deans and department chairs if enrollments are rising why the allocation of faculty lines went to that growing unit. In order to "flatten" the academic governance system at the institution and make it more responsive, it is well worth the provost's time to work with the CIO in order to produce new reports and to share them as widely as possible online. More than almost any other element discussed in this chapter, this advance will put in place the necessary foundation for interactive academic governance.

Since 2000, forces outside of higher education have been calling for increasing accountability from universities and colleges. Of growing interest to the CAO and others charged with governance leadership are budget dollars and where they go. Financial allocations rarely survive without semi-annual, or even monthly, adjustments. But the more that can be done on the basis of shared data, the more those adjustments will be accepted by faculty and students. Over the past two decades, some critics have complained that costs to students have risen while administrations have increased in size and scope unnecessarily and that institutions have become more focused on doing research at the expense of teaching. These are all items a chief academic officer is likely to be asked to explain, particularly to the world beyond the campus. Presidents are under this pressure every semester, but when it turns to the core business of the institution, the provost is now likely to be called upon to provide the explanation. As a start, developing extensive data and distributing it to faculty where feasible will characterize cohesive academic governance.

6. Learn governance from students

Some inexperienced CAOs lead as if students have no role in institutional governance. It is easy to forget about the students in this context, in part because a provost often has little daily or weekly connection to the students she or he oversees. A famous example is outlined in Richard Light's *Making the Most of College: Students Speak their Minds.*[3] Light describes how students at Harvard College were advised to take their core classes and other requirements as first-year students to get them "out of the way." This left many undergraduates hungry for more direct professor-student interaction in fields that they found rewarding and in which they wanted to major. Students that rated the college experience with the highest satisfaction were the ones who had formed early mentoring relationships with faculty in their areas of interest. This outcome seems intuitive now, but one can see how well-meaning administrators and faculty could have designed a first-year curriculum that was highly efficient for them in registering students but not optimal for students as learners.

How does an administrator address this kind of problem? Provosts usually have little difficulty finding time for faculty, but their time in direct student contact is often limited, and there are governance lessons to be learned from this. When today's CAOs were students, few if any had the mobile technologies in which almost every undergraduate is now fluent. Few provosts can text like an undergraduate, yet the interconnectivity and speed of response produced by texting are goals that academic

The Single Most Important Piece of Advice for a New Provost on the First Day in the Position

■ Teams are critical to high-end institutional accomplishment, and to build them you must be genuinely yourself. People recognize guarded behavior and wonder what you may be hiding.

governance needs to implement in order to maintain an influential role on campuses of the next generation. CAOs need to grasp this fluidity and familiarity among their students and utilize it in designing shared governance formats.

7. Trust the senate

In governance matters, the senate will be the provost's greatest challenge and greatest support, sometimes simultaneously. Often composed of administrators, staff members, and students as well as teaching faculty, it will reflect the institution as a whole, academically and politically. In the senate, it is not curricular approvals that cause CAOs difficulty, since these operations are usually well digested in lower level committee meetings. Instead, what presents the deepest complexities are, appropriately, issues involving the well-being of the faculty and students, such as authority over the classroom, curriculum, and educational policies. At some institutions, especially those without collective bargaining, questions of salary increases, teaching loads, and changes in tenure policy will also produce significant debate.

One of the many assignments the provost must accept is to learn the new and ongoing factors influencing the senate's decision making. If things are handled smoothly and thoughtfully, the CAO will not be viewed as an unwelcome force in the senate but rather as a provider of information and as a dependable, balanced resource for initiatives that advance the college or university while protecting its students and supporting its faculty.

Final Thought: Remember What Governance Is Not

Even an effective governance process is fundamentally asymmetrical. For the CAO, it involves working with a single president while serving as the head of what is always the largest unit under that president's authority. In response, some provosts view governance principally as a military command structure, while others see it as a more

Lessons Learned: The CAO and Academic Governance

BY MARK EDELSTEIN

1. *Don't Talk Too Much.* You need a clear vision for your institution's future, but you do not need to keep talking about it. Your institution may require a major transformation of its academic culture and basic practices, but to express this can appear dismissive of the institution's history and of all the goals to which your faculty have dedicated themselves prior to your leadership.

2. *Link the Future to the Past.* However bold and innovative your ideas for the future, be sure to tie them to the traditions of the past. Framing a new initiative as yet another step in the consistent development of the college or university can mute some of the opposition that changes in governance almost always inspire.

3. *Sympathy Matters.* Listen carefully and sympathetically to all suggestions and complaints shared with you. Some may strike you as wrong-headed or ill-informed, but you will gain little to nothing by arguing and trying to set people straight. CAOs sometimes learn the hard way that they do not need to solve every problem. However, they do have to show respect for all who share those problems.

4. *Governance Depends on Constituencies.* Build your own constituency among faculty and staff members. While you should always respect the college's governance structure, the authority of the president to whom you report, and the authority of the deans who report to you, nothing prohibits you from building strong professional relationships with people at every level of the institution. Their support may become critical at a later date.

Mark Edelstein wrote the chapter on the CAO and academic governance in First Among Equals: The Role of the Chief Academic Officer *(1997). Now retired, Edelstein served as president of Lakes Region Community College (NH) and Diablo Valley Community College (CA).*

flexible marriage of colleagues. Whatever the analogy and reality, this chapter is about the roles and responsibilities of the leader at the center of this web of formal agreements and the understandings that guide an institution forward while offering coherence and meaning for the lives within.

NOTES

1. Robert Birnbaum, "Education Policy and Leadership," University of Maryland, http://www.education.umd.edu/EDPL/faculty/birnbaum.htm.

2. Jonathan Haidt, *The Righteous Mind: Why Good People Are Divided by Politics and Religion* (New York: Vintage Books, 2012).

3. Richard Light, *Making the Most of College: Students Speak Their Minds* (Cambridge, MA: Harvard University Press, 2001).

II

Essential Partners

CHAPTER ELEVEN

The CAO and the Chief Financial Officer: Managing a Critical Connection

James Gandre and Miroslava Mejia Krug

Establishing effective relationships with a variety of individuals and con-stituents—the president, deans, vice presidents, faculty, and, more broadly, the college or university community—is critical to the achievement of any chief academic officer. To be successful, the provost must manage up, down, and to both sides each day. Although all of these relationships have importance, two of the most important relationships in a CAO's professional life are those with the president and the chief financial officer. Indeed, if an institution is to flourish, the triumvirate of president, provost, and CFO must hold a clear and strategic vision for the institu-tion. Their relationship must be characterized by openness, candor, and walking in step for the good of the present and future institution.

Establishing a Solid Foundation

Earlier in this book, R. Michael Tanner presented best practices in the relationships among the president, provost, and board of trustees. In this chapter, we will focus on the critical team of provost and CFO. Given the breadth and depth of these two central figures as well as their interdependency, the need for starting this relationship out right and con-tinuing in good stead is more than obvious. When that happens, the re-sults are positive and powerful, helping to fully serve the mission of the university or college and its individual stakeholders. Yet all too often, the CAO-CFO relationship is laden with misunderstanding, mistrust, power plays, and day-to-day tension. When this is the reality, the insti-tution suffers and the two individuals will, more personally, have less-than-rewarding experiences in their positions. As well, the president will be saddled with a fractured executive team and burdened with having

The Thing I Very Much Wish I Had Known on My First Day as CAO

- I wish I had realized and been clearer with colleagues that the annual budget persuasively reflects the real values of the institution and that it is important to clarify and align those values before starting the numbers process.

to broker many, if not most, important institutional decisions involving the CAO and CFO.

Interestingly, the American Council on Education (ACE) and the National Association of College and University Business Officers (NACUBO), along with the Lumina Foundation, have been paying close attention to the importance of this relationship and the sometimes inevitable presence of "bad blood" between the CAO and CFO. Together, these organizations created the annual CAO/CFO Collaboration Workshop, designed to explore "the dynamics between CAOs and CFOs," to strengthen this relationship, to develop "a common understanding for working together effectively" and a "shared action agenda," and to find "solutions to challenging problems they face individually and collectively."[1]

Anne Huot, former provost and vice president for academic affairs at the State University of New York College at Brockport and now president at Keene State College in New Hampshire, says:

> [When] the relationship between the provost and CFO is good, the two will make things happen for the institution that are important. When you have a real partnership, you understand and feel the satisfaction of making things happen over and over again. You work through the institutional problems and challenges. You set aside your differences and work to bring factions together and find needed resources so the institution can achieve its goals, it mission, and vision. And, through this work, the relationship continues to grow stronger, like any close relationship, opening up more and more opportunities for success as the relationship matures.[2]

We will use ourselves as an example of such a relationship. The two of us started in our respective positions eight months apart and worked together for more than four years. Gandre had been a long-serving dean of one college within Roosevelt University and had most recently served concurrently as an interim dean of another. As CAO, he had responsibilities as chief academic and chief operating officer and had to function more comprehensively than as a college dean. He now had responsibility for the academic mission of the university as a whole, including oversight of all five, eventually six, colleges and their unit deans; direct contact and work with the board of trustees; accreditation, assessment, and program review for units, programs, and the university as a whole; oversight of all sponsored research and grants; and much of government and civic engagement and partnerships. In addition, he had to work with Krug, as CFO, and the Planning and Budget Committee, composed primarily of faculty, to develop the annual budget. Their first budgets included significant departures from previous standard budgets at Roosevelt, including appropriations for a new College of Pharmacy, the restart of intercollegiate athletics, and the beginning projections for the institution's new 32-story multipurpose building. Krug, an experienced CFO, had worked earlier in her career in finance and budgeting at United Airlines and the Chicago Housing Authority, but she now had to learn the significantly different culture of higher education, and quickly. Together, we not only learned our individual jobs side by side, but we also taught and helped each other.

Starting simultaneously, and learning to trust and respect experience, leadership styles, and differing perspectives served to build a strong and durable working relationship. Kathleen Enz Finken, provost at California Polytechnic University, underlines the need for faith and confidence in the experience and skills of the other partner:

> The relationship between the provost and CFO must be one of tremendous trust, respect, and integrity if it is a good one. Both parties must believe in the other's background, their readiness for the job at hand, and what they bring to the table. They do not need to agree on everything, indeed having different perspectives on issues is often a major plus when discussing tough challenges, but ultimately, if it is a good relationship, each must know they have the other's back no matter what.[3]

A successful CAO–CFO relationship can help colleges and universities address major challenges, particularly those involving student outcomes assessments, student loan defaults, and the rising cost of a college degree.

Best Practices in CAO-CFO Relationships

- Adopting a public, united posture
- Scheduling and following through on a regular weekly meeting just for the CAO and CFO
- Scheduling a regular meeting for the CAO and CFO with the president

The Weekly Routine: Creating a United Approach and Working Successfully with the President

Before discussing the most important activity that the provost and CFO can do together—leading the planning for and construction of the annual budget—it is appropriate to discuss how to develop a shared, successful weekly routine, and how to work effectively with the president. As the CAO and CFO, we knew our positions came with what Peter G. Northouse calls "position power,"[4] but we also knew that "position power" alone normally does not have much longevity in higher education. Colleges and universities are highly relational places, and we also wanted to build what Ronald A. Heifetz calls "informal authority."[5] In our respective positions, and as a team, we knew that informal power and authority hold more lasting influence if they come from being viewed as open and knowledgeable, as good listeners, and as administrators whose word can be trusted. We could then use our position power and informal authority with trustees, faculty, and staff colleagues to initiate strategic movement toward the key goals of serving students and their ultimate success, and supporting the faculty and staff in their professional development.

As we began to assess how our relationship would function and how we would achieve our common goals, we agreed that we had to shape the public image of a united pair that worked together efficiently and collegially. One simple example of this was that we made sure we were seen together publicly whenever appropriate, deliberately walking into and sitting together at open forums and all-university events. We also agreed that to remain united we had to commit to a scheduled weekly meeting to review issues directly related to each other's operations and also to common issues relating to the faculty, the trustees, the president, and the other vice presidents and their staffs. Considering how busy every provost and CFO are on a daily basis, we knew this weekly appointment would be difficult to work into our schedules, but we eventually found that this time together was one of the most important parts of creating and sustaining a strong relationship. This session also fostered discussions about many other issues outside of our direct responsibilities that would never have taken place if we had not pledged ourselves to this scheduled time.

Isiaah Crawford, provost at Seattle University, believes in this kind of work as well. He has worked with two CFOs during his six years as provost. With the first CFO he had lunch two or three times a month or a brief meeting after work. He now meets twice a month with his new CFO colleague and twice a month with the president, CFO, executive

Keys to Effective, Collaborative Budget Development

1. Transparency
2. Close linkage between the budget and the institutional mission
3. Multiple constituency participation and buy-in
4. Streamlined process and meeting agendas
5. One clearinghouse planning and budget committee
6. Significant information sharing with the committee and the community
7. Year-round budget planning and development activities
8. A strategic as well as financial focus

vice president and the university counsel as a group. He holds fast to the concept that "Nurturing these key relationships is paramount to successful efforts on behalf of the faculty, students, and staff of the university. I need their help and they mine. Our importance to each other is obvious. We are a team that bases its success on transparency and collaboration."[6] Another part of our strategy and operational plan was to meet with the president regularly. These standing appointments allowed us to discuss pressing issues and future planning, and they also allowed for time to talk more generally about higher education trends and topics affecting the university.

Best Practices in Preparing a Collaborative Budget

The annual budget process at every college or university is central to its proper and strategic operation, yet this core institutional activity often goes astray, shrouded in secrecy, and confirming for many faculty members that the administration cannot be trusted. Any annual budget is a guide to what an institution values. Upon a thorough evaluation of any budget, one can see where money is, and where that money is betrays institutional identity and values.[7] A good budget is one that clearly delineates plans for student success and faculty and staff professional development to ensure student success. In a less-than-optimal budget, one will find numerous pet projects of a president, dean, faculty group, and even alumni, along with historical artifacts that are connected to culture, or political compromises made to appease individuals or power groups. Expenditures like these—and every institution has some—are difficult to eliminate unless there is a shared strategic mandate that budgets are to serve the core mission of educating students and providing the experiences and environment in which they can succeed. Expenditures that do not meet that requirement should be cut and replaced with others that are in concert with the university or college's mission, values, and current strategic plan. This critical piece of the budget—the consistent use of principles of identity and values to guide the process of developing an appropriate budget—can and should be guided by a strong and candid CAO-CFO partnership. These two officers can help illuminate their own perspectives to one another as well as to the president, and they can also lead sometimes difficult discussions with faculty members, deans, and, increasingly, student stakeholders.

After our first year as a team at Roosevelt, we immediately noted that our annual planning and budget processes needed updating. The first thing we acknowledged was that the process was cumbersome and disjointed. We had both a Planning Committee (made up of five faculty members, one from each college, the CAO, and CFO) and a Budget Committee (made up of three faculty members, the CAO, and CFO). These two committees operated independently, with the Planning Committee holding no budgeting responsibility or authority and yet evaluating annual presentations by academic and non-academic units before sending numerous recommendations and endorsements to the Budget Committee. The Budget Committee then had to wade through and review this large volume of recommendations, which were in the form of printed materials and the verbal recollections of the CAO and CFO, and make recommendations to the president and board of trustees. The process seemed inefficient and dated to us, and it was replaced with a more strategic, high-functioning committee holding combined planning and budgeting responsibilities.

We proposed to replace these two committees with an overall Planning and Budget Committee consisting of eight faculty members as well as the university provost, the CFO, and the recently created suburban campus provost. We also planned to make available greater amounts of financial information for faculty on the newly designed committee. The new structure and our greater openness brought more transparency to the process, building trust in the greater community and more support for the final decisions to follow. We took this plan to the University Senate, the faculty as a whole, and ultimately to the board of trustees, revising the faculty's constitution to incorporate the new model. The restructured committee operates throughout the full academic year, rather than simply the spring semester. With more time as a group and with the provost and the CFO as part of the group, committee members grasp the budget on a far deeper level than members of either of the previous committees did in the past. Additionally, committee members now have the opportunity to take advantage of opportunities that are

Presidential Observations on the CAO-CFO Relationship

BY CHARLES R. MIDDLETON

1. *Never forget that you hired them and retained them.* While every senior position at the college is a critical hire, the president's ability to oversee the finances and the academic enterprise are largely dependent on the success of these two officers. Shaping their collaborations and joining them regularly for three-sided conversations about major issues is an essential use of the president's time and a key component of successful leadership.

2. *The CAO and the CFO need your leadership.* They also can help the president provide it to other officers who will respond best when the messages from all three of you are consistent and collegially developed. The president has an obligation to the academy to nurture talented future leaders, and doing so with the CAO and CFO is one way to accomplish that broader goal while strengthening his or her institution.

3. *Set your expectations for collaboration between these two officers and then work to help them attain it.* It is wise in the hiring process to introduce this expectation as a condition of employment. If the annual evaluation faithfully includes an assessment of how well the two are working together, there will be an incentive to do so successfully.

4. *Remember that you need their guidance as much as they need yours.* It is difficult for the CAO and CFO to deliver tough advice to the boss. They will think long and hard before doing so. Successful presidents learn that there are times when they may not be completely convinced.

5. *Do not pick sides when they disagree during policy debates.* However, do be clear about your priorities so that both of them can work to achieve them within and across their own divisions. Open give and take in meetings models an expectation for respectful discourse, especially when there are differences of opinion. They will take their cue from you.

Charles Middleton has served as the president of Roosevelt University since 2002 and supervised James Gandre and Miroslava Mejia Krug at the time of writing their chapter. Middleton was one of the founders of the organization, LGBTQ Presidents in Higher Education, in 2010.

strategic rather than simply reactive. Finally, this empowered group of faculty also serves as formal and informal ambassadors to the rest of their colleagues, which has been especially important and influential during the past few years when financial constraints have required budget cuts and reallocations.[8]

Budget constraints have affected nearly every higher education institution in the United States since 2008, even institutions with significant endowments, robust annual fundraising, and steady tuition revenues. At the University of Chicago, for instance, President Robert Zimmer asked Provost Thomas Rosenbaum and Vice President for Administration and CFO Nim Chinniah to work together to deal with the fiscal constraints the recent national economic crisis brought to the university's budget. Their approach was to implement a values-based and cost-containment process. One key values-based decision was to continue the university's longstanding need-blind admissions policy. Taking a "need-conscious" approach to admission, even for a short period of time, would have been a relatively easy thing to do and could have filled the institution's budget hole, but the institution's values would have been compromised and the option was rejected. Rosenbaum and Chinniah decided that the most difficult decisions would be made together, rather than one administrator proposing and the other accepting or denying. Rosenbaum worked with each dean, who then worked with their various faculty members and departments; Chinniah worked with the other vice presidents. Each dean and vice president was charged with bringing back plans for values-based decisions and budget reductions that would do the least harm to the unit. They did not impose any specific cuts, since all of the units had to buy into the process and, ultimately, its results. Working together, the provost and CFO achieved the desired outcome: a balanced budget, 2 to 4 percent decreases in academic units, 6 to 9 percent decreases in non-academic units, and general buy-in across the university.[9]

Additional Leadership Opportunities for the CAO-CFO Team

The CAO and CFO, by virtue of their professional portfolios, cross into nearly every aspect of a college's operations and life, and they often perform duties outside their direct administrative purviews. An example of this might be their combined work with student services when a residence hall is being built and there is the need to design it within budget while at the same time providing attractive amenities as well as features conducive to learning communities, faculty engagement, and increased retention. Another example might be working creatively with the human resources office on new models of faculty sabbatical and research leaves.

The Single Most Important Piece of Advice for a New Provost on the First Day in the Position

■ To be successful as provost over the long term, it is most important to build unambiguously open, honest, and close relationships with the president and the CFO. Without these, a CAO will be less effective and will be out of the job in a shorter time than anticipated.

Perhaps the most common example of this work on campuses is in the area of enrollment management. The CAO and CFO normally have a large role in this area because recruitment and admission units cannot run without quality academic programs to market and the proper staffing and budget underpinnings to make their work possible. The CAO, CFO, and chief enrollment officer will often work collaboratively to set enrollment goals by major, student mix, and geographic reach as well as strategically set the tuition discount rate.

A closer working relationship will also be beneficial when there are abnormal challenges to an institution's enrollment that ultimately affect the fiscal health of the institution. During the past several years, institutions of nearly all kinds have seen changes in their normal enrollment patterns. Yield has been dropping as students apply to greater numbers of institutions. Many private colleges, and more recently four-year public ones, are seeing declining enrollments as students either delay or forego a bachelor degree, or decide to go to a community college to save money on tuition and residence costs. Roosevelt University has not been immune to this phenomenon and has been hit with its own enrollment challenges over the past several years. During the second and third years of the recession, enrollment sagged after years of steady growth. However, additional growth was still required to finance the significant expansion of Roosevelt's facilities already well underway if the university was to continue full funding of its current activities and priorities.

In addition to leading discussions of budget cuts with the president, board of trustees, and the Planning and Budget Committee, the provost and CFO also engaged the vice president for enrollment management and student services to begin to address recruitment and retention efforts as globally as possible at the institution. After two years of working collaboratively on this issue, the university experienced significant increases in new undergraduate students and has put in place the beginnings of a more systemic retention program with the appointment of two

Lessons Learned: The CAO-CFO Relationship

BY MICHAEL GALLAGHER

1. *Understand How to Focus on Priorities.* The annual budget process too often places its focus on short-term budget priorities and can result in weak or no support for longer-term objectives. Priorities should be developed from strategic thinking about why and how institutions function. Realistically, however, time and financial constraints can affect the viability of all programs and activities. Although several factors can be critical to maintaining financial viability and, ultimately, institutional success, perhaps the most important among these is the CAO's ability to understand, lead the development of, and maintain focus on academic priorities.

2. *Understand the Role of the Chief Financial Officer.* CAOs and even presidents can abdicate their responsibilities in financial decision making and provide the chief financial officer with a key vote in virtually all college and university decisions. However, the appropriate role of the CFO in setting institutional priorities is to provide assistance in maximizing resources available to accomplish objectives and to outline the financial outcomes of various alternatives. The CAO, thus, has the central responsibility to lead the development of academic priorities that promote the institutional mission while providing direction for financial planning. After appropriate priorities have been developed, detailed budgets of income and expenditures at all levels can be developed. The CAO should establish academic priorities that lead, not follow, the budgeting process.

3. *Understand That Budgets Are Simply Plans.* The minute the new annual budget takes effect, it is out of date. Adjustments to both income and planned expenditure levels will need to be made. New accounts will be created, resources will be consolidated, and funds will need to be transferred between accounts during the year. These actions can create an environment often described as "finding the money" and may foster the perception that the CAO or CFO is holding back a mysterious unallocated amount of money somewhere inside or outside the budget. In fact, rarely does a CAO "find" money. More often, he or she transfers funds from lower priority activities to higher priority needs that have emerged. To promote understanding and avoid the perception that the CAO or CFO can find new money, a clearly defined, priority-based rationale should accompany transfers of funds that occur during the budget year.

Michael Gallagher wrote the chapter on effective relationships between the CAO and the CFO in First Among Equals: The Role of the Chief Academic Officer *(1997). Now retired, Gallagher was the president of the now-named Colorado Mesa University and interim president of Idaho State University.*

retention officers, one in academic affairs and one in enrollment management and student services. This ongoing work of bringing together a comprehensive set of experiences and perspectives has demonstrated that venturing out of normal operations for the CAO and CFO have tangibly helped produce a turnaround in enrollment trends.

Conclusion: What Lies Ahead for CAOs and CFOs

Many higher education leaders believe that the current tensions affecting college and university stability may be simply a warm-up for even greater dislocations to come. Some concerns are coming from the public because of higher education's exponentially rising costs relative to inflation. Others are coming from the government and accrediting agencies calling for more transparency, accountability, and outcomes data to prove the value of a baccalaureate degree. It appears that the determination of those questioning higher education leaders will continue to grow. In responding to these calls for change and improvements, the CAO and CFO can play a key role in helping to guide the larger on-campus conversation. Working with the president and other vice presidents to address structural changes and to develop enhanced financial models, the CAO-CFO team can also be instrumental in the resolution of trustee questions and student concerns.

Another change with implications for both CAOs and CFOs is the "greying" of the American college presidency and the unprecedented rate of turnover projected over the next several years.[10] If current trends persist, fewer of these positions will be filled by the most traditional source in the past—sitting provosts. In a recent American Council on Education study on chief academic officers, only 30 percent of provosts were intending to apply for a presidency. Another 25 percent were unsure about whether to seek the position, and almost half had decided not to pursue a presidency at all.[11] While sitting presidents, provosts, and deans still constitute the majority of those who go on to become presidents, there have been indications from various sources, including the ACE study of CAOs, that suggest American higher education presidencies will increasingly be filled by those in four distinct groups: chief advancement officers, chief financial officers, chief student affairs officers, and those outside of higher education. If these indications become the status quo, the role of the provost will certainly change as a result. In some cases, if the president is a non-academic, the role of the provost could be enhanced because the president will rely more heavily on the campus-based knowledge and experience of the CAO. Conversely, with other presidents, the provost's position could diminish as the chief executive officer looks more often to the leadership of the CFO or the chief advancement officer while viewing the functions of a chief academic officer more narrowly. Whatever the institutional leadership dynamic, our view remains that the CAO-CFO team is a critical pairing and force for good on every campus. When the partnership is authentic, the reward can be enormous for an institution, its president, its students, and the faculty.

NOTES

1. American Council on Education, "CAO/CFO Collaboration: Building Collaborative Opportunities Together" (Washington, DC: American Council on Education, 2008). http://www.acenet.edu/leadership/programs/Pages/CAO-CBO -Workshop.aspx.

2. Anne Huot, conversation with author, 16 August 2012.

3. Kathleen Enz Finken, conversation with author, 2 August 2012.

4. Peter G. Northouse, *Leadership Theory and Practice, Third Edition* (Los Angeles: SAGE, 2013), 10–13.

5. Ronald A. Heiftez, *Leadership Without Easy Answers* (Cambridge, MA: The Belknap Press of Harvard University Press, 1994), 101.

6. Isiaah Crawford, conversation with author, 10 August 2012.

7. Richard L. Morrill, *Strategic Leadership in Academic Affairs* (Washington, DC: Association of Governing Boards, 2002), 44–45.

8. James Gandre and Miroslava Mejia Krug, "Dynamics on the Double." *Business Officer Magazine* (July/August 2011): 64–65.

9. Nim Chinniah, conversation with author,12 October 2012.

10. Bryan Cook and Kim Young, *The American College President 2012* (Washington, DC: American Council on Education, 2012), 49–50.

11. Peter G. Eckel, Bryan J. Cook, and Jacqueline E. King, *The CAO Census: A National Profile of Chief Academic Officers* (Washington, DC: American Council on Education, 2009), 18–21.

CHAPTER TWELVE

The Academic Ask: Partnering Academic Affairs and Institutional Advancement

Bradley W. Bateman, Wesley R. Fugate, and Julia Beyer Houpt

No matter what the size of your college or university, one thing that will always be true is that lots of people want lots of things. Faculty will typically want more tenure lines and more support for their research. Coaches and athletic directors will want new facilities and more staff members. Almost every office on campus will want more enterprise software to help them with their work. Everyone wants more space. Unfortunately, the resources to achieve these ends may be scarce. Presidents quickly learn that there is no way to achieve everything they want to do to improve the institution. Time is scarce, the development staff is never as large as it needs to be, and the number of donors changes every year. In response, chief executives have to make difficult choices and focus sometimes limited resources.

This chapter argues that the CAO plays a critical role in designing successful plans to accomplish fundraising goals. CAOs are most importantly responsible for the faculty and curriculum. So why ask them to get involved in fundraising too? The answer is simple: because they are finally responsible for so much of what happens in the college or university, they need to be full partners in the development process at every stage in order to help the institution succeed consistently.

Viewing Academic Productivity in New Financial Terms

Effective institutional planning is the foundation of effective fundraising. A well-defined and broadly communicated set of strategic priorities ensures that the board, the administration, faculty members, staff, alumni, and students all know where the college or university is heading and how it intends to get there. In this way, savvy institutions let strategic priorities drive their fundraising efforts. Another factor for long-term success is the relationships among cabinet members, and especially between the CAO and the chief advancement officer. Working together, these two individuals can match the college's academic aspirations with donor interests. Keys in this relationship are working together to develop common strategic goals, to identify potential donors who can help the institution achieve those goals, and to enlist others—the president, trustees, faculty, and volunteers—to assist in making the case to those prospective donors.

The president sets a collaborative vision and agenda for the institution and is the primary solicitor of large gifts. Many major donors, in fact, expect the president to be the person to ask for their significant investment, but the CAO plays an important role as well. While some CAOs still balk at accepting fundraising responsibilities, this chapter focuses on two priorities: clarifying the role of the CAO in the fundraising process, and describing how a CAO and a vice president for advancement can collaborate to maximize opportunities for success. As we noted above, a well-defined, clearly articulated strategic plan will provide the necessary foundation to achieve eventual fundraising success. A variety of methods are used to develop such a plan: the process can utilize existing committees and organizations on campus; a high-profile group of trustees, senior faculty, and administrators can be appointed, signaling the importance of the process; or a less-visible group can be appointed to address planning issues as part of the institution's regular business.[1] Whatever the approach, it is very important that the process engage all major institutional constituencies so that a variety of perspectives are represented and the constituencies feel they were consulted and are invested in the process and the plan. A plan that is simply handed down from the trustees or president is less likely to be successful than one that reflects broad and collegial involvement. This more collaborative process also enables those involved to grasp the larger institutional picture and to understand, even if they do not agree, that choices were made to advance the entire college, sometimes at the expense of a department or program.

Whatever type of planning method and organization is used, the CAO and other vice presidents will be asked to contribute comments from their units or divisions. In these instances, the faculty needs to be at the center of the strategic planning process.[2] It will be wise to include senior professors, since their stature will give the final plan weight and will help to ensure acceptance by the faculty as a whole. Engaging professors and allowing them to express their hopes for the institution's future is a critical first step in developing a successful strategic plan, and the CAO is the person who can best work to ensure this. Next, the CAO and the chief advancement officer need to consult about what the institution's priorities are as they begin the actual strategic planning process.

The board, the president, the CAO, the chief advancement officer, and other vice presidents will eventually discuss the ideas, and each department or college will have its own way of deciding what become their components of the final strategic plan. The plan will have the best chance of success if it engaged the entire community along the way, and there is no better way to generate enthusiasm and legitimacy for that plan than to have listened carefully to the whole community in its early stages of formulation.

Once strategic goals and priorities are identified and the plan developed, questions will arise as to how much these priorities will cost and how they can be funded. Certainly, some objectives can be achieved without additional funding by assessing current budgets and shifting funds as appropriate or by eliminating programs that are no longer necessary. Some objectives can be achieved by raising tuition or fees from other sources such as rental fees for conferences or summer programs, but often the plan will require a significant fundraising campaign in order to achieve its objectives. This is where the chief advancement officer can provide practical information and perspectives regarding the realistic potential for success.

In the case of Denison University, the leadership invested in a development program that raised several million dollars annually in operating funds through the Annual Fund.[3] In this sense, fundraising and stewardship are ongoing efforts and not something that the university stops and then starts every eight to ten years. Once the Denison board approves a strategic plan, it then invests in a consulting team to help develop a campaign plan and strategy. The team conducts a feasibility study that tests the strategic plan and fundraising goals with forty to fifty key donors and constituents. For one of Denison's recent campaigns, the results of the study indicated that while prospective donors were very enthusiastic about much of the plan, some of the objectives were not of interest and, most importantly, that its target number—$200 million— was too high. In response, the administration and the board listened to

Keys to an Effective CAO–Chief Advancement Officer Partnership

1. Collaborative identification of strategic goals annually
2. Joint, strategic approach to prospective donors
3. Successful engagement of the president, trustees, faculty members, and volunteers in priority projects.

the consultants' recommendations and donor feedback and scaled back its aspirations accordingly. Consequently, two needed building projects, a major renovation to an outdated chemistry building and a significant renovation of the university's natatorium, were cut from the campaign. Other fundraising goals were rethought in response to donor feedback as well, and when the quiet phase of the campaign began, its goal was set at $160 million and its objectives reflected a greater emphasis on people and programs and less on facilities and technology infrastructure.

In retrospect, sustained faculty involvement in the process and a commitment to ongoing collaboration between the CAO and the chief advancement officer helped to maintain institutional focus on combined academic and financial success. In the case of Denison, this included the CAO listening closely to the chief advancement officer and learning new information about the college's donors in preparing for and running several campaigns, and then agreeing that certain building projects were an attractive goal. We had learned that while we could raise money for buildings, it was still much more difficult than raising funds for people and programs. Still, there were several construction projects that clearly supported the academic program, including the once-delayed chemistry building and natatorium upgrade. Once these two items had been added to the list, the CAO needed to turn to other academic priorities and determine what was reasonable to add from those lists.

While it may appear to donors that a college or university is constantly in a capital campaign, that is not always the case. Prior to a successful campaign, it is crucial for a college or university to determine its most important needs. In the case of the then-named Randolph-Macon Woman's College, the institution's 2006 strategic plan had identified financial sustainability as a core goal, with one of the primary tactics to achieve this being the transition from a single-sex to a coeducational institution.[4] Not surprisingly, the environment was not right for a capital campaign immediately after this decision. Alumnae had to become used to the addition of men to the campus culture and the change of the name of the institution to Randolph College before a capital campaign could be started.

Instead of a campaign, priorities were identified from the strategic plan that would assist the newly named college in its efforts to grow enrollments as one of the primary reasons for becoming coeducational in the first place. Toward this end, the CAO worked with the chief advancement officer to identify academic needs that could have a direct impact on enrollment. The college incorporated some of these priorities into the annual budgeting process, while others were identified as potential gifts that donors might consider making above and beyond their annual fund giving. In particular, donors enjoyed making larger than normal annual fund gifts that directly benefited the academic experience. For example, the college developed the Randolph Innovative Student Experience (RISE) program to afford every junior and senior at the College up to $2,000 for a research, creative, or study-abroad experience that would enrich their academic program. Donors were particularly enthusiastic about making annual funds gifts that would support this program that the college also views as an important recruitment and retention tool.

The Advantages of Saying Yes to the CAO

In November 2011, the authors were invited to make a presentation at the annual meeting of provosts and deans of the Council of Independent Colleges (CIC) about the best practices between chief academic and chief advancement officers. We were joined by Katie Conboy, then provost, and Francis Dillon, vice president for advancement, at Stonehill College. Stonehill had recently successfully completed its own campaign, and Conboy and Dillon offered useful examples of how the relationship can work efficiently in shaping a college's future. As Stonehill entered its campaign, its board of trustees decided that it wanted to construct a new building to house the college's business program. The board wanted business to receive more emphasis in the curriculum and believed that a new classroom and office building would attract more students. The vice president for advancement believed that money could be raised for a new building, but the provost thought that the greatest need for the college was not a new business building but rather instructional spaces for the laboratory sciences. Stonehill had a long history of success at educating undergraduates for medical school and attracted many students because of this success, but the provost knew that their main laboratory facilities needed renovation and expansion if Stonehill were to continue its prominence in this area.

The vice president for advancement and the provost then worked together to make this case to the trustees. One factor central to their efforts was that the vice president for advancement trusted the CAO's judgment

Counter-Intuitive Methods to Raise Money

1. Say *yes* to the CAO's most important project.
2. Say *no* to a donor when there are good reasons for it.
3. Say *maybe* to a faculty member when appropriate with the rationale that the proposal was excellent and it should be saved for the next campaign.

and was willing to work to create an awareness in the planning process for board members to see other needs beyond their primary target of a new building for the business program. While there are usually layers of decision making involved, the board will, of course, always hold the final authority regarding what priorities are the highest, but there are also likely to be committees of the board that will have differing degrees of influence in the deliberations. During this process, experienced CAOs and vice presidents for advancement will collaboratively work across these various constituencies and keep the channels of communication open. In this case, the board voted for the science building option after the CAO organized tours of the existing facilities led by members of the science faculty. They were the best people to carefully explain how crowded the labs were and what kinds of new facilities were needed to be able to keep the college in the forefront nationally. The CAO also provided useful statistics about the enrollments in pre-med courses and the numbers of science majors, while the faculty themselves articulately made the case for what advancements could occur in the classroom and in their research with a new facility.

Another example of collaborative partnerships between a CAO and chief advancement officer can often be found with an institution's grant officers. For a number of years, the development office at Centre College[5] had only one staff member in corporate and foundation relations.[6] This single position simply could not handle the needs of the advancement staff as well as faculty grant needs. In fact, the chief advancement officer had long sought additional personnel in this area. The current staff member was spending a considerable amount of time reporting back to those organizations that had provided the college a grant rather than using that time to identify additional sources of support. Having been unsuccessful in creating a new position, he approached the CAO seeking a partnership through which a new staff member might spend half of her or his time working with faculty on their grants. The CAO agreed to the plan, and the collaborative approach worked in helping to secure the new position, which has been helpful to both vice presidents to increase funding directly the institution and to faculty research.

The Advantages of Saying No to a Donor

One of the most counter-intuitive requirements for successful fundraising is the ability to say no to a prospective donor. The need to do so may arise for many reasons, but the central principle behind the need to say no remains the same: resources for advancement are scarce, as are the resources for implementing new programs. Once priorities have been defined for the strategic plan and the campaign, the CAO will be working against her- or himself by becoming involved in projects that are not

core items in either that plan or the campaign. This problem emerged at
Denison during the most recent capital campaign. One priority that had
been collaboratively developed was to create new space for a University
Learning Center equipped with new levels of instructional technology.
The advancement office knew of someone who had interests in learning
and technology, so the CAO and the chief advancement officer started
explaining to the prospective donor what the university needed and why.

Almost immediately, however, the CAO and the chief advancement
officer discovered that the donor had very strong ideas about the importance of technology to the future of American education. Her main
interests were in how America could remain competitive in world labor
markets, and her ideas drew heavily from work done in this area by people outside the university. During preliminary discussions, the donor began by focusing on future changes in the university's curriculum with
an emphasis on preparing graduates for the new world of work. The potential for a gift was clear, but it would not be in support of the university's established strategic priorities. There was little doubt in the minds
of the CAO and the chief advancement officer that the donor had identified an area of concern for future American workers—and Denison
graduates—in an increasingly global and "flat" world economy.[7] Still,
as talks continued, it became clear that she was interested in trying to
effect changes in the curriculum and establish a center significantly different than the one the CAO and chief advancement officer jointly had
in mind when approaching her.

Eventually, the costs of going forward proved to be too high. Even
as vice presidents of the university, the CAO and chief advancement officer had no mandate in the campaign to change the university's curriculum, and they were already strongly and publicly committed to the priorities the institution had established for fundraising. The donor had both
interesting ideas and good intentions, but in order to provide a major
gift, she wanted to move the curriculum in a direction that the faculty
did not support. Reluctantly, the CAO and the chief advancement officer decided to decline this opportunity and to continue looking elsewhere
for the support that was needed.

Saying no to a donor need not mean loss of a gift. Sometimes the
explanation of other institutional priorities can stimulate a donor to take
interest in funding another key goal. At Randolph College, a commitment
had been made to a scholarship fund that was a priority in the capital
campaign at an earlier point. Years later, after a new strategic plan had
been developed, that priority was not as important to the institution. The
strategic plan and facilities master plan had called for a renovation to the
existing science and mathematics building. Faculty in these departments

had long argued to the CAO that with recent changes in the curriculum and enrollment growth, their programs were running out of laboratory space. Already an environmental science lab had to be located in another building, nor could the environmental science faculty offices be located with the other scientists. Exactly what type of space was needed in this new facility, however, needed to be further explored.

The CAO advocated this growing need frequently to his fellow members of the senior administration. The chief advancement officer recognized this priority and encouraged a donor to consider using a portion of the gift committed to the scholarship during the last campaign to help fund a consultant to visit campus to review the current space and meet with faculty to help the college gain a better understanding of the needs required in a new or renovated facility. The donor was pleased to assist with this strategic priority of the college, and the full gift committed during the previous campaign was realized.

The Advantages of Saying Maybe to a Faculty Member

Despite best efforts to listen to all constituencies during a strategic planning process, some faculty will learn that their proposals were left behind when the formal campaign commences. At Denison, one enterprising teacher informed the CAO and chief advancement officer that she wanted to raise money for her program even after it failed to make it onto the campaign. She asked for meetings with the provost, the president, and the vice president for advancement, and she offered to meet with potential donors and make calls to foundations. While it was easy to view her behavior as helpful and positive when she started, it became harder to view it that way as time passed and her efforts came to be seen as counterproductive. However, her faculty colleagues did not agree. From their point of view, this professor led a popular program, she had identified potential donors, and she was offering to help Denison with its advancement work. All the university needed to do was cooperate with her.

Ways to Earn Faculty Buy-in to College Fundraising Campaigns

1. Invite senior professors to lead the way.
2. Involve all faculty members, including adjuncts, in the planning process.
3. Share large amounts of information.
4. Establish and adhere to realistic timelines.
5. Expect the CAO to be a faculty advocate.
6. Share the final report with the faculty.

   Similar to the example of the prospective donor who wanted the university to accept and implement her ideas about how to prepare our students for the technological demands of the twenty-first century, this case
represented a challenging problem for university human relations. Both
the CAO and the vice president for institutional advancement were finding themselves spending time on a project that was not going to help
them attain shared institutional goals that were also the result of a comprehensive strategic planning process. In the short term, we decided to
tell the faculty member that no more resources could be spent on her
proposal because it was not a core element of the strategic plan. However, while *no* was the short-term response, *maybe* was the longer term
understanding reached with her. We carefully explained that the strategic plan and campaign were underway but that maintaining a positive
relationship with this individual and with the faculty as a whole was crucial because the university would shortly be starting plans for the *next*
campaign, and we were inviting her to submit her proposal at the front
end of that process to increase the likelihood of its approval. In the context of this "maybe," time and advice would also be offered to the faculty member to help her strengthen her eventual submission.
   "Maybe" can also mean asking a faculty member to envision her or
his needs in different ways. At Randolph College, both the psychology
department and biology department had, unbeknownst to each other,
included the need for similar pieces of equipment to aid in their classroom instruction in their budget requests. The biology department's
equipment had long been outdated and, with the addition of a new popular major in sports and exercise studies requiring more students to take
its physiology course, the need had become urgent to move forward in
securing new equipment. The psychology department had wanted to use
the new equipment to reinvigorate a course that standing faculty had not
taught for a dozen years—obviating an outdated animal facility in favor
of sophisticated monitoring equipment. Generally, the senior administration supported the need to purchase the equipment, and the chief advancement officer believed funds could be raised for such a system. If donor
funding could be secured, the then-president was comfortable moving forward, with one caveat: the college could only purchase one system.
   The CAO, seeing the potential to assist both departments, worked
to find ways to achieve their needs through the purchase of one system
that would have the flexibility of being used by both departments. Thus,
the response to this request for equipment was "maybe" if there was a
way to achieve synergies through a shared purchase. Thanks to the work
of the CAO, one department did in fact alter its needs. The chief advancement officer found a potential donor who was intrigued by the idea

of helping two different departments, and in the end, the equipment was secured.

Conclusion

No matter whether the answer to a donor or faculty member is yes, no, or maybe, effective responses can best be developed through successful cooperation between a CAO and the vice president for advancement. The most successful cooperation between the two positions begins with a shared approach to institutional planning. In turn, effective fundraising is based on the ability first to listen to potential donors and then to tell them persuasively why you need their support. In most cases, this work will be centered in the current strategic plan and a campaign based on that planning. Whatever the stage of the process, it is most important for the chief academic and chief advancement officers to trust each other and to share knowledge and expertise on a weekly basis. The CAO will continuously identify the most pressing needs for the college or university's academic programs, and the vice president for advancement will monitor the full donor base and the possibilities for support that lie within it. Together, they form an under-leveraged resource to move the institution forward.

NOTES

1. William L. Picket, "The Long-range Planning Process," in *The Successful Capital Campaign*, ed. H. Gerald Quigg (Washington, DC: Council for Advancement and Support of Education, 1986), 12.

2. Ibid., 8–9.

3. Denison University is a small liberal arts college in central Ohio, founded in 1831 by Northern Baptists from Brown University who sought to found a new college on the western frontier. With 2,200 undergraduates (and no graduate students), Denison is slightly larger than the typical mid-western liberal arts college, but not enough larger to make a significant difference in the scale of its operations or the nature of its curriculum. The college operates with a 10:1 student/faculty ratio and offers a traditional set of 33 majors divided into four academic divisions (science, humanities, fine arts, and social sciences).

Like Harvard, Denison's name derives from an early donor who left a large estate to secure the prospects of the college. Thus, like most liberal arts colleges, Denison has been dependent on successful fundraising since its inception. At $660 million, Denison's endowment ranks among the top 135 in the nation among all colleges and universities, large and small. (We would not be so keenly aware of this if it were not for the fact that several years ago Senator Charles Grassley requested information from those 135 colleges and universities when he was weighing legislation mandating the annual pay-out from college endowments. Grassley's effort seems to have been abandoned following the 2008 financial crash and the sudden fall in endowment values that it caused.) This endowment sets Denison apart from many other colleges of its kind: with 30 percent of its annual operating budget covered by the funds generated from the endowment, Denison has the ability to meet student financial need and thus draws a student body that is unusual in its socioeconomic diversity. The endowment also provides stability in the operation of the college; during the global financial crisis in 2008–09, Denison increased funding for scholarships by $2 million without cutting funding for any program, academic or co-curricular, and without cutting or freezing staffing levels.

4. Founded in 1891 as Randolph-Macon Women's College and becoming co-educational in 2007, Randolph College is a small private liberal arts college in central Virginia. With approximately 700 students, almost all of which are undergraduates, Randolph is smaller than nearly all of its peers. It operates with a 9:1 student/faculty ration and offers 30 majors divided into three academic divisions (arts and letters, natural sciences, social and behavioral sciences).

With a $133 million endowment, Randolph has a strong endowment per student. It has been overly reliant on this endowment to provide operating funds each year, with nearly 37 percent of its annual budget coming from endowment spending. This over-reliance on endowment to balance operations is particularly difficult during down economic times.

5. Centre College, a private liberal arts college located in central Kentucky, is slightly smaller than most of its peers, with 1,350 undergraduates (no graduate students). The college has a student faculty ratio of 11:1 and offers 33 majors in three divisions (humanities, social studies, and science and mathematics). Its endowment is modest for its size at approximately $213 million.

6. Phone conversation with Centre College Vice President for College Relations Richard Trollinger, 16 January 2014.

7. See, for instance, Thomas Friedman, *The World Is Flat: A Brief History of the Twenty-first Century* (New York: Farrar, Straus, and Giroux, 2005).

CHAPTER THIRTEEN

Working Effectively with the Senior Student Affairs Officer

Penny Rue and Suresh Subramani

A new chief academic officer quickly needs to become an expert about a world of concerns that rarely surface for the typical faculty member. When this occurs, he or she will find a ready partner in the chief student affairs officer who recognizes the primacy of teaching and learning and strives to create an organization dedicated to student success. The following chapter identifies areas of significant overlap and shared interest and provides a roadmap for successful partnerships between the CAO and the CSAO.

A Natural Partnership to Create Student Success

The CAO can rely on student affairs professionals to know that growth occurs when students are stretched to try new things and learn new concepts and skills, but not stretched so far that they are inclined to retreat. Support services, one of the best areas to design a partnership between Academic Affairs and Student Affairs, can make a difference by allowing students to achieve the greatest degree of "stretch" and learning possible. From the inception of student services as an area of study, journal articles and national meetings of student affairs administrators have focused on assessing the effect of student support services on academic outcomes. Thus, for a new provost or dean, the strongest partnership is likely to be with a CSAO who possesses an understanding of different student learning styles. The CSAO, along with associates in Counseling, Career Development and Residence Life, can be a key colleague in understanding and translating the factors that produce student success. CSAOs also play a central role in ensuring that students manage the joys and stresses of college life in a balanced fashion. This chapter will explore ways in which CAOs can ask for support from CSAOs to create "seamless learning environments" that foster student learning and development, provide a rich array of out-of-class learning experiences, and manage student crises in ways that minimize disruption to their learning environment.[1]

Meaningful institutional differences abound, and Joan Hirt, in her research on different types of universities and colleges, notes that the nature of student affairs practice varies from focused personal work at small liberal arts colleges to highly bureaucratized functions at complex research universities.[2] Not all student affairs departments are configured in similar ways, and the size of an institution will have a significant impact on the level of organizational complexity. At the largest universities, in fact, there now appears an unfortunate trend, described by the Association of Public and Land Grant Universities as "mineshafts, where most of the mineworkers, i.e., professionals, are intent on the task of deepening their mines without giving much thought to the need to build corridors connecting the shafts."[3] With that caveat, there still can, and should, be meaningful alliances between Academic Affairs and Student Affairs that enhance the holistic student learning experience.

Opportunities for Partnership Development

Certain core responsibilities underpin the work of Student Affairs, and these often are the areas that present ideal opportunities for partnerships:

1. Admissions and Orientation

The recruitment and enrollment of appropriately qualified students prepared to take advantage of institutional offerings is a strategic necessity. For private, tuition-driven colleges, Admissions is often the most critical function to ensure the institution's economic viability. At public universities, it represents the outward facing dimension of the university and often the one most subject to scrutiny. While faculty at even the most competitive schools will bemoan the lack of motivation and commitment of the students they teach, a significant portion of a university's reputation does derive from student selectivity.[4]

Typically, the CAO will be keenly aware of faculty perspectives on student preparedness, since it is a standard topic of departmental conversations. Still, asking for a thorough and non-anecdotal briefing on both the recruitment and the evaluation process can give a new provost an insider's view of how a class is "built" and how selection criteria are applied fairly to a large applicant pool in a public university. Reciprocally, it should be the CAO's duty to provide the CSAO with fresh information about the strengths and future plans of the academic programs in

Core Partnership Areas between Student Affairs and the CAO
1. Admissions and orientation 2. Student mental health 3. Student retention and persistence 4. Inclusion, equity, and diversity issues 5. Assessment and learning outcomes activities

order to answer queries that spring up in the minds of prospective students and their families. The yield of admitted students also is a shared priority, and a concerted partnership to highlight both academic and student life experiences may provide an excellent opportunity for the CAO and CSAO to collaborate to improve the campus's selectivity and ranking.

2. Student Mental Health and Critical Incident Management

The CAO will rely on the CSAO to be the institution's lead crisis manager as it relates to students, whether a campus event has gone awry, a hurricane is on the way, or some students are stranded abroad in a foreign country. Perhaps most importantly, in the wake of multiple fatal shooting incidents such as those at Virginia Tech in 2007 and Northern Illinois University in 2008, are the risks presented by persons with serious mental health challenges on campus. Arguably, the most critical role for Student Affairs is that of overseeing the health and well-being of students. It has been documented that students today come with a complex array of mental health challenges,[5] and federal disability law requires that universities provide accommodations that allow each student to be fully engaged in the life of the college. The CAO can depend on the CSAO's expertise in assisting suicidal students, conducting or managing threat assessment procedures, working with faculty to recognize signs and symptoms of distress, and understanding pertinent legal requirements.

Since a disruptive student may have widespread impact, the dean and especially inexperienced faculty will benefit from the breadth of services and expertise embedded in most college counseling centers. National data show that 6.4 percent of students consider suicide sometime during the academic year, and another 1.1 percent actually attempt suicide—amounting to hundreds of students at almost any large university.[6] While completed suicides are not uncommon on college campuses, they are a small fraction of those attempted, thus showing the efficacy of emergency response and counseling services. One essential partnership in which the CAO can collaborate is in the creation of resources to help faculty identify the signs and symptoms of student distress and manage disruption in the classroom.[7] Virginia Tech developed state of the art behavioral intervention and crisis management services as well as critical incident response protocols in 2008 following the events on their campus in 2007. At times of individual crisis, particular attention must also be paid to international and domestic non-resident students who are far away from families and may feel lonely, isolated, and lost.

3. Student Retention

The academic success of a campus is often judged by the public through its retention and graduation rates. These statistics are typically linked to the quality of incoming students, and top tier universities and colleges are routinely recognized for their outstanding retention and graduation rates. Students leave institutions for dozens of reasons, and efforts to improve retention can be best served by proactive, collaborative strategies between Academic Affairs and Student Affairs. Books, conferences, and articles about retention strategies are readily available. Research tells us that meaningful engagement outside the classroom has the greatest impact on a student's likelihood of persistence to graduation.[8] The University of California, San Diego, for example, employs an Academic Affairs–Student Affairs partnership to diagnose and correct impediments to student retention, and individuals from both teams work cooperatively to address ongoing issues that impact graduation rates.

4. Inclusion, Equity, and Diversity

Closely related to retention is the overall climate of the institution. Do all students feel a sense of belonging? Is the campus free from racial or gender-based harassment or exclusion? While perfection is impossible, campus climate is a composite of factors that students perceive on a continuum from welcoming to unwelcoming. The development of a positive campus climate, culture, and atmosphere is a broadly shared responsibility, even though most assessments and interventions designed to improve the climate occur within Student Affairs. Sylvia Hurtado and colleagues, synthesizing a body of work on campus climate and student retention, have created a framework that highlights academic validation in each classroom, a curriculum of inclusion, and integration of learning as key factors in supporting a diverse learning environment.[9] Indiana University, for instance, employs Incident Teams to assist and support students who report an incident of discrimination in finding a resolution. Institutions that encourage a respectful, open though sometimes difficult dialogue about their campus climate stand a better chance of navigating the challenges therein, and a united CAO-CSAO approach can lead those dialogues more effectively.

5. Assessment and Learning Outcomes

One of the strongest trends within higher education since the late 1990s has been a move to a student learning outcomes approach. While decades have elapsed since the first mentions of co-curricular learning, the past ten years have brought significant progress in adoption of measurable learning outcomes, thanks to the work of accrediting agencies, the Association of American Colleges and Universities (AAC&U), George Kuh, Trudy Banta, and others. In particular, AAC&U's Liberal Education and America's Promise Project (LEAP) has developed broadly applicable essential learning outcomes and high-impact educational practices that create a framework for rich learning partnerships between the CAO and CSAO.[10] Using national data from the National Survey of Student Engagement (NSSE), AAC&U has identified the engagement opportunities most likely to spur student development toward the essential learning outcomes. As examples, the University of Michigan Arts of Citizenship program embeds community-based research in the undergraduate curriculum, and Pomona College creates engagement with diverse viewpoints in its Core Commitments program. Perhaps even more importantly, this project has identified which students participate in these high-impact experiences by key variables such as full-time or part-time, native first-year or transfer, first generation status, and ethnicity. While these national data may mask meaningful institutional differences, they also illuminate that white students are most likely to participate in almost every high-impact practice except service learning, for which African-Americans top the list. Also, first-generation and part-time students are disadvantaged in participation across every measured practice, and Chicano/Latino students are *least* likely to do research with a faculty member. A nuanced understanding of who participates in these high-impact practices is useful to a CAO who is developing strategies to reduce educational disparities.

Student affairs professional associations such as Student Affairs Administrators in Higher Education, known as NASPA, have also developed increasingly sophisticated support programs and materials that help practitioners develop expertise and capacity in assessing student learning outcomes outside the classroom.[11] With a growing recognition that learning and development are intertwined, CSAOs are increasingly expecting of their provosts that programs and engagement opportunities for students align with campus learning frameworks, that they articulate expected learning outcomes for participants, and that they include a means of assessing the extent to which they have been achieved. While widespread adoption of such rigorous practices takes time, some campuses have challenged themselves to move ahead in this regard: the State University of New York (SUNY) at Albany has an assistant vice president dedicated to student success, and the programs developed for this purpose are recognized as having achieved congruence among strategic goals, learning outcomes, and assessment efforts.[12]

High-Impact Practices and Academic Collaboration

The CSAO provides leadership for an array of specific programs on campus, many of which can be of strategic interest to the CAO, and several of which are defined as high-impact practices by AAC&U. The programs described below are particularly useful for collaboration.

1. Learning Assistance

One of the most frequent ways that an academic vice president can expect support from her or his CSAO is in the area of learning assistance. On many campuses, one or more of these services, including academic advising, developmental instruction, tutoring, writing centers, and study skills support rest within Student Affairs. If the CAO is concerned about retention, for example, a careful analysis of courses with high failure rates, or the identification of under-preparation of incoming students, can provide a clear direction for the development of targeted support services to address these specific concerns.

2. Academic Integrity

The need to educate students and faculty alike about their responsibilities in maintaining academic integrity has been a rising concern on many campuses over the past decade, and few issues cut across the student and faculty experience as directly. Electronic tools, many via the cellphone, allow for new forms of academic shortcuts, and faculty members are now challenged to develop more sophisticated techniques to identify cheating and plagiarism. A newly appointed academic dean is probably familiar with the necessity of such efforts but may not have thought of these issues from a systemic perspective before. Student Affairs is often responsible for the adjudication of academic misconduct and for the education of students found to have committed such acts. A solid Student Affairs–Academic Affairs partnership in this area can build programs and guidelines that help faculty prevent and respond to violations of academic integrity.

High-Impact Practices and Academic Collaboration: Eight Examples

1. Learning assistance
2. Academic integrity
3. Student conduct
4. International programs
5. Service learning
6. Career counseling and development
7. Undergraduate research and scholarship
8. Technology and new media

The International Center for Academic Integrity (ICAI) is an institutional membership organization whose leadership spans faculty and administrators from both Academic Affairs and Student Affairs. ICAI provides a menu of resources designed to predict, describe, and address issues related to academic dishonesty and gives faculty and administrators the tools they need to develop a culture of integrity.[13] At some colleges, students are now taking the lead to promote integrity among their peers through honor councils and advisory boards. An experienced dean for student life can serve as a key resource for a newly promoted academic dean who would like to raise faculty awareness of these issues.

3. Student Conduct

Non-academic misconduct is a central responsibility of Student Affairs, and the CSAO will most likely be personally engaged in policy formation; compliance with system, state, and federal changes in law and policy; and the resolution of complex cases. While the bulk of conduct violations each year, no matter what campus, involve underage use of alcohol, many academic deans also acknowledge that more troublesome behaviors, often coupled with mental health challenges, are on the rise. Classroom disruption, threatening behavior, stalking, and bullying have all increased over the past decade. Rarely do these problems confine themselves to the residence hall, and faculty members are increasingly involved as victims or witnesses to forms of institutional disturbance. While even experienced professors may expect that a disruptive student be summarily removed from a classroom, due process and mental health accommodations can make such a rapid outcome unlikely. Since the CSAO is often the final appeal for any disciplinary sanction on campus, he or she will not become personally involved in a case until near the end, but the CSAO will be prepared to assist a provost or dean in understanding how the system works and making sure that the involved faculty members are well supported in the conduct process.

4. International Programs

Support for international students coming to American campuses and advising and support of students planning to study abroad may rest within Student Affairs, depending on institutional history and practice. Within these programs, staff members offer a combination of highly technical academic advising to ensure that study abroad does not extend the time to obtain a degree along with focused counseling of students to determine how much cultural stretching is optimal for their growth and development. An additional challenge embedded in the admissions process is to identify international students who have the potential to thrive in a foreign environment. These concerns regularly cross Academic and Student Affairs reporting lines, and a flexible partnership is essential to manage risk and ensure student success.

5. Service Learning

One of the most natural partnerships between Academic Affairs and Student Affairs is in the field of service learning because it incorporates the curriculum and the co-curriculum. The field arose, in part, through recognition that the traditional higher education tripartite mission of teaching, research, and service calls for an outward focus, and that service to the community is an integral part of what it means to be a college or university. Students strive to resolve questions encountered in their service experiences with answers discovered in the classroom, and they have pressed institutions to be more engaged in issues and concerns beyond the campus perimeter. Students become goodwill ambassadors for their campus in the larger community, helping to generate positive press about campus engagement. The Haas Center for Public Service at Stanford University provides an excellent model. Housed in Student Affairs, it provides substantive opportunities for faculty engagement in creating service-learning courses and conducting community-based research in addition to high-impact student involvement opportunities.

6. Career Counseling and Development

Most higher education institutions, especially high cost ones, are under increasing scrutiny to demonstrate the return on investment of a bachelor's or master's degree. Students and parents alike now view higher education as a ticket to a well-paying job or a prestigious graduate program.

At the center of many of these expectations is the staff in Career Services. Part academic advisor, part counselor, and part career-developer, a talented career services professional can help students identify strengths, develop skills through professional internships and undergraduate research, and market their assets to targeted employers. Provosts are constantly interested in the job placement rates and graduate school acceptance rates of their disciplines, and they will advertise these successes to parents and alumni.

7. Undergraduate Research and Scholarship Preparation

The opportunity to collaborate with faculty in conducting research has become a distinctive form of experiential learning. While faculty members design the opportunities, CSAOs can serve as a main link in creating the program to identify the most promising candidates, to match faculty and student participants, and sometimes to extend the learning experience to the student living environment. In the process, these students receive a head start in applying for national fellowship opportunities such as Rhodes, Truman, and Marshall scholarships. Competitive candidates will receive essay critiques, interview advice, and perhaps even wardrobe consultations from a faculty-staff scholarship committee. Georgetown University's Fellowship Secretary provides a leadership model in this area that reflects the shared goals under discussion.

8. Technology and New Media

Just as technology has changed the face of teaching and learning, so too it has altered the multiple ways in which the Office of Student Life communicates with students. Handbooks, directories, and mailings have been almost completely replaced by websites, chat functions, and portals. E-mail, for the last fifteen years the primary means of communication with students, is now described as "for old people," and some schools no longer assign an institutional e-mail address.[14] Universities struggle with developing sophisticated web resource navigation tools using device-neutral responsive design principles while trying to deliver student services that match Amazon-style customer service expectations. Texting and tweeting are the new communication media for today's students, and future classes will only be attracted with the most sophisticated marketing techniques. The CSAO should take responsibility for staying current with and utilizing the most effective ways to reach students and should frequently communicate changing needs and expectations with the provost. These skills can be critical in a crisis, when rapid, efficient communication with students is essential.

What CAOs Don't Get about Student Affairs

BY KEVIN KRUGER

- Do not confuse student affairs staff with party planners. Their role is to create a campus environment and experiences that facilitate learning in and outside the classroom, to prepare graduates for successful employment, and to develop civic-minded individuals.
- Student Affairs is three things simultaneously: a business (housing, student union, recreation); a support network (counseling and health center, crisis response); and a key partner in the student learning process (career development, service learning, leadership development).
- Student Affairs is not a fiscal competitor or an example of administrative bloat. Student Affairs staff members are critical to all retention, persistence, student success, and learning initiatives on campus.
- The next time you think Student Affairs may not be delivering on that Return On Investment (ROI) calculation, recall that effective, professional student affairs practice is about all that stands between a provost and his or her name on a lawsuit in today's regulatory environment.

Kevin Kruger is the first executive-level president of NASPA—Student Affairs Administrators in Higher Education. He assumed that role in 2012 after more than fifteen years as NASPA's associate executive director. In his position, Kruger is a national advocate and the primary spokesperson for student affairs administrators in higher education.

Conclusion: Strengthening the Partnership with Student Affairs

One of the hottest topics at national meetings for CSAOs continues to be how to strengthen their partnership with the provost and the Office of Academic Affairs. Given the new calls for accountability in higher education and the increasing resource constraints facing almost all institutions today, aligning resources and programs to meet the academic goals of the college or university while supporting individual student success is of critical importance.

Like the CAO, student affairs officers are accountable to numerous stakeholders. While the CAO devotes considerable attention to issues of faculty governance, the CSAO may also answer to multiple faculty expectations, and the CAO can be a useful partner in navigating these relationships. Professors may sit on a governance or oversight committee for student affairs. Or, while leadership for a reaccreditation process will likely fall to the provost, a team approach is often utilized to write the report and prepare the campus for the site visit. The CSAO can serve as a well-positioned co-chair of the overall endeavor. As accrediting bodies have increased their emphasis on evidence of learning outcomes, CSAOs are likely able to provide numerous examples of substantive outcomes from out-of-class environments that complement the institutional mission. The Western Association for Colleges and Schools (WASC), for example, has fully integrated co-curricular learning into its accreditation model and expects to see evidence of student learning outside the classroom in the accreditation process.[15] Evidence of collaboration in aligning curricular and co-curricular learning outcomes demonstrates tangible progress towards a seamless learning environment.

In sum, many of the challenges facing American higher education are too complex and multifaceted to be addressed without jointly leveraging the resources of the CSAO and the CAO. Pockets of Academic Affairs and Student Affairs collaboration already exist at almost every institution. Mapping those connections, conducting a gap analysis, and enhancing existing relationships provides a basic roadmap. In each case, the provost needs a partnership with a CSAO who supports the primacy of the teaching and learning mission. Both are invested in student learning and the creation of engaged and dedicated alumni, and both have skills to contribute to the handling of sensitive campus issues. As a result, each can be more successful by participating in a mutually supportive partnership that sets the tone for the overall institution.

NOTES

Suresh Subramani wishes to acknowledge that although this chapter reflects contributions from both authors, Penny Rue was primarily responsible for the initial organization and assembly of the manuscript.

1. Ernest T. Pascarella and Patrick T. Terenzini, *How College Affects Students,* 2nd ed. (San Francisco: Jossey-Bass, 2005).

2. Joan B. Hirt, *Where You Work Matters: Student Affairs Administration at Different Types of Institutions* (Lanham, MD: University Press of America, 2006), 186–94.

3. Kellogg Commission on the Future of State and Land-Grant Universities, *Returning to Our Roots: Toward a Coherent Campus Culture* (Washington, DC: National Association of State Universities and Land-Grant Colleges, 2000), 28.

4. US News Rankings, "Best Colleges, Best Graduate School, Best Hospitals, and Best Health Insurance Companies," *US News & World Report,* http://www.usnews.com/rankings.

5. Richard Kadison and Theresa Foy DiGeronimo, *College of the Overwhelmed: The Campus Mental Health Crisis and What To Do About It* (San Francisco: Jossey-Bass, 2004); Sherry A. Benton and Stephen L. Benton, "Distressed and Distressing Students: Creating a Campus Community of Care," *College*

Student Mental Health: Effective Services and Strategies Across Campus (Washington, DC: NASPA, 2006), 15–30.

6. American College Health Association, *American College Health Association National College Health Assessment,* http://www.achancha.org/reports_ACHA-NCHAII.html.

7. Counseling and Psychological Services, "Resources for Faculty and Staff," University of California, San Diego, 2012, http://caps.ucsd.edu/faculty-staff.html.

8. UCLA Diversity Research Institute from Higher Education Research Institute, "Understanding the Campus Racial Climate," conference presentation, University of California, Los Angeles, August 3, 2010.

9. Sylvia Hurtado, L. Arellano, M. Cuellar, and C. Guillermo-Wann, "Diverse Learning Environments Survey Instrument: Introduction and Select Factors," conference presentation, Diversity Research Institute from University of California, Los Angeles, August 6, 2010.

10. George D. Kuh, *High-impact Educational Practices: What They Are, Who Has Access to Them, and Why They Matter* (Washington, DC: Association of American Colleges and Universities, 2008); Carol Geary Schneider, introduction to *High-impact Educational Practices,* by George D. Kuh (Washington, DC: Association of American Colleges and Universities, 2008).

11. Richard P. Keeling, ed., *Learning Reconsidered 2: A Practical Guide to Implementing a Campus-wide Focus on the Student Experience* (Champaign, IL: Human Kinetics, 2006).

12. Michael Weisman, email to author, 16 April 2012.

13. International Center for Academic Integrity, "Academic Integrity Assessment Guide," http://www.academicintegrity.org/icai/ resources-1.php.

14. Dan Carnevale, "E-mail Is for Old People," *Chronicle of Higher Education,* October 6, 2006, http://chronicle.com/article/E-Mail-is-for-Old-People/4169/.

15. Western Association of Schools and Colleges, *Handbook of Accreditation 2008,* WASC Accrediting Commission for Senior Colleges and Universities, http://wascsenior.org/files/Handbook_of_Accreditation.pdf.

CHAPTER FOURTEEN

What Provosts Need to Know About Enrollment Management

Robin Mamlet, David W. Pershing, and Sheila Murphy

Enrollment management—or the purposeful creation of synergies among admissions, financial aid, student records, marketing, strategic planning, pricing, modeling, institutional research, student accounts, and student success services—influences all operational aspects of a college or university and especially the success of its academic core. The delicate interplay among academic quality, number, and distribution of students; deployment of student financial assistance; and student retention programs that lies within the purview of the chief enrollment officer is central to the intellectual life and reach of a higher education institution. The art and science—and it is both—of enrollment management have never been more critical to what a provost can achieve as chief academic officer.

From College Admissions to Enrollment Management

The ground has shifted under higher education in fundamental ways over the past two decades, and one of the operational areas most significantly affected has been the enrollment function. The public has steadily become more involved in the world of admissions. From neighborhood cocktail parties to the White House, everyone seems to have an opinion about who gets admitted to which university and why. Dozens of new books guide students and parents through the process, while an industry of private consultants contracted by parents to guide the process has gotten large and established enough to form its own professional association. The cost of a bachelor's degree now annually shocks politicians, parents, and the public at large.

Enrollment operations often compete aggressively with institutional advancement offices for non-instructional budget allocations to support their expanding programs. Faculty members weigh in with their own informal assessment of the success of the enrollment operation based on their perception of the academic readiness of the students in their classrooms. Student life staff members wonder why such a disproportionate number of matriculants arrive at orientation showing the after-effects of familial instability and financial stress. In the midst of all this, it should not be forgotten that enrollment management is still a relatively new approach, especially for many public institutions.

Some colleges—though fewer and fewer—have not (yet) consolidated enrollment management under a single individual. However, institutions are beginning to aggregate undergraduate and sometimes graduate functions together, with or without international enrollment in the mix; others manage undergraduate enrollment without recognizing the gains that can be achieved when strategic enrollment constructs are applied to the graduate realm. Overall, in our view, consolidating under one administrator at least some of the possible enrollment related functions is more efficient and positions the college or university to capitalize on a broader set of opportunities.

A provost should begin by asking her- or himself, "Do I have as strong a partnership with the chief enrollment officer as I need?" Sometimes the chief enrollment officer sits within the academic structure, and other times outside it. It does not matter, in our experience, since the trust and confidence behind the partnership are more important than its location within the institutional structure. The weekly give and take between chief academic and enrollment officers must be constant and substantial, and in this chapter, we offer seven concepts, or drivers, that a provost should consider when shaping a mutually supportive relationship with the senior enrollment officer. Whether the CAO or enrollment head is new or seasoned, the institution will benefit if their relationship is intentional, candid, and strong. In practice, enrollment management is still a young field with no formal training other than national association conferences, on-the-job experience, and a few relatively new formal degree programs. Traditional graduate degrees can help discipline one's thinking and improve the likelihood of success, and they can increase the likelihood of an enrollment officer's being more respected within a higher education environment, but no established graduate degree can, at present, fully prepare a young administrator for this leadership role.

With this in mind, the following observations address the changing nature of the role of chief enrollment officer and its value to the institution's academic operations.

Seven Drivers Shaping Enrollment Management and the Provost's Connection to It

1. Prepare for a changed world demographically

Long gone are the days when an enterprising college band director whispered to a veteran admissions dean that he needed strength in the horn section, or the football coach invited the dean to lunch in order to point out what a difference a freshman running back could make "for all of us." In fact, university and college enrollment management is now based on new technologies, commitments to globalization, public awareness, public skepticism, increased institutional accountability for retention, legislative oversight, and a shifting legal context among other influences.

Realities within the college enrollment world are changing dramatically, and shifting demographics have become key. In 2012, for example, the number of international students at American colleges and universities increased by 6.5 percent over 2011 to a total of 764,495.[1] More than a quarter of all current students are now in at least one developmental course.[2] By 2015, 37 percent of those in college will be minority students of color. This has significant implications for admission programs vis-à-vis language proficiency and cross-cultural competency for the whole campus. CAOs will need to look at curriculum, faculty development, and necessary services for these new populations of students. Provosts and academic vice presidents need to be well-informed, strategic partners with their chief enrollment officers to insure the best possible retention and graduation outcomes for their institutions.

2. Expand your research capacity

Extensive, constant research—asking good questions and assessing continuously—produces effective enrollment management. Structuring

---

Seven Drivers Shaping Enrollment Management and the Provost's Connection to It

1. Prepare for a changed world demographically.
2. Expand your research capacity.
3. Share strategic information with the enrollment manager.
4. Learn your levers.
5. Engage in recruitment and retention efforts.
6. Shape your institutional messaging for the next generation.
7. Share the work of enrollment management.

the questions and methods of research provides another important partnership opportunity between the provost and chief enrollment officer. The enrollment officer may wish to examine time-to-degree within the graduate population, for example, factoring in a range of variables such as program, academic background, financial background, age, gender, ethnicity, and work status. A comprehensive examination might lead to the identification of documented differences that bear further discussion and examination by the CAO regarding program delivery and course sequencing. Similarly, the enrollment head may also consider the academic preparation of applicants and any patterns that emerge, and this could lead to further examination of recruiting approaches, admission policies, and factors affecting yield. Well-done assessment yields a culture of continuous improvement, and openness to using the results of reliably conducted research is a critical enrollment management strategy.

There is virtually no part of the enrollment arena that should be left out of a collaborative review with the chief academic officer, because there are useful observations and assessments to be shared in both directions. Some enrollment managers track conversion rates based on which classes and faculty members student visitors encounter. Others track the residence halls in which visiting admitted students are hosted. The options are numerous, and while one would not claim causal relationships from these studies, it is important that examination be continuous and rigorous and that methodology, data, conclusions, and potential improvements be discussed regularly with a variety of academic administrators as well as the provost or academic dean.

3. Share strategy information with the enrollment manager

Experienced academic vice presidents understand that their enrollment colleagues need to be kept up to date on what is happening in Academic Affairs. It is essential that they share a common vision and goals as well as such things as news of full-time hires, of promising research, and of the success stories that enable admissions officers to grasp the evolving texture and details of academic life at their institution and strengthen their presentations and recruiting materials. They share anticipated faculty issues so that their enrollment colleagues are not taken by surprise, and they always discuss any ideas or plans for new degree programs well in advance, inviting suggestions and comments from their enrollment colleagues. The current economic climate in higher education suggests that universities may need to restructure, and in some cases close, academic programs where there is little to no demand. Significant institutional damage can be done when an uninformed admission representative is out recruiting students for an academic program that is unlikely to survive for the undergraduate's four-year stay.

4. Learn your levers

Every college has levers, and they do not all reside in the financial aid office. While financial aid is of course a critical tool, enrollment is more nuanced than financial aid alone. There are multiple areas for study and numerous opportunities to think creatively. An overall pricing strategy, for example, is a different and more complex entity than a simple discount rate. Differential pricing, perhaps in the form of differential tuition, can be an extremely effective method for some institutions to enhance the funding available in high-demand areas like business without hurting applications in less popular majors. Leveraging public and/or external support for program development that enhances the regional economy is another strategy employed by many schools. Some upper-tier colleges can still benefit from the 1980s "Chivas Regal" strategy: "If it costs this much, it must be really good." However, growing consumer sentiment to go to a lower-cost public undergraduate institution and then invest more heavily in a higher-priced elite graduate program is creating a seismic shift under many of the country's most costly undergraduate institutions. One solution is to know and then use your institutional levers strategically to position the college advantageously in upcoming enrollment initiatives. News of an exciting new program such as computer game development, a high-profile service learning site, or the hiring of a faculty star can make a tangible difference in meeting September enrollment goals.

5. Engage in recruitment and retention efforts

CAOs can lead the way in modeling for deans and faculty leaders that they are critical to the enrollment effort and that their full participation is expected and will be rewarded. Few institutions can afford to have key members of its community uninvolved in and ignorant of a major sector of its operating budget. More than one president has quietly pointed out to us that every time a university staff or faculty member goes out of his or her way to greet a visitor warmly or pick up a piece of trash, it helps someone else in making an enrollment decision. Prospective students and faculty can quickly sense the mood of a campus, so it is essential that the people on the front line present an upbeat, positive image of the school.

Many faculty members now realize that they cannot simply do their scholarship and teaching and leave the recruitment and care of current students to others. They are significant participants in admissions programs, not as a sales force but as the people who most directly shape and illustrate the student academic experience. Perhaps the most critical CAO–enrollment manager collaboration occurs in setting the target number and academic parameters for an incoming class. This should be an iterative discussion with alternative models and their academic and fiscal implications clearly outlined in each scenario. The net tuition revenue projected, the discount rate, and the overall size of the student body are all within the institution's control in a well-planned enrollment operation. But permutations are still possible, and the CAO and chief enrollment officer should engage in a frank discussion of the costs and benefits for each potential scenario. They must also collaboratively discuss the impact of external factors such as a booming (or collapsing) job market for certain degrees (e.g., law) and the resulting changes this may necessitate.

Finally, student success is increasingly under the legislative and public microscope. When the institutional leadership team becomes too insulated from new opportunities to enhance the experience of students, the college community is diminished. For example, some academic vice presidents pair budgetary resources with departmental success in student enrollment and student persistence, attaching financial incentives both to overall enrollment and, more specifically, to program retention. Others may provide direct financial incentives tied to graduation rates. By doing so, the chief academic officer sends a clear message that he or she intends to invest the institution's resources in the most high-performing units as measured, in this instance, by enrollment, retention and graduation.

What Students Really Think: A Deeper Look at the Millennial Generation and Beyond

BY PAUL STILLMANK AND JAMES DAVIDSON

Chief academic officers and admission directors, in particular, are learning that the students now entering their institutions are significantly different from those of just a few years ago. Our recent work with higher education institutions has clarified these changes.

Key Concepts
- Social is the default state for Millennials.
- Millennials rely on social-user-generated content for all major financial decisions.
- Millennials share good and bad information freely.

(cont'd)

- Millennials place a high value on reputation derived from social communities.
- The college or university experience is the bridge to the emerging social business workplace.
- Millennials absorb and manage information differently than previous generations.
- Colleges and universities that create their own open communities have a much greater degree of credibility with Millennials.
- Social business enablement in higher education demonstrates an immediate, measurable impact on reputation.

What We Know

Two of the greatest challenges American higher education now faces are adapting to how Millennials live, interact, and learn, and properly preparing students for the emerging social business workforce. Millennials need to be viewed through the prism of three social personas:

- *Personally Social.* Students and employees are actively involved on social networks like Facebook, Twitter, and Google+. They are connected to people like themselves and are using social media to find, subscribe, and connect with people and businesses in new ways and to make key life decisions.
- *Academically Social.* When Gen Y or Xs enter an academic setting, there is a thud effect as they are forced to work within disparate systems, web 1.0 sites, and antiquated systems and processes. They are used to social platforms like Facebook but are still forced to use systems like Blackboard to manage their on-campus experience. They also have access to an almost limitless number of academic sources, often posted online by institutions like Stanford for free. Traditional institutions are no longer the only conduit for educational advancement, and students have now become customers that freely share their opinions.
- *Professionally Social.* Once students graduate and become alumni, they are active on networks like LinkedIn to find and apply to jobs and stay in touch with their institutions.

College-age Millennials currently comprise Gen Y but will soon include Gen Z, the first digital natives. Millennials are a unique constituency since "social" is their default state, and they share freely, in part because they are not concerned with their digital footprint. Millennials continually demonstrate a "prove it to me" attitude toward institutions and leaders, so community reputation is very important to them. Consequently, they rely heavily on their social networks and user-generated content to inform and guide their decisions.*

How They Decide

- 22% of Millennials buy products or services based on input from social channels.
- 51% of Millennials vs. 34% of Boomers state that user-generated content from strangers is more influential than their personal networks.
- 42% of Millennials share their good experiences on social media.
- 32% of Millennials share their bad experiences on social media.
- Most Millennials consider companies that include customer feedback on their websites honest and credible.
- More than 60% of Millennials say companies should offer more ways to share their opinions online.

The reliance of Millennials on social networks and user-generated content for making major purchasing decisions has huge implications for provosts and admissions directors when these students choose a college or university. Millennials see themselves as customers, even in an academic setting, and freely share information on ratemyprofessor.com and other social sites that influence the decisions of others.

Putting What We Know into Action

Their tools and the ability to be connected constantly also distinguish Millennials:

- 80% use Facebook
- 49% use YouTube
- 28% use Twitter
- 25% use Google+

This creates a unique challenge for higher education, especially in creating a bridge to the emerging social business workforce. Graduating Millennials not only experience a substantial transition in their core knowledge and understanding but also in how they use social tools, behaviors, and networks. Two opportunities for higher education are to demonstrate an understanding and ability to help students make that transition and to keep them engaged afterward.

Socially enabled colleges and universities will grow their market share by implementing a more holistic social business model as higher education integrates social concepts and practices more effectively into its recruiting, teaching, and learning processes with the goal of improving intake, yield, performance, and retention of Millennial students.

Paul Stillmank is president and CEO of 7Summits. James Davidson is the organization's vice president for digital strategy. 7Summits is a social business agency founded in 2009 to help Fortune 1000 brands become more socially connected through an approach they describe as Applied Social Media.

* http://www.bazaarvoice.com/files/whitepapers/BV_whitepaper_millenials.pdf.

6. Shape your institutional messaging for the next generation

The chief enrollment officer should invite the CAO to share in crafting the college or university's ongoing institutional messaging. Every CAO should annually assign a colleague or an age-appropriate friend or relative to play the part of a prospective undergraduate or parent and review the website. Ask for candid feedback on what is new and exciting as well as what is confusing and hard to locate. Despite the hundreds of hours of thought that can go into crafting a message and its delivery, one must remember that many of the website's visitors, young and old, will scan it with distracted attention, flipping between the college's pages and Facebook, talking, texting, and listening to music while they casually investigate an institution's identity. In this regard they will be typical students, reflecting much higher levels of comfort and trust in technologies than the makers of the messages on most campuses. As a strategy, the provost should scan the website to confirm that there are at least as many photographs of classrooms, laboratories, and interactions between professors and students as there are of athletes, outdoor adventures, and shots highlighting the campus's proximity to the ocean or a major city. The provost will make a powerful statement if he or she also volunteers to supply a fresh pool of academic photographs for consideration.

Even though speaking to the next generation is critical, the influence of parents must not be neglected. Provosts must recognize that they are going to encounter parents who are extremely involved with their student's decision—perhaps too involved in some cases (so-called helicopter parents)—and they will expect sophisticated, detailed information. Other parents will have no understanding of higher education and may not even speak English well enough to read university materials.

Finally, does the admissions staff have new and timely examples of academic and intellectual engagement in their presentations about the institution? The CAO can help with this by meeting annually with the recruiting staff and tour guides to update all information about academic programs and buildings. The chief enrollment officer can, in turn, reinforce the concept that the enrollment process is best viewed as an infinite loop; that is, creative, positive messages about the college or university will attract the students who will be best prepared to thrive there. By retaining them to graduation, institutional selectivity and reputation will rise, drawing more applications and driving up selectivity and reputation further in coming years. Students who graduate are also far more likely to become major donors decades hence.

7. Share the work of enrollment management

Managing enrollment is shared work. Experienced CAOs learn over time that admissions staff members, sometimes even the youngest ones, may be the first to know where the potential lies for a new master's program, a post-graduate certificate program, or an overlooked way to expand offerings that can increase selectivity and market share. Having the chief enrollment officer in the loop when new degree programs are considered can intentionally result in fresh approaches to academic planning. Similarly, drawing on the enrollment management team to help orient new faculty can provide a fuller picture of current student lifestyles and expectations that will influence the classroom experience.

In these ways, admissions and enrollment personnel can lead the way in helping the faculty recognize that contemporary students are quite different from undergraduates of ten or fifteen years ago, and much of this stems from their dependence on technology. Students now access information differently, and they value visual experiences far more than did their parents and many of their teachers. Skilled enrollment managers realize this and reach out to provosts to share strategies.

Conclusion: Enrollment Realities for Provosts

In closing, we offer four summary thoughts on the changing nature of campus life for veteran CAOs and on the benefits of sharing information and resources with the chief enrollment officer:

1. *The New Student Experience.* Applying for and enrolling in a college or university has changed so much in one generation that many provosts express concerns about simply keeping up with the intricacies of the admissions process. They seem to realize that the model calls for the chief academic officer and the faculty to think about enrollment and how it is achieved in new ways, but they do not always grasp that these new ways may not be attractive to long-term academics. Just as some professors became familiar, if not comfortable, with talking about "marketing to student consumers," they are now asked to establish Twitter accounts and invite their students to follow their commentary about scholarship and college life. In fact, students have finely tuned antennae for evidence to trust amidst the daily saturation of Facebook and other social media, and the provost will be wise to remain in close contact with the enrollment management team for trends and developments.

2. *Creation of an Institutional Dashboard.* It is essential that the provost and the enrollment officer agree on the metrics for success and

then closely monitor them to ascertain which programs are helping them achieve their goals and which ones need attention. One
effective method to do this is to create an institutional dashboard—
a highly graphic data display of the major metrics over time. Making this available, either to leadership or across the institution, allows everyone involved in the process to see the progress throughout
the year as well as on a year-to-year basis.

3. *Increased Competition.* Even as they design outreaches to new student markets, if the college or university is struggling to meet its
enrollment goals, the CAO and chief enrollment officer should join
forces and conduct an examination of the reasons. In these instances, it is wise to pay particular attention to the responses from
admitted but non-enrolling students. Institutions that systematically engage in program review pay close attention to market forces
and continuously follow the activities of competitors who are the
best positioned to respond to early warning signs of declining interest. Also, after spending much of each fall semester on the road
recruiting, admissions staff members typically return with much
useful information about what students and parents around the
country are asking for, and expecting, if they enroll. A late fall de-
briefing with these professionals can educate senior members of
the faculty and the provost regarding degree programs to consider
and new strategies to remain competitive.

4. *A Collegial, Collective Approach.* In small institutions, the CAO
should encourage each department chair to invite the chief enrollment officer to a department meeting at least once a year to hear
news of program initiatives, faculty presentations and publications,
and other time-sensitive developments that the enrollment officer
can integrate into the college's story for multiple audiences. The
CAO and enrollment manager should also have a plan in place in
case bad news breaks about the institution locally or nationally
and without warning. Most important will be agreed-upon procedures for quickly developing a response, approved by college counsel, that is fair, accurate, and lets prospective students and their
families know what they can realistically expect over the coming
year or longer.

Finally, the provost has both an opportunity and an obligation to
model a collegial relationship with the chief enrollment officer, encouraging faculty conversation and participation in admission activities,
sharing data about applicant profiles, and honestly discussing the options

available and the implications of each one, in establishing a reasonable, sustainable discount rate. In our view, a college or university derives significant benefits from candid discussions between chief academic and chief enrollment officers that move beyond cordial information sharing to institutional decision making.

NOTES

1. Institute of International Education, "Fast Facts," in *Open Doors Report on International Education Exchange,* http://www.iie.org/en/Research-and-Publications/Open-Doors.

2. Columbia University Graduate School of Arts & Sciences *Teaching Center,* "The Future of Higher Education," http://www.columbia.edu/cu/tat/pdfs/future%20 0f%20higher%20ed.pdf.

CHAPTER FIFTEEN

Increasing Accountabilities: The Provost's Role in Intercollegiate Athletics

George H. VanderZwaag and William Scott Green

If a sociology professor were accused or suspected of the type of actions that Jerry Sandusky was at first just suspected of, and if the heads of the University were about to move against that sociology professor, and the head of the sociology department said, "You know, I don't think so. I don't think you should report this to child protective services. I think the compassionate thing to do would be to just talk to the sociology professor and then ease him out." Would he have that kind of influence? Would he be able to obscure good judgment that way? I don't think so.

—Bob Costas

We have grafted a multi-billion dollar entertainment industry onto higher education. It is inherently discordant with the mission of the university. It is inherently corrupting. . . . Big time football has no business on college campuses.

—George Will

The epigraphs above—provoked by the crisis at Penn State in 2011—graphically capture some of the troubling ideas and practices that affect athletics in American higher education. Though its focus is on "big time football," George Will's comment reflects a widely held view that athletic programs are both irrelevant to and "inherently discordant with" the educational missions of colleges and universities. Bob Costas's hypothetical

Athletics and Academic Mission: Four Observations

1. Athletics have a legitimate place in higher education and are a valuable form of experiential learning.
2. On campuses, athletics play a unique role in shaping campus culture and defining the student body.
3. Many higher education institutions are still confused about the relationship between athletics and academic mission.
4. To eliminate this confusion, the CAO should establish a clear academic rationale for athletics and then monitor its regulatory compliance.

but wholly accurate example shows the consequence of that view: athletic programs are an exception to standard academic practice, and rules that apply to professors do not necessarily apply to coaches. The crisis of oversight at Penn State crystallizes a longstanding uncertainty about athletics in higher education and shows why provosts and academic deans must care about and be actively engaged in their school's athletic program.

Our argument has four parts: First, athletics have a legitimate place in higher education and are a valuable form of experiential learning. Second, as a matter of practice, athletics play a unique role in shaping the campus culture and defining the student body in American colleges and universities. Third, as an industry, American higher education seems confused about the place of athletics in its mission and its structure, which leads to inconsistent oversight and goal-setting for athletics and can yield the sorts of lapses and excesses that led to the Penn State crisis. Fourth, to eliminate this systemic confusion, the CAO should establish a clear educational rationale for athletics and should monitor and support consistent regulatory compliance and management of all athletic programs.

Athletics and Institutional Identity: What Works Best

In nearly every culture, athletics—both formal and informal—are a routine part of growing up. Little League Baseball, founded in the late 1930s, has nearly 200,000 teams in all fifty U.S. states and in eighty countries.[1] Pop Warner Football, which began in 1929, claims 425,000 young people ranging from ages 5 to 16.[2] Soccer and lacrosse leagues are increasing in many regions across the country. Almost all high schools sponsor interschool athletic competition, and the visible and influential role of professional athletics in American society requires no elaboration. The value and virtue of teamwork—essential skills for athletes on teams—is undisputed. Indeed, for many students, it is in athletics that they first learn to work with people of different backgrounds and heritages toward a common goal. Authentic athletics, as in all forms of learning, is ultimately about improvement and excellence. Student athletes are relentlessly assessed in practice and on the field or court. No Family Educational Rights and Privacy Act (FERPA) legislation masks their performance or makes it confidential. In athletic competition, students play or sit on the bench, succeed or fail, in public. Athletics have the potential to teach the importance of both collaboration and accountability, traits essential in higher education for building community and addressing complex tasks.

In fact, it is not widely understood that on many Division III campuses, student athletes are the largest subgroup of undergraduates. At over half of Division III schools—the division, in principle, least susceptible to the pressures of athletics—at least half of the student body are student athletes on intercollegiate teams, and in the rest of the division, it is not uncommon for at least one-quarter of the student body to play on intercollegiate teams. Although credit-bearing activities are what tuition pays for, almost every residential college testifies that its campus is a theatre of comprehensive learning and growth, both in and out of its classrooms, and few would seriously question the capacity of intercollegiate athletics to generate institutional loyalty and school spirit, both of which shape the larger campus community. At the University of Miami, for example, orientation for first-year students includes both a distinguished academic lecture and a spirit event in which students are addressed both by the university president and the varsity coaches.

Collegiate athletics also affects a wide range of non-sports issues, as the institutional admissions process illustrates. Athletic teams, like orchestras, require members with different skills and talents. No school wants to impose mediocrity or failure on its students; therefore, schools need to admit students with the talents to give their athletic teams a reasonable possibility of success. This means that athletics will legitimately add criteria to some admissions decisions along with grades and SAT scores, and these considerations increase with a greater percentage of athletes in the undergraduate population. Together and individually, the authors of this chapter have witnessed meaningful academic achievement by student athletes whose high school grades and test scores made admissions officers hesitant. A recent study by Michael L. Anderson claims that for some institutions, "football success increases alumni athletic donations, increases the number of applicants . . . increases the average SAT scores of incoming classes, and enhances a school's academic reputation."[3]

Gut Check for Sheltered Provosts

BY JIM DONALDSON

- Take your head of out the sand. The NCAA loves to refer to its "student-athletes." The reality, in too many cases, is that they are athletes first, and students only secondarily. As a dean, you have chosen a life in higher education, so act like an academic: Do your utmost to make academics more important than athletics while remaining aware that it could cost you your job.

- Take a stand against the "one-and-done" syndrome that is now prevalent in major university basketball. It is simply a pre-professional program for the NBA. The players who come to college to play a season before turning pro have no intention of ever graduating and, consequently, are never serious students. Once the season ends, so will their class attendance. For a university to pretend this is anything other than using a player to win games and increase revenues is self-delusion.

- Understand the priorities of the institution at which you work. If it is primarily a football factory, get with the program. If this offends you—and it should—leave the institution.

- The football coach and basketball coach have much higher profiles than the chief academic officer. They earn higher salaries too. If the president pays more attention to them than he does to you, do not be surprised.

Jim Donaldson has been a sports columnist and reporter for The Providence Journal *since 1979. His principal beat has been the New England Patriots, and he wrote one of the first books ever published on the subject of fantasy football in 1984.*

This study demonstrates how athletics can positively impact a college or university' educational mission.

Despite some evidence to the contrary about athletics, many in the academy still harbor doubts about its educational relevance and administrative oversight. As Suzanne Estler observes: "Athletics often lie at the center of campus dynamics related to academic standards, race, gender, reputation, finance, community relations, politics, priorities, legal responsibilities and liabilities, and ethical responsibilities. Yet athletics are rarely reflected in the literature of higher education related to these areas."[4]

The sometimes undecided status of athletics in higher education also becomes apparent in the inconsistent reporting structure of athletics departments. Reporting models will vary considerably among different types of institutions. At most Division I schools, athletics reports to the president. In Divisions II and III, athletics reports to various offices. These statistics for Division III reporting relationships are illustrative:

Chief Student Affairs Officer	47.6%
Chancellor or President	17.7%
Chief Academic Officer	17.0%
Other	13.1%
Chief Financial Officer	4.6%[5]

The fact that athletics departments typically do not report to the chief academic officer heightens the belief among some that athletics and academic priorities are essentially unrelated, even oppositional. These uncertainties about the best place for athletics in the organizational structure reflect a blurred identity at some institutions.

Two Key Roles for Provosts

There are multiple reasons for chief academic officers to engage with—and care about—athletics and athletic competition at their institutions even if these activities fall outside of their formal management responsibilities. Athletic directors and coaches are subject to relentless internal and public pressures to win, and engaged, supportive academic leadership can counter-balance some of those pressures by acknowledging athletics' distinctive value and its integration into the institution's broader education priorities. It is easy for some scholars to describe athletics as marginal, yet we argue that this perception unfairly discounts athletics' legitimate contributions to the learning process and weakens the overall educational experience.

Two areas in particular benefit from the chief academic officer's professional expertise: the hiring and evaluation of athletic directors and coaches, and the regulatory compliance and educational integrity of each program.

1. Establish quality athletics personnel management

Chief academic officers need to hire coaches who are educators and help the director of athletics maintain educational standards for hiring and evaluation. Coaches are agents of significant experiential learning, and they will exert considerable influence on the lives of the students on their teams. Perhaps no other adult on campus has as much daily contact with students as a coach does. To reinforce these positive aspects, the CAO should insist that coaching is educational work and support athletic directors in treating it as such. In turn,

Evaluating Coaches beyond Their Won-Lost Records: Ten Criteria

1. Ability to teach fundamental techniques
2. Support for academic commitments
3. Ability to evaluate talent
4. Ability to motivate talent
5. Effectiveness as a communicator
6. Effectiveness as an administrator
7. Capacity to teach strategic thinking
8. Willingness to enforce discipline
9. Recognition of ethical decision making
10. Ability to serve as a mentor

coaches need to publicly affirm the values of the institution and highlight their roles as educators. However, since winning is too easily rewarded and losing is the basis for losing one's job, provosts should realize that they need to offer constant reinforcement and support of coaches' full educational mission.

Coaches should be evaluated on their abilities to recruit the right students, to build winning teams, and to carry out their educational roles. In addition to winning and losing, the following criteria are integral to the evaluation process:

- Knowledge of the sport and the ability to teach fundamental techniques

- Support for academic commitments

- Ability to evaluate and motivate talent

- Effectiveness as a communicator

- Effective administration and practice planning

- Capacity to teach team strategy and develop a game plan

- Promotion of team discipline, sportsmanship, and ethical behavior

- Ability to mentor and serve as a role model

As they do for other instructors, students should provide regular feedback on how a coach is performing in the role. The criteria listed above should be used along with other pertinent information to provide a full view of a coach's educational effectiveness.

2. Preserve the educational integrity of athletics

Given the pressures to build winning teams at all institutions, a second important role for CAOs is to protect the integrity of the athletic enterprise. This hinges on two primary factors: compliance with intercollegiate rules, and student athletes completing their courses of study within the institution's normal time frame for non-athletes. The ways athletes select majors and how they perform relative to other students is important; however, it is also fair to say that normal progress toward a degree signals to almost all constituents that students admitted with athletic talent as a factor are prepared to do college-level work. Metrics such as probation, retention, and graduation rates can and should be used to monitor how athletes are performing.

The NCAA rules under which an institution operates are extensive and complex. Thus, it is wise for the CAO to understand the general compliance structure and ensure that appropriate people and systems are in place to monitor compliance. Sometimes a question of integrity can be even more complicated from an internal standpoint. The faculty's support will be a crucial validation of the educational value of athletics, and multiple factors can shape their perceptions. Obviously, the quality of students in the classroom is foremost among them. If the athletics department appears to endorse the admission of student athletes incapable of meeting normal academic demands, a serious credibility problem will result and may place a provost or dean in jeopardy. As the chief academic officer, this individual is charged with helping the faculty understand exactly what is happening within the athletic context on campus.

A professor may point to missing one class for a game as a problem with the institution's athletic culture and assume that student athletes care more about their team identity than about their academic commitments. In our experiences at several universities, the majority of athletes with whom we have worked contribute additional hours to manage their schedules and fulfill their commitments on both academic and athletic fronts. Missing a class is not a sure signal that an athlete lacks intellectual curiosity or preparation, nor is it a function of not caring. It may simply be the result of trying to meet an expected set of educational objectives while fulfilling a time-sensitive commitment to a team. Many colleges and universities have adopted an academic policy that excuses student athletes from class in the case of a game conflict while holding them accountable for the work of the missed session. Such a policy helps to link the educational relevance of athletics with the priority of academic engagement. At institutions lacking such a policy, the provost should take a leadership role in helping the faculty to devise one and address some faculty concerns while strengthening the integrity of the athletics program.

While athletics rules—and reputations—are now inescapable elements of American higher education, we have also observed that few provosts and deans are adequately trained to manage them. Academic mentoring may teach a faculty member how to evaluate scholarship and student learning outcomes, but few experiences can prepare a new vice president for academic affairs to oversee a major athletics program. Athletics is understood as one of the most highly regulated areas within higher education, and chief academic officers now need to understand the major compliance pitfalls embedded in it. The general lack of preparation about an issue such as this helps to explain why many colleges and universities cannot achieve a consensus about where athletics belongs within their institutional structures.

Conclusion: Make Leadership Visible

Even if it is thoughtfully managed, the athletics department will still present numerous leadership challenges for a chief academic officer. It is therefore important for the CAO to visibly link this enterprise to the institutional mission, to play a central role in hiring effective coaches and athletic directors who appreciate and advance key educational goals, and to hold those individuals who develop the annual academic and performance plans in each sport accountable. A failure to realize the educational advantages of athletics in these ways can lead to a failure on the part of the college or university in achieving its own broader goals. While the historic events at Penn State in 2011 are extreme examples of a destructive loss of institutional and programmatic integrity, far less dramatic and newsworthy corruptions can build up more quietly and then swiftly damage an entire program.

To advance the educational mission, the athletics program will require the support and respect of the faculty. No other campus leader is as well-positioned to translate the educational value of athletics to the faculty and to ensure that the faculty's educational values inform the athletic enterprise as the chief academic officer. This will require provosts and deans to take the time to know their coaches and directors and to affirm student athletic performance through attendance at games, matches, and other competitions. The impact and value of this kind of visible support cannot be overstated.

ACKNOWLEDGMENT

Donna E. Shalala, president of the University of Miami, reviewed an earlier draft of this paper and made many insightful suggestions. We are grateful for her help.

NOTES

Epigraphs. Bob Costas: "Meet the Press," *NBC News*, http://www.msnbc.msn.com /id/3032608/vp/48189038#48189038. George Will: "This Week," *ABC News*, http://abcnews.go.com/ThisWeek/video/james-carville-suspend-penn-state-football -16782104.

1. Pop Warner, Little League® Baseball and Softball, "History of Little League," http://www.littleleague.org/learn/about/historyandmission.htm.

2. "History of Pop Warner," Pop Warner Little Scholars, Inc., http://www.pop warner.com/About_Us/history.htm.

3. Michael L. Anderson, "The Benefits of College Athletic Success: An Application of the Propensity Score Design with Instrumental Variables," working paper, National Bureau of Economic Research, June 2012, 3.

4. Suzanne E. Estler with Laurie J. Nelson, *Who Calls the Shots? Sports and University Leadership, Culture, and Decision Making* (ASHE Higher Education Report: 30/5, 2005), 11.

5. National Collegiate Athletic Association, "2008 NCAA Division III Membership Survey," Indianapolis, IN, 2008, 7.

CHAPTER SIXTEEN

Keep Your Friends Close and College Counsel Closer: New Developments in Higher Education Law

James E. Samels and James Martin

Introduction: Educate, Regulate, Enforce

Over the past twenty-five years, several new specialty areas of higher education law have emerged, and chief academic officers are partnering more closely with college counsel to address them proactively before damage control is needed. The most complex challenges include academic consumer protection, intellectual property, identity theft, plagiarism, social media censorship, multi-site licensing, and the changing nature of faculty appointments. Facing this array of new decisions, CAOs need to develop strong relationships with their college or university's legal advisors, and their advice is especially important when the services being provided are by outside counsel instead of in-house attorneys practicing law on campus every day.

As a wise starting point, each fall semester the provost should invite legal counsel to a faculty professional development workshop to share recent changes in the law and their impact on campus both inside and outside the classroom. For instance, it frequently falls to the CAO to protect the institution and its students from breaches in the security and privacy of academic and financial data systems regulated by federal and state authorities as well as college or university policies. Since 2000, data breaches resulting in the theft of student and employee social security numbers, driver's license numbers, bank account numbers, and student academic information have mushroomed, and social network identity theft has become one of the fastest growing crimes on campus. One notable example occurred in Hawaii in 2010. In the case of *Gross v. University of Hawaii,* approximately 98,000 University of Hawaii students, faculty, alumni, and employees were affected by five data breaches beginning in 2009. This class action data breach lawsuit resulted in a settlement that was historic as the largest class action suit filed in Hawaii and also the first data breach settlement in Hawaii.[1]

Another example occurred at Maricopa Community Colleges in Arizona, where a data breach exposed the personal information of 2.4 million current and former students and employees. The breach was not disclosed for seven months while the district spent time investigating the extent of the exposure. The district's governing board is spending up to $7 million to notify and offer credit monitoring services to those potentially affected. In each of these examples, a candid, trusting relationship between the CAO and college counsel can position the institution advantageously when a major decision must finally be made. In turn, an institution can limit its liability exposure for data breach by keeping its preventive measures current with the industry standard in utilizing firewalls and otherwise taking necessary measures to safeguard sensitive information.

The Benefits of a Preventive Legal Audit

Chief academic officers should invite campus counsel to conduct an annual legal audit—a proactive tool for avoiding untoward liability exposure. The audit can be combined with a preventive law workshop for full- and part-time faculty to clarify past and current practices and implement changes to conform to the changing legal landscape. Each academic year, the provost or dean should request from counsel a review and update of applicable academic policies, rules, regulations, standards, processes and procedures that could affect the fulfillment of institutional mission. Overall, the objectives of a legal audit and preventive law workshop are "not to constrain the institution, but rather to identify incipient campus legal problems and to highlight recent legal trends or new developments in the law of higher education."[2]

What follows are illustrative opportunities to avoid, mitigate, or transfer risk exposure through the deployment of the audit.

1. A Plan for Catastrophe

Some may question why the CAO needs to be prepared to be on the front lines addressing a campus disaster, but this preparedness is essential because in many institutions, when crisis strikes and the president is absent or unavailable, the provost needs to step into the president's role. It is also wise to remember that the CAO is often responsible for investigating the factual circumstances leading up to and surrounding the disaster and may be called upon to act as the institution's representative with the media. The points that follow constitute a Disaster Management Plan that can address crises of many types and causes.

- Develop worst case, best case, and likely case strategies.

- Establish multiple early warning systems.

- Define "due diligence," then exercise it.

- Pick one spokesperson.

- Emphasize candor and honesty.

- Protect institutional privacy.

- Eradicate perceptions of impropriety as strenuously as impropriety itself.

- Conduct a post-crisis review.[3]

In addition to these points, CAOs should take advantage of new technologies and all available means of communication throughout the crisis to ensure that the university or college employs multiple, instantaneous methods to share information when doing so could mean saving lives.

Although the fatal shootings at Virginia Tech in 2007, at the University of Northern Illinois in 2008, and at the University of Alabama in Huntsville in 2010 heightened national attention on violent campus crimes and the preparedness of higher education security forces, the American public may not have realized that in 2013 alone there were fatal shootings associated with at least three additional schools: Hazard Community and Technical College in Kentucky in January, the University of Central Florida in March, and Santa Monica College in June. These shootings collectively resulted in ten deaths. This provides a useful segue to address liability exposure precipitated by CAO misjudgments about when and how to document events properly.

Even with states like Virginia passing laws requiring four-year colleges to set up threat assessment teams, chief academic officers need to plan and do more than they have in the past to ready their schools for a violent, even fatal event.[4] Working with attorneys to develop a comprehensive disaster plan that incorporates annual updates can offer the institution a valuable roadmap during chaotic moments. In fact, administrators at Virginia Tech found in 2008 and 2009 that the amount of basic planning and work necessary to bring the campus back on track was immense.[5]

In the wake of a disaster such as those above, some administrators may fear breaching confidentiality, yet college counsel can advise that confidentiality yields under both Family Educational Rights and Privacy Act (FERPA) and, for social workers and mental health practitioners, state law where there is an imminent threat of harm to self or others.[6] Additionally, an imminent threat of harm to self or others justifies utilizing an interim suspension process through which an institution may act immediately and provide process later. Institutions may mandate that a student be involuntarily committed for an evaluation, and in appropriate cases schools may implement behavioral contracts mandating frequent counseling sessions as a condition of continued enrollment. All of these elements can be incorporated into the disaster management plan during the audit process.

2. When Distance Learning Becomes Distance Litigation

As institutions attempt to expand their missions and markets into multiple states, CAOs are learning that the process will move more smoothly if the university's attorneys are involved from the initial planning session. Along with the preventive audit process, provosts may also decide to hire a consulting team with legal and strategic planning experience in multi-state academic planning to produce a preliminary feasibility study.

Distance learning has the advantages of reaching students in remote areas and increasing enrollments while reducing overhead and demands on facilities. A downside is that national and global enrollments may also lead to national and global litigation. All too frequently, there is a gap between the distance learning "lip and cup," and deans need to ensure that staff members have gotten the latest waivers as well as indemnification, confidentiality, and noncompete stipulations and agreements in order to avoid costly challenges at later dates. In *Johnson v. Walden University* (2011),[7] a student who had been enrolled in an online doctoral program in Japan brought suit in Connecticut after being barred from taking the state licensure exam because he did not have a clinical degree. He used the doctrine of diversity jurisdiction to select a state with stronger consumer protections than the institution's state of incorporation. An institution may attempt to minimize the chances of litigation in multiple forums by utilizing enrollment contracts that contain clauses for both governing law and choice of forum. In addition, the institution could mandate alternative forms of dispute resolution such as arbitration or mediation. Without such limits, the burden and expenses of long-distance litigation may consume any revenues the institution realizes from its distance learning ventures.

3. The Changing Nature of Faculty Employment

Gone are the days when the majority of faculty members were full-time employees who convened at monthly faculty senate meetings. Utilization of part-time adjunct faculty means that many teachers work without health insurance, retirement plans, and other benefits, and they are unable to claim the protections afforded by collective bargaining agreements. Institutions need to balance the priority to be cost conscious with the societal implications of a shrinking full-time professoriate. As Audrey Williams June reported in the *Chronicle of Higher Education* in 2012: "About 70 percent of the instructional faculty at all colleges is off the tenure track. . . . Change has occurred more rapidly on some campuses, particularly at regionally-oriented public institutions and mid-tier private universities . . . [and] community colleges have traditionally relied heavily on non-tenure-track faculty, with 85 percent of their instructors in 2010 not eligible for tenure."[8] What this means in practical terms is that CAOs should work through the audit process with legal counsel to create a reasonable balance for their specific institutional culture that includes tenure-track, non-tenure-track, multi-year, and employment at-will contract options.

While it is clear that "a public college professor dismissed from an office held under tenure provisions . . . and college professors and staff members dismissed during the terms of their contracts . . . have interests in continued employment that are safeguarded by due process," the situation is less clear for faculty members whose contracts are expiring or tenured faculty up for review.[9] When in doubt, it is safest to provide procedural protections, such as a hearing, in which the faculty member is provided with a meaningful opportunity to be heard. Failure to do so could result in terminations being overturned even if they were otherwise justified. Prior to proceeding with a termination, college counsel should be consulted since constitutional protections apply if it is a public institution and a liberty or property interest is deemed to exist, or if a constitutional right such as free speech has been breached. Other rights may adhere based on collective bargaining agreements, faculty handbooks, faculty contracts, and even past practices if applied in an inconsistent and disparate manner. Furthermore, if the employee had recently filed a workers compensation claim, an application for family medical leave, or a sexual harassment or other complaint, then issues of possible prohibited retaliation or whistleblowing can make defending a termination even more complex.

In addition, universities that lay off or terminate senior faculty as lacking in current curriculum competencies and technological skills may find themselves in a morass of age discrimination litigation, particularly when the layoff or termination is followed by a wave of hiring new, younger faculty. The chances of withstanding an age discrimination challenge to a layoff are strongest when an institution can establish the following factors: that it is faced with financial exigency; that older faculty have not been disproportionately affected; that the layoffs are not followed by creation of new positions with the same or significantly overlapping job responsibilities; and that, if such positions are created, they are not filled by younger, less-experienced applicants with lesser credentials. Thinking proactively, a best practice would be to provide faculty with professional development, sabbatical, and other continuing education opportunities that enable them to keep their academic expertise and technological skills current. To the extent that a faculty member may be unable to adapt to the changing needs of the time, rather than a layoff, the better course of action may be to pursue progressive discipline by period performance evaluations no less than annually, documenting performance deficiencies, counseling, job performance goals with deadlines for compliance, and consequences of noncompliance that could include *termination for cause* based on poor job performance.

Since 2000, not only has the composition of tenured, contract, and adjunct faculty been altered, but so have the means and methods of faculty recruitment. Recruitment via the Internet allows even a small college to reach an electronic national and global audience instantly. This allows the institution to achieve diversity in its faculty without the time constraints and costs that an equivalent national and global print media campaign would require. This form of recruitment can also create a new model of adjunct faculty via faculty mentors providing supervision of internships, field practicum, and work co-ops nationally and internationally. Strategically, however, CAOs need to employ and enforce the risk management contracts discussed earlier in this chapter.

4. Compliance: Connecting the Legal Dots

Provosts with senior operations responsibility will often need to lead in the absence of the president. This requires a wide range of expertise in academic management, program development, academic master planning, and faculty governance. Superimposed on this list of responsibilities is the need to be actively managing federal, state, and local licensing, regional and specialty accreditation, and environmental and financial compliance requirements. CAOs need to be proactive in ensuring that their institution satisfactorily fulfills its broad range of compliance and reporting obligations. Toward this end, compliance calendars have been developed as a means to track federal, state, disclosure, and other reporting requirements.

In one case, Washington and Lee University developed such a calendar, organized by department, that is interactive and contains links to more detailed information.[10] For a first-time dean or provost, acronyms like USDE, FERPA, and IPEDS can seem like a new language, but veteran CAOs learn to implement the regulations promulgated by these state

Six Reasons for an Annual Legal Preventive Audit

1. Create a campus disaster management plan
2. Prevent distance learning from becoming "distance litigation"
3. Stay current with the changing nature of faculty contracts
4. Fulfill multiple institutional compliance obligations
5. Avoid educational malpractice challenges
6. Update the institution's intellectual property policy

and federal licensing and enforcement agencies in the development of a culture of compliance that enables all faculty and staff members to play an active role in the advancement of their campus.[11]

5. Educational Malpractice: Many Paths, Many Pitfalls

Over the past twenty years, educational malpractice claims have been recognized and rejected by the courts, depending, for the most part, on a particular state's regulatory and educational consumer statutory framework.[12] In general, the judiciary has been loath to second guess academic judgments made by faculty and chief academic officers. For example, the cause of a student's failure to learn is inherently complex, and the courts do not view it as their role to determine at what point a student who has failed to learn has met his or her responsibility to study, or at what point a teacher has failed in his or her obligation to teach. Reasons the courts have articulated for refusing to recognize educational malpractice claims include these, among others:

- There is no satisfactory standard of care by which to measure an educator's conduct.

- The cause of the student's failure to learn is inherently uncertain, as is the nature of damages.

- Permitting such claims would flood the courts with litigation and would thus place a substantial burden on educational institutions.

- The courts are not equipped to verse the day-to-day operation of educational institutions.[13]

That said, experienced CAOs have learned that claims against an educational institution for academic failings or misconduct may sometimes be successful. Thus, colleges and universities may not abandon their fundamental legal responsibilities with impunity. In certain educational consumer cases, courts may enforce representations from a college or university as a contract, and the primary document enforced will be the institution's catalogue.[14] Representation in advertisements, application forms, brochures, and course descriptions may also be enforced.[15] In addition, courts have considered institutional publications that describe policies or procedures as the bases of agreements between students and institutions.[16] In this context, quasi-contractual analysis is often used to analyze whether institutions are "delivering the goods" they promise to students.

Proprietary colleges and their provosts may be particularly vulnerable because for-profit professional organizations sometimes promise students they will acquire specific skills, licenses, or other forms of certification upon completion of their program. For-profit educators point out that retention rates between for-profits and public community colleges are not significantly different and that public institutions have the advantage of both direct government subsidies and indirect subsidies through Title IV financial aid, while for-profits have only the indirect subsidy. Admittedly, there have been cases of abuse among for-profits; however, it is also unfortunate that, as a category, these institutions are being painted with such a broad brush, since this harms many for-profit colleges and universities that are legitimately addressing unmet needs via quality programs not offered by public and non-profit institutions.

6. Intellectual Property: Who Owns It?

With the advent of distance learning, the stakes involved in intellectual property ownership have risen dramatically. This issue was less controversial when classroom learning occurred face-to-face. Now that the classroom has gone global, potential earnings from online education can generate major revenues. On one side of the issue, faculty intellectual property may be treated as a work for hire when it is backed by institutional resources and created as part of a faculty member's workload. The work-for-hire provision allows an employer to assert ownership over materials prepared by its employees acting within the "scope of their employment."[17] As one court noted:

"[W]hether any particular creative work of a faculty member constitutes a work for hire will depend on whether . . . it is the type of work the faculty member was hired to create; whether it was created substantially within the time and space limits of the job; and whether it was motivated by a purpose to serve the university employer."[18] From an institutional perspective, college administrators have a fiduciary duty to develop and enforce intellectual property policies that best protect the educational interests of their students. As well, rising operating expenses and indirect costs coupled with shrinking endowments may be driving some institutions to claim a bigger piece of the intellectual property "pie."

Conversely, if campus administrators expect professors to produce innovative online courses, their efforts to produce quality materials should be rewarded. If a university is not willing to provide adequate incentives for faculty to create online works, the institution may lose a competitive edge in the marketplace as talented faculty members seek new opportunities.

Institutions may attempt a fair allocation of intellectual property rights by means of an intellectual property policy. However, in *Forasté v. Brown University*, the court found that an allocation of ownership to faculty via an intellectual property policy was insufficient to overcome a statutory presumption that works created by employees within the scope of employment belong to the university.[19] Therefore, although it is commendable for an institution to address allocation of intellectual property rights within a policy, the safer course would be to require a written agreement signed by both the institution and employee allocating ownership rights, particularly in cases where the allocation contravenes a statutory presumption.

The allocation of rights must be considered within the context of the individual institution. For example, "universities with sufficient endowments may find it expedient to allocate all copyrights to faculty creators, while other universities may decide to fund the production of expensive, technologically complex works with a share in the revenue produced by such works."[20] An option to be avoided is joint ownership of property. This is not recommended because in the event that the parties have a falling out, this has the potential to halt the use of the intellectual property, sometimes indefinitely until the merits get sorted out through lengthy litigation. The better practice is for one party to own the property and for the other party to have a nonexclusive license for use.

Finally, institutions need to have policies in place that put students on notice that there will be sanctions for violating the intellectual property rights of the college or university and its faculty members. Students can be enticed by financial incentives into posting course materials and lecture notes on commercial sites. The institution's code of conduct can list this as prohibited. In addition, faculty members can be provided with templates to include in course introductory materials, syllabi, and online materials defining acceptable use as personal use only and setting forth parameters of prohibited use.

Conclusion: Leading from the Center

Today the role of campus counsel is first to *educate*, next to *regulate*, and, at the end of the day, failing voluntary compliance, to *enforce* through discipline and sanctions appropriate to the level of wrongful conduct. By educate, we mean forming a regulatory framework to guide and inform campus expectations and behavior. That said, sometimes it may take catastrophic events like those at Virginia Tech in 2007 to challenge academic leaders and university counsel to provide campus-based preventive legal education. In some cases, an annual audit can address and eliminate what could become an immediate source of conflict for the leadership team. In other instances, a long-term collaboration emphasizing shared resources and data can serve as a powerful tool for positive change. Whatever the circumstances, CAOs are wise to partner with college counsel in developing creative ways to lead from the center of their institutions.

NOTES

1. U.S. District Court for the District of Hawaii Case No. CV1000684ACKLEK.

2. James E. Samels, "Preventive law 'graduates' to higher education despite initial resistance,' " *Preventive Law Reporter,* June 1989.

3. Stanley Z. Koplik, James L. Martin, and James E. Samels, "In a Crisis Count to 10," *Trusteeship* 4, no. 1 (1996): 22–23, 24–26.

4. In 2008, Virginia passed a law requiring its four-year colleges to set up threat assessment teams after a mentally unstable student who had been sending out warning signs shot and killed 32 people. §23-9.2:10 Code of Virginia as amended. See also Kay Heidbreder, *Virginia Law on Threat Assessment in Public Institutions of Higher Education,* Virginia Department of Behavioral Health and Developmental Services, 2013, https://www.dmhmrsas.virginia.gov/documents /ThreatAssessment%20in%20Higher%20Ed%202013.03.28.pdf.

5. Danielle Dellorto, "Therapists walk fine line in reporting violent plans," *CNN,* 2 August 2012, http://www.cnn.com/2012/08/02/health/therapist-violence.

6. 20 U.S.C. § 1232g; 34 CFR Part 99 Family Educational Rights and Privacy Act ("FERPA" and otherwise known as the Buckley Amendment) (20 U.S.C. § 1232g; 34 CFR Part 99).

7. 839 F.Supp.2d 518.

8. Audrey Williams June, "Adjuncts Build Strength in Numbers," *Chronicle of Higher Education,* November 5, 2012, http://chronicle.com/article/Adjuncts-Build -Strength-in/135520.

9. *Board of Regents v. Roth,* 408 U.S. at 576–77 (1972).

10. See Washington and Lee University Compliance Initiatives at http://www .wlu.edu/general-counsel/answer-center/compliance-initiatives.

11. USDE is the United States Department of Education; IPEDS is Integrated Postsecondary Education Data System, the primary source for data on colleges, universities, and technical and vocational postsecondary institutions in the United States; and FERPA is the Family Educational Rights and Privacy Act, which governs disclosure of educational rights.

12. See, for example, *Ross v. Creighton University,* 740 F.Supp. 1319 (ND. Ill. 1990).

13. See *Moore v. Vanderloo,* 386 N.W.2d 108 (Iowa 1986).

14. See *Russell v. Salve Regina College,* 938 F.2d 315, 316 (1st Cir.1991).

15. See *Lyons v. Salve Regina College,* 565 F.2d 200. 202.

16. See *Mangla v. Brown University,* 135 F.3d 80 (1St Cir. 1998).

17. See Ownership of Copyright, 17 U.S.C. §101; Definitions, 17 U.S.C. §201.

18. *Pittsburgh State University Kansas National Education Association v. Kansas Board of Regents/Pittsburgh State University and Public Employee Relations Board,* Supreme Court of the State of Kansas No. 91, 305, November 10, 2005.

19. 248 F.Supp.12371 (D.C.R.I.2003).

20. Laura G. Lape, "Ownership of Copyrightable Works of University Professors: The Interplay between the Copyright Act and University Copyright Policies," 37 Vill.L.Rev.223 (1992): 267.

CHAPTER SEVENTEEN

Building Bridges beyond the Quadrangle: The CAO and the External Community

Mark B. Lapping

The traditional president–CAO relationship has been viewed as an inside-outside agreement wherein the president plays an increasingly public set of roles while the CAO is the quintessential "inside player." However, the growing complexities of the higher education environment have caused a rethinking of this paradigm. The distance between these two positions and their roles continues to narrow, and a clear alignment has become critical in the context of external relationships. It is no longer possible to talk of the president as having the outside portfolio of responsibilities and the CAO the inside portfolio. Successful presidents will maintain a strong and engaged internal profile while, increasingly, the CAO must assume a robust, visible, external presence.

Perhaps, the most obvious rationale to justify a growing external orientation for the CAO lies in the fact that he or she must be prepared to act in place of the president when the latter is absent from the campus. The CAO is almost always the individual designated as the acting president in the absence of the chief executive officer. Thus, a knowledge of and appreciation for the external responsibilities of the president must be part of the portfolio of any provost or academic dean. When the president of an institution is away and the CAO acts in his or her place, the CAO must be prepared to maintain external relationships in the public policy arena, with the local business community, and among current and potential funders and alumni. One of the best ways to be prepared to act effectively on the outside is for the provost to be updated on key relationships through regular briefings from the president specifically focused on the status of external connections that need to be maintained and cultivated. Contemporary communications technologies make it relatively easy for the president to be in contact with the campus community, but there will still be times when the presence of the CAO as the physical stand-in for the president will be necessary and appropriate.

External demands on collegiate communities have grown over the past two decades in number, complexity, and sensitivity. While traditional town-gown issues remain salient, institutions are now embedded in increasingly complex and nuanced social environments, and the varied roles of the CAO in external affairs have evolved in a corresponding fashion. Two decades ago, for example, it was much easier for colleges to erect new or expanded facilities. As buildings have grown more sophisticated, sustainable, and expensive, especially in the science and medical fields, working with the perceived and real concerns of the external community has become a necessity. Often it falls to the CAO, who must not only explain to multiple constituencies why new facilities are necessary now but also why such work is critical to future students and faculty of the institution. Provosts must now become conversant—if not expert—in dealing with planning and zoning issues and the management of both real and perceived risk. Multiple university and college administrations have foundered on their failure to work early and closely with the local community when new facilities are proposed. When handled poorly, town-gown interface issues can create or extend a climate of conflict and mistrust, even of hostility. If the core issue is, in fact, an expansion of the campus footprint, the academic dean or provost may find him- or herself in the middle of a controversy with a critical leadership role to play.

Build a Flexible Town-Gown Connection

Connected to this have been attempts by colleges and universities to enhance their connection with local communities through public-private partnerships, endowment investments that seek to expand local businesses, and the provision of quality housing options and other amenities. Such activities must be administered with skill and reflect a commitment to justice and equity that may not benefit the institution initially but have the potential to pay enormous dividends over the following decade

The CAO beyond the Campus: Four Responsibilities

1. Build a flexible town-gown connection
2. Leverage legislative friends
3. Externalize the curriculum
4. Manage institutional image

The Thing I Very Much Wish I Had Known on My First Day as CAO

- Faculty members will take almost anything I say and assume it is official policy.

and more. These values must be articulated and supported by the CAO even as the president leads such efforts.

While the initial impetus for such investments might be to make the college more attractive to potential applicants, the reality is that enhancing the quality of life for local neighbors returns significant dividends to the college community. An example is provided in the Suzanne Vitale Center at Western Kentucky University that brings together university and community resources to address the needs of disabled persons in the local community.[1] Here a variety of services are brought under one roof to provide people with disabilities opportunities and support that otherwise might not be easily accessible. Partnerships can bring the college to the community and the community to the college in a highly beneficial way. A recently published piece by Mike Ross, "Seeding University Communities," points out how former President Judith Rodin of the University of Pennsylvania led university efforts to significantly enhance the West Philadelphia neighborhood in which the university is situated.[2] Local businesses have benefited from Penn's "buy local" preference and similar economic development initiatives. Likewise, as Ross points out, Northeastern University in Boston has generated substantial funds to support business and job creation in the long-time depressed Roxbury neighborhood of that city.

Leverage Legislative Friends

Local and state governments have also been proactive partners in the growth and development of multiple colleges and universities. Through various mechanisms, the public sector has played an important role in helping to support collegiate initiatives, especially as they relate to local and regional economic development. As universities are viewed as engines of growth, the provost will typically be asked by the president or board to help the public understand how higher education institutions propel growth in jobs and employment and sustains a region's "creative economy." As a growing trend, colleges now spend resources to develop economic impact statements on the net effect of institutions on their local and regional economies.[3] Where such documentation does not exist, the CAO should convene campus representatives to develop relevant data and information, and he or she should also invite state and federal legislators to join this conversation and bring resources from their own networks. Newly elected officials sometimes fail to understand the impact that colleges and universities have on their communities, and such studies can be effective in gradually changing perceptions.

Understanding and appreciating the issues before a state legislature or a town council can be especially useful to a CAO in navigating the external interests of the college or university. While larger institutions will typically have a governmental affairs specialist on staff, it often falls to the provost to provide the factual basis that an institution may take relative to a particular bill or proposal before a public body. In a rising number of regions, legislators are learning the benefits of helping their local college and universities contribute substantially to the regional economy and enhance the overall attractiveness of an area. In the high tech sector, it is impossible to imagine the Silicon Valley without Stanford and San Jose State Universities, or the Route 128 Corridor surrounding Boston absent more than thirty proximate Massachusetts universities, or the Research Triangle in North Carolina minus the contributions of UNC Chapel Hill, Duke, North Carolina State, and Northern Carolina Central Universities.

The American retirement industry, another growth sector in many regions, strategically builds strong connections with colleges and universities because of the amenities they directly and indirectly provide for retirees. An expanding number of institutions are taking advantage of maturing alumni by developing retirement communities closer to campuses to respond to the growth of this influential demographic. The national Osher Lifelong Learning Institutes (OLLI) is a notable campus-based model that serves the retirement community.[4]

Three Emerging Trends

1. The public does not understand what faculty members do, so use opportunities as the CAO to explain to the outside community.
2. There is a growing suspicion of science and technology among the general public. As CAO, do not hesitate to address this.
3. Partnerships are vital to long-term institutional health.

Externalize the Curriculum

Over the past two generations of students, college and university curricula have steadily become externalized as the campus quadrangle and its traditional boundaries are no longer viewed as the sole location of learning and instruction. Through internships, placements, field stations, and laboratories, the external community—variously defined—is now an integral locus for the production and acquisition of knowledge. This is perhaps most clearly seen in the emergence of service learning as a transformative element of the undergraduate curriculum. Service learning places the student in a context where real-world situations combine with theory to provide an educational experience that could not occur solely in a traditional classroom. From the perspective of the institutional community, the CAO, working with faculty to embed service learning and experiential education in tenure and promotion criteria, sends a clear message about the institution's commitment to new definitions of the classroom experience and the value of external relationships.

Manage Institutional Image

Effective provosts translate the value of higher education to the larger community. They convey the faculty's role in creating, generating, and transmitting knowledge and skills. Together with the president, the CAO must also serve as an aggressive advocate beyond the campus for the place that higher education plays in the economic and social development of our society. One mechanism for doing this is to provide venues through which the public comes to understand more clearly what faculty work includes. For many people, daily faculty activities remain a mystery.

Early in my career as a vice president for academic affairs, I designed a public access television program that highlighted faculty scholarship and creative work for viewers in the state of Maine. I used an interview format to discuss new academic initiatives along with the direct benefits students at the university would receive from them. In bringing the work of teachers and staff members to a broader cross-section of the local com-

The Single Most Important Piece of Advice for a New Provost on the First Day in the Position

- Walk around each day and listen: a CAO's visibility and curiosity are infectious and can raise morale and build trust.

Lessons Learned: The CAO and External Relations

BY JON STROLLE

1. *Government relations.* Learn the culture and speak the language of elected officials. Consider running for office at some point.

2. *Legislative delegations.* Meet all key staff members and learn the committees your legislator attends.

3. *Grants.* Read with precision the Request For Proposals and answer every question in the exact order asked. Think like the evaluator.

4. *Reinvention.* Bend the future around the strength of your institution's resources. No university or college is universal.

Jon Strolle wrote the chapter on the CAO and external relations in First Among Equals: The Role of the Chief Academic Officer *(1997). He is a Fellow of the National Foreign Language Center and was for many years associated with the Monterey Institute of International Studies, including as dean and associate provost.*

munity, I was conveying what people on the campus actually did and why such things as sabbaticals, academic freedom, and professional research are essential. As a CAO, I did this in part because I had observed that publications highlighting research work by faculty were designed for peers at higher education institutions. While these had their value, they did practically nothing to strengthen ties for colleges and universities with their local communities, and this was a missed opportunity.

A Final Word on the Power of Partnerships

As resource-challenged colleges and universities utilize external partnerships as a strategy to build new facilities, especially student housing, and as major universities employ them to deepen their institutional research capacity, relationships with non-academic partners can still be complex. Whether they involve laboratory animal care policies, developing a swampy tract of land, or intellectual property ownership, these initiatives can demand a set of skills that many CAOs need to develop while still remaining consistent with their institutional mission.

As provosts and deans are offered these opportunities for leadership outside their institutions, they will need to balance carefully the sometimes conflicting expectations of student consumers, faculty skeptics, and trustee bottom-liners back on campus.

NOTES

1. Suzanne Vitale Clinical Education Complex, "CEC Programs," Western Kentucky University. http://www.wku.edu/wkucec/programs.php.

2. Mike Ross, "Seeding University Communities," *Boston Globe*, 23 December 2013, http://www.bostonglobe.com/opinion/2013/12/23/seeding-university-neighbor hoods/y6qK9dzVXoen3gIkZEoljP/story.html.

3. Michael C. Carroll and Bruce W. Smith, "Estimating the Economic Impact of Universities: The Case of Bowling Green State University," *Industrial Geographer* 3, no. 2 (2006): 1–12.

4. Osher Lifelong Learning Institutes, "National Resource Center," The Bernard Osher Foundation, University of Southern Maine, http://usm.maine.edu/olli.

Bibliography

ABC News. "This Week." http://abcnews.go.com/ThisWeek/video/james-carville
-suspend-penn-state-football-16782104.

Altbach, Philip. "Academic Salaries and Contracts: What Do We Know?" *International Higher Education* 68 (Summer 2012).

———. "It's the Faculty, Stupid!—The Centrality of the Academic Profession." *International Higher Education* 55 (Spring 2009).

American Association of State Colleges and Universities. "Academic Affairs Summer Meeting 2012, July 26–28." Washington, DC: American Association of State Colleges and Universities. http://aascu.org/meetings/aa_summer12/.

American Association of University Professors. "New Report on Contingent Faculty and Governance." 2013. http://www.aaup.org/AAUP/newsroom/2012webhigh light/congovreport.htm.

American Council on Education. "CAO/CFO Collaboration: Building Collaborative Opportunities Together." Washington, DC: American Council on Education. http://www.acenet.edu/leadership/programs/Pages/CAO-CBO-Work shop.aspx.

Anderson, Michael L. "The Benefits of College Athletic Success: An Application of the Propensity Score Design with Instrumental Variables." Working paper, National Bureau of Economic Research, June 2012.

Association of Governing Boards of Universities and Colleges. "Effective Governing Boards: A Guide for Members of Governing Boards of Public Colleges, Universities, and Systems." Washington, DC: AGB Press, 2010.

Austensen, Roy. "First Among Equals: The Current Roles of the Chief Academic Officer." In *First Among Equals: The Role of the Chief Academic Officer,* James Martin, James E. Samels, and Associates, 21–40. Baltimore: Johns Hopkins University Press, 1997.

Bailey, Jonathan. "Is Academic Plagiarism Truly on the Rise?" *Plagiarism Today,* 22 May 2012. http://www.plagiarismtoday.com/2012/05/22/is-academic-plagiarism -on-the-rise/.

Blumenstyk, Goldie. "One-Third of Colleges Are on Financially 'Unsustainable' Path, Bain Study Finds." *Chronicle of Higher Education*, 23 July 2012. http://chronicle.com/article/One-Third-of-Colleges-Are-on/133095/.

Burgan, Mary. *What Ever Happened to the Faculty?* Baltimore: John Hopkins University Press, 2006.

Carnevale, Dan. "E-mail is For Old People." *Chronicle of Higher Education*, 6 October 2006. http://chronicle.com/article/E-Mail-is-for-Old-People/4169/.

Carroll, Michael C., and Bruce W. Smith. "Estimating the Economic Impact of Universities: The Case of Bowling Green State University." *Industrial Geographer* 3, no. 2 (2006): 1–12.

Christensen, Clayton M., Michael B. Horn, Louis Caldera, and Louis Soares. "Disrupting College," Executive Summary. Washington, DC: Center of American Progress, Innosight Institute, February 2011. http://cdn.americanprogress.org/wp-content/uploads/issues/2011/02/pdf/disrupting_college_execsumm.pdf.

Coalition on the Academic Workforce. *A Portrait of Part-time Faculty Members*. June 2012. http://www.academicworkforce.org/CAW_portrait_2012.pdf.

The College and University Professional Association for Human Resources. "Who We Are." In *About Us*. http://www.cupahr.org/about/index.aspx.

Collins, George, and John G. Flores. USDLA Research: Distance Learning Accreditation, 2011. www.usdla.org.

Collins, Tracy, Scott Slough, and Hersch Waxman. "Lessons Learned about Mentoring Junior Faculty in Higher Education." *Academic Leadership* 7, no. 2 (2009): 1.

Columbia University Graduate School of Arts & Sciences Teaching Center. "The Future of Higher Education." http://www.columbia.edu/cu/tat/pdfs/future%20Of%20higher%20ed.pdf.

Common Core State Standards Initiative. "In the States." The National Governors Association Center for Best Practices and the Council of Chief State School Officers. http://www.corestandards.org/in-the-states.

Cook, Bryan, and Kim Young. *The American College President 2012*. Washington, DC: American Council on Education, 2012.

Council for Advancement and Support of Education. "Development for Deans and Academic Leaders." Washington, DC: CASE. http://www.case.org/Conferences_and_Training/DALW12.html.

Council of Independent Colleges. "2011 Institute for Chief Academic Officers and Chief Advancement Officers, November 5–8." Washington, DC: Council of Independent Colleges. http://www.cic.edu/meetings-and-events/Annual-Conferences/CAO-Institute/2011-CAO-Institute/Pages/default.aspx.

Counseling and Psychological Services. "Resources for Faculty and Staff." University of California, San Diego. http://caps.ucsd.edu/faculty-staff.html.

Davidson, Adam. "Smart Jobs: A Special Report." *Wired* 19, no. 6 (June 2011): 124.

Davies, Anna, Devin Fidler, and Marina Gorbis. *Future Work Skills—2020*. The Institute for the Future for the University of Phoenix Research Institute, 2011. http://cdn.theatlantic.com/static/front/docs/sponsored/phoenix/future_work_skills_2020.pdf.

Denneen, Jeff, and Tom Dretler. "The Financially Sustainable University." *Bain Brief*, 6 July 2012. http://www.bain.com/publications/articles/financially-sustainable-university.aspx.

Department of Education. "A First Look as Gainful Employment Data, by Program and Institution." *Chronicle of Higher Education,* 25 June 2012. http://chronicle.com/article/A-First-Look-at-Gainful/132589/.

Diamond, Daryl, Mary T. Kolesinki, and Evelyn Nelson-Weaver. *Digital Solidarity in Education: Promoting Equity, Diversity, and Academic Excellence through Innovative Instructional Programs.* New York: Routledge, 2014.

Eckel, Peter D., Bryan J. Cook, and Jacqueline E. King. *The CAO Census: A National Profile of Chief Academic Officers.* Washington, DC: American Council on Education, 2009.

Estler, Suzanne E., with Laurie J. Nelson. *Who Calls the Shots? Sports and University Leadership, Culture, and Decision Making.* ASHE Higher Education Report 30, no. 5 (2005): 11.

Fairweather, James. "Beyond the Rhetoric: Trends in the Relative Value of Teaching and Research in Faculty Salaries." *Journal of Higher Education* 76, no. 4 (2005): 401–22.

———. *Faculty Work and the Public Trust: Restoring the Value of Teaching and Public Service in American Academic Life.* Boston: Allyn and Bacon, 1996.

Ferren, Ann, and Wilbur Stanton. *Leadership through Collaboration: The Role of the Chief Academic Officer.* Westport, CT: American Council on Education/Praeger Publishers, 2004.

Flores, J. "White Paper: Enabled By Broadband, Education Enters a New Frontier." United States Distance Learning Association, November 2010. http://www.heartland.org/policy-documents/enabled-broadband-education-enters-new-frontier.

———. "White Paper: Expanding the Classroom: Mobile Distance Learning across America." United States Distance Learning Association, August 2011. http://www.usdla.org/assets/pdf_files/USDLAWhitePaper.English.FINAL.9.15.pdf.

Friedman, Thomas, *The World Is Flat: A Brief History of the Twenty-first Century.* New York: Farrar, Straus, and Giroux, 2005.

Gabriel, Trip. "Plagiarism Lines Blur for Students in Digital Age." *New York Times,* 1 August 2010. http://www.nytimes.com/2010/08/02/education/02.cheat.html?pagewanted=all.

Gandre, James, and Miroslava Mejia Krug. "Dynamics on The Double." *Business Officer Magazine* (July/August 2011): 64–65.

Gappa, Judith M., Ann E. Austin, and Andrea G. Trice. *Rethinking Faculty Work.* San Francisco: Jossey-Bass, 2007.

General Education Program, "Purpose of the General Education Program." University of Illinois at Chicago. 2011. http://www.uic.edu/depts/oaa/gened/purpose.html.

Goldstein, Michael G. "Cracking the Egg: Preserving the College While Protecting the Core." *Trusteeship* 18, no. 1 (January/February 2010): 24–29.

Goleman, Daniel, Richard Boyatzis, and Annie McKee. *Primal Leadership.* Boston: Harvard Business School Press, 2002.

Green, Kenneth C., with Scott Jaschik and Doug Lederman. *The 2011–2012 Inside Higher Ed Survey of College and University Chief Academic Officers.* Washington, DC: Inside Higher Ed, 2012.

Groves, Robert. "The land Between the Disciplines." *The Provost's Blog,* 16 July 2014. https://blog.provost.georgetown.edu/between-the-disciplines/.

———. "But What Do the Faculty Think about It?" *The Provost's Blog,* 9 October 2013. https://blog.provost.georgetown.edu/but-what-do-the-faculty-think-about -it/.

———. "Diversity of Another Sort." *The Provost's Blog,* 9 January 2013. https:// blog.provost.georgetown.edu/diversity-of-another-sort/.

———. "An Evolution of Joint Appointments." *The Provost's Blog,* 25 September 2013. https://blog.provost.georgetown.edu/an-evolution-of-joint-appoint ments/.

———. "The Instructor as Director of a Play." *The Provost's Blog,* 11 December 2013. https://blog.provost.georgetown.edu/the-instructor-as-director-of-a -play/.

———. "Joint, Inter-Disciplinary, Multi-Disciplinary, Trans-Disciplinary." *The Provost's Blog,* 3 April 2013. https://blog.provost.georgetown.edu/joint-inter-disc iplinary-multi-disciplinary-trans-disciplinary/.

———. "Learning Adaptive Learning." *The Provost's Blog,* 31 July 2013. https:// blog.provost.georgetown.edu/learning-adaptive-learning/.

———. "Navigating the Academy." *The Provost's Blog,* 12 June 2013. https://blog .provost.georgetown.edu/navigating-the-academy/.

Hartley III, Harold V., and Eric E. Godin. *A Study of Chief Academic Officers of Independent Colleges and Universities.* Washington, DC: Council of Independent Colleges, 2010.

Heidbreder, Kay. *Virginia Law on Threat Assessment in Public Institutions of Higher Education.* Virginia Department of Behavioral Health and Developmental Services, 2013. http://www.dbhds.virginia.gov/documents/ThreatAssessment%20 in%20Higher%20Ed%202013.03.28.pdf.

Heiftez, Ronald A. *Leadership Without Easy Answers.* Cambridge, MA: Belknap Press of Harvard University Press, 1994.

Hentschke, Guilbert C. "For-Profit Sector Innovations in Business Models and Organizational Cultures." In *Reinventing Higher Education: The Promise of Innovation,* ed. Ben Wildavsky, Andrew P. Kelly, and Kevin Carey. Cambridge, MA: Harvard Education Press, 2011.

Hirt, Joan B. *Where You Work Matters: Student Affairs Administration at Different Types of Institutions.* Lanham, MD: University Press of America, 2006.

Howard, Jennifer. "Laura Czerniewicz Is Educating by Phone," in "Rebooting the Academy: 12 Big Ideas." *Chronicle of Higher Education* 58, no. 26 (2012): A12. http://www.wku.edu/wkucec/programs.php.

Hurtado, Sylvia, L. Arellano, M. Cuellar, and C. Guillermo-Wann. "Diverse Learning Environments Survey Instrument: Introduction and Select Factors." Conference presentation, Diversity Research Institute from University of California, Los Angeles, 6 August 2010.

Hutchings, Pat. *Opening Doors to Faculty Involvement in Assessment.* National Institute for Learning Outcomes Assessment, 2010.

International Center for Academic Integrity. "Academic Integrity Assessment Guide." http://www.academicintegrity.org/icai/ resources-1.php.

Jayakumar, Uma M., Tyrone C. Howard, and Walter R. Allen. "Racial Privilege in the Professoriate: An Exploration of Campus Climate, Retention, and Satisfaction." *Journal of Higher Education* 80, no. 5 (2009): 538.

Kadison, Richard, and Theresa Foy DiGeronimo. *College of the Overwhelmed: The Campus Mental Health Crisis and What to Do About It.* San Francisco: Jossey-Bass, 2004.

Kahn, Joseph P. "Generation Broke." *Boston Globe,* 29 May 2012, 12G.

Kaplan, Andreas M., and Michael Haenlein. "Users of the World, Unite! The Challenges and Opportunities of Social Media." *Business Horizons* 53, no. 1 (January/February 2010): 59–68.

Katz, Stanley. "Beyond Crude Measurement and Consumerism." *Academe* 96, no. 5 (2010). http://www.aaup.org/AAUP/pubsres/academe/2010/SO/feat/katz.htm.

Kazar, Adrianna, and Cecile Sam. "Understanding the New Majority of Non-Tenure-Track Faculty in Higher Education: Demographics, Experiences, and Plans of Action." *ASHE Higher Education Report* 36, no. 4 (2010): 78.

Keeling, Richard P., ed. *Learning Reconsidered 2: A Practical Guide to Implementing a Campus-wide Focus on the Student Experience.* Champaign, IL: Human Kinetics, 2006.

Keim, Marybelle C., and John P. Murray. "Chief Academic Officers' Demographics and Educational Backgrounds." *Community College Review* 36, no. 116 (October 2008).

Kellogg Commission on the Future of State and Land-Grant Universities. *Returning to Our Roots: Toward a Coherent Campus Culture.* Washington, DC: National Association of State Universities and Land-Grant Colleges, 2000.

Keynes, Pauline E. "New Paradigms for Diversifying Faculty and Staff in Higher Education: Uncovering Cultural Biases in the Search and Hiring Process." *Multicultural Education* 14, no. 2 (2006): 65–69.

Kotkin, Joel. "Generation Screwed." *Newsweek* 160, nos. 4 and 5 (2012): 42.

Kuh, G. D., J. Kinzie, J. H. Schuh, E. J. Whitt, & Associates. *Student Success in College: Creating Conditions That Matter.* San Francisco: Jossey-Bass, 2005.

Kuh, George D. *High-impact Educational Practices: What They Are, Who Has Access to Them, and Why They Matter.* Washington, DC: Association of American Colleges and Universities, 2008.

Lape, Laura G. *Ownership of Copyrightable Works of University Professors: The Interplay between the Copyright Act and University Copyright Policies.* 37 Vill. L. Rev. 223, 1992.

Light, Richard. *Making the Most of College: Students Speak their Minds.* Cambridge, MA: Harvard University Press, 2001.

Marthers, Paul, and Jeff Parker. "Small Colleges and New Faculty Pay." *Academe* 94, no. 4 (2008): 45–49.

———. "The Greening of the Provost." *Trusteeship* (March/April 1999): 18.

Martin, James, James E. Samels, and Associates, eds. *First Among Equals: The Role of the Chief Academic Officer.* Baltimore: Johns Hopkins University Press, 1997.

Martin, Robert E. "College Costs Too Much Because Faculty Lack Power." *Chronicle of Higher Education,* 5 August 2012. http://chronicle.com/article/College-Costs-Too-Much-Because/133357/.

McCormick, Alexander. "The Complex Interplay between Classification and Ranking of Colleges and Universities: Should the Berlin Principles Apply Equally to Classification?" *Higher Education in Europe* 33, no. 2/3 (2008): 209–18.

McMillin, Linda. "Through the Looking Glass: Faculty to Administration." *Chronicle of Higher Education,* 16 October 2011. http://chronicle.com/article/Through-the-Looking-Glass-/129417/.

McMillin, Linda, and William G. Berberet. *A New Academic Compact.* Boston, MA: Stylus Press, 2002.

Middlehurst, Robin. "Investing in Leadership Development: The UK Experience." *International Higher Education* 67 (Spring 2012): 16.

Moden, G. O., R. I. Miller, and A. M. Williford. "The Role, Scope, and Functions of the Chief Academic Officer." Paper presented at the annual forum of the Association of Institutional Research, Kansas City, MO, May 1987. (ERIC Document Reproduction Service No. ED293441).

Monk, James. "Who Are the Part-time Faculty?" *Academe* 95, no. 4 (2007): 33–37.

Morrill, Richard L. *Strategic Leadership in Academic Affairs.* Washington, DC: Association of Governing Boards, 2002.

Nelson, Cary. "Reforming Faculty Identity." *Academe* 97, no. 4 (2011): 56.

Nelson, Stephen J. "Balance Wheels: College Presidents in the Crucible of the 1960s and the Contests of Today." *Bridgewater Review* 31, no. 1 (June 2012): 26.

Northouse, Peter G. *Leadership Theory and Practice,* 3rd ed. Los Angeles: SAGE, 2013.

Paradise, L. and D. Kimya. "New Peril for the Provost: Marginalization of the Academic Mission." *About Campus,* 12 April 2007.

Pascarella, Ernest T., and Patrick T. Terenzini. *How College Affects Students,* 2nd ed. San Francisco: Jossey-Bass, 2005.

Porter, Dave. "Assessment as a Subversive Activity." *AAUP Journal of Academic Freedom* 3 (2012): 14.

Presidents' Climate Commitment. "Celebrating Five Years of Climate Leadership." American College & University Presidents' Climate Commitment, 2012. http://www.presidentsclimatecommitment.org/reporting/annual-report/five-year-report.

Presley, John Woodrow. "Chief Academic Officers and Institutional Change: The Example of Community Engagement." *Teacher-Scholar—the Journal of the State Comprehensive University* 2, no. 1 (Fall 2010): 21.

Rice, R. Eugene. "Future of the Scholarly Work of Faculty." In *Faculty Priorities Reconsidered,* ed. KerryAnn O'Meara and R. Eugene Rice. San Francisco: Jossey-Bass, 2005.

Rios-Aguilar, Cecilia, Manuel Sacramento González Canché, Regina Deil-Amen, and Charles H. F. Davis III. "The Role of Social Media in Community Colleges." Tucson: The Center for the Study of Higher Education at the University of Arizona and Claremont Graduate University, 2012.

Ross, Mike. "Seeding University Communities." *Boston Globe,* 23 December 2013. http://www.bostonglobe.com/opinion/2013/12/23/seeding-university-neighborhoods/y6qK9dzVXoen3gIkZEoljP/story.html.

Samels, James E. "Preventive Law 'Graduates' to Higher Education Despite Initial Resistance." *Preventive Law Reporter,* June 1989.

Schmidt, Peter. "Survey of Chief Academic Officers Raises Concerns about Diversity and Longevity," *Chronicle of Higher Education,* 12 June 2009. http://chronicle.com/article/ Survey-of-Chief-Academic-Of/1518/.

Schuster, Jack, and Martin Finkelstein. *The American Faculty.* Baltimore: John Hopkins University Press, 2006.

Slaughter, Anne-Marie. "Why Women Still Can't Have it All." *Atlantic Monthly,* July/August 2012. http://www.theatlantic.com/magazine/archive/2012/07/why-women -still-cant-have-it-all/309020/.

The Sloan Consortium. "Changing Course—10 Years of Tracking Online Education in the U.S." Babson Survey Research Group and Quahog Research Group, LLC, 2013. http://www.onlinelearningsurvey.com/reports/changingcourse.pdf.

Song, Wei, and Harold V. Hartley III. *A Study of Presidents of Independent Colleges and Universities.* Washington, DC: Council of Independent Colleges, 2012.

State Council of Higher Education for Virginia. "Council Agenda Item 10." *Agenda Book* 10 (July 2007): C24. http://www.schev.edu/SCHEV/AgendaBooks/Agenda BookJuly07/AgendaBookJuly07.pdf.

Tierney, W. G., and G. C. Hentschke. *New Players, Different Game.* Baltimore: Johns Hopkins Press, 2007.

Trower, Cathy. "A New Generation of Faculty: Similar Core Values in a Different World." *Peer Review* (Summer 2010): 27–30.

Turner, Caroline, Viernes Sotello, Samuel L. Myers Jr., and John W. Creswell. "Exploring Underrepresentation: The Case of Faculty of Color in the Midwest." *Journal of Higher Education* 70, no. 1 (1999): 27–59.

UCLA Diversity Research Institute from Higher Education Research Institute. "Understanding the Campus Racial Climate." Conference presentation, University of California, Los Angeles, 3 August 2010.

US News Rankings. "Best College, Best Graduate School, Best Hospitals, and Best Health Insurance Companies." *US News & World Report.* http://www.usnews .com/rankings.

Van Der Werf, Martin, and Grant Sabatier. *The College of 2020: Students.* Washington, DC: Chronicle Research Services, 2009.

Vedantam, Shankar. "Lessons in Leadership: It's Not About You. (It's About Them)," *NPR,* 11 November 2013. http://www.npr.org/2013/11/11/230841224/lessons -in-leadership-its-not-about-you-its-about-them.

Vedder, Richard. "12 Inconvenient Truths about American Higher Education." *Trusteeship* 20, no. 3 (May/June 2012).

William, Damon, Joseph Berger, and Shederick McClendon. *Toward a Model of Inclusive Excellence and Change in Postsecondary Institutions.* Washington, DC: Association of American Colleges and Universities, 2005.

Williams June, Audrey. "Adjuncts Build Strength in Numbers." *Chronicle of Higher Education,* 5 November 2012. http://chronicle.com/article/Adjuncts-Build-Strength -in/135520.

Wilson, Robin. "Why Are Associate Professors So Unhappy?" *Chronicle of Higher Education,* 3 June 2012. http://chronicle.com/article/Why-Are-Associate-Professors /132071/?sid=at&utm_source=at&utm_medium=en.

Contributors

JAMES MARTIN has been a member of the Mount Ida College faculty since 1979. Now a professor of English, he served for over fifteen years as the college's vice president for academic affairs and provost. An ordained United Methodist minister, he was awarded a Fulbright Fellowship to study mergers in the University of London system. Martin is also a senior academic advisor at The Education Alliance.

With his writing partner, James E. Samels, Martin has co-authored five previous books available from Johns Hopkins University Press: *Merging Colleges for Mutual Growth* (1994), *First Among Equals: The Role of the Chief Academic Officer* (1997), *Presidential Transition in Higher Education: Managing Leadership Change* (2005), *Turnaround: Leading Stressed Colleges and Universities to Excellence* (2009), and *The Sustainable University: Green Goals and New Challenges for Higher Education Leaders* (2012). He co-writes with Samels a column on college and university issues, "Future Shock," for *University Business Magazine*. Martin and Samels also co-hosted the nation's first television talk program on higher education issues, *Future Shock in Higher Education*, from 1994 to 1999 on the Massachusetts Corporation for Educational Telecommunications (MCET) satellite learning network. A graduate of Colby College (A.B.) and Boston University (M.Div. and Ph.D.), Martin has written articles for the *Chronicle of Higher Education*, *London Times*, *Christian Science Monitor*, *Boston Globe*, *Trusteeship*, *CASE Currents*, and *Planning for Higher Education*.

JAMES E. SAMELS is the founder and CEO of both The Education Alliance and the Samels Group, a full-service higher education consulting firm. He is also the founding partner of Samels Associates, a law firm serving independent and public colleges, universities, and non-profit and for-profit higher education organizations. Samels has served on the faculties of the University of Massachusetts and Bentley College and as a guest lecturer at Boston University and Harvard University. Prior to his appointment at the University of Massachusetts, Samels served as the deputy and acting state comptroller in Massachusetts, special assistant attorney general, Massachusetts Community College counsel, and general counsel to the Massachusetts Board of Regents.

Samels holds a bachelor's degree in political science, a master's degree in public administration, a juris doctor degree, and a doctor of education degree. He has written and co-written a number of scholarly articles, monographs, and opinion editorials appearing in the *Chronicle of Higher Education, AGB Trusteeship, Christian Science Monitor, London Guardian, Boston Globe, Boston Herald, Boston Business Journal, Journal of Higher Education Management,* and *Planning for Higher Education.* He is the co-author, with James Martin, of *Merging Colleges for Mutual Growth* (1994), *First Among Equals: The Role of the Chief Academic Officer* (1997), *Presidential Transition in Higher Education: Managing Leadership Change* (2005), *Turnaround: Leading Stressed Colleges and Universities to Excellence* (2009), and *The Sustainable University: Green Goals and New Challenges for Higher Education Leaders* (2012), all from Johns Hopkins University Press. Samels has previously consulted on projects and presented research papers at universities, colleges, schools, and ministries of education in China, Canada, Great Britain, France, Korea, Sweden, Thailand, and Turkey.

MICHAEL A. BAER is a vice president and partner at Isaacson, Miller, a national executive search firm that recruits exceptional leaders for mission-driven organizations. His practice is in higher education, where he has recruited presidents, provosts, and deans. He joined Isaacson, Miller in 2005 after serving as senior vice president at the American Council on Education (ACE). At ACE, Baer oversaw all campus-based programs, including those that identified and prepared individuals to move into senior administrative positions, international education, workforce preparation, and adult learning.

Prior to joining ACE in 1998, Baer served Northeastern University for eight years as provost and senior vice president for academic affairs. A political scientist, Baer began his academic career at the University of Kentucky, where he was a professor and department chair before serving for nine years as dean of the College of Arts & Sciences. He is the co-author of *Lobbying: Interaction and Influence in American State Legislatures,* and co-editor of *Political Science in America: Oral Histories of a Discipline.* Baer's undergraduate degrees in chemistry and political science are from Emory University, and his M.A. and doctoral degree in political science are from the University of Oregon.

BRADLEY W. BATEMAN was appointed president of Randolph College in 2013. Prior to arriving at Randolph, Bateman had served as provost of Denison College since 2007. During his tenure at Denison, Bateman fostered conversations on campus concerning undergraduate writing, faculty advising, and assessment of the entirety of the Denison learning experience within and without the classroom. He was successful in winning support from the Andrew W. Mellon Foundation to initiate faculty conferences on the liberal arts and was involved in efforts to find additional financial support for the Denison Museum and for the college's performing arts programs.

Prior to his post as Denison's provost, Bateman was the associate dean of the college at Grinnell College in Iowa (2005–2007). After joining the Grinnell faculty in 1987, Bateman also served as the Gertrude B. Austin Professor of Economics, the chair of the Department of Economics, and the acting director of the Center for Prairie Studies. Earlier in his career, he was an assistant professor of economics at Simmons College and an instructor of economics at the University of Kentucky. Bateman holds a Ph.D. and M.A. from the University of Kentucky and a B.A., with honors, from Alma College.

MEREDITH S. BILLINGS is a graduate student research assistant and doctoral candidate in public policy in postsecondary education in the School of Education at the University of Michigan.

BRYAN J. COOK was formerly the director of the Center for Policy Analysis at the American Council on Education. The Center conducts and commissions research on federal and national higher education policy issues of interest to ACE members, policy makers, other higher education associations, and the media. Topics on the Center's agenda include student financial aid, college costs, improving college readiness, student outcomes, demographic trends in higher education, the provostship, and the presidency.

Cook managed several ACE initiatives, including a three-year project that looked at ways of ensuring academic success for low-income adults and a two-year project focused on programs and services for military service members and veterans in higher education. He was a leader of the ACE CAO census project and has authored other publications on a wide array of higher education topics, including higher education diversity, student enrollment and persistence trends, educational attainment, and college finance. He is currently the senior vice president for Institutional Capacity Building at the American Dental Education Association. Cook received his Ph.D. and M.A. from the Center for the Study of Higher and Postsecondary Education at the University of Michigan. He received his B.A. in urban planning from Miami University of Ohio.

RICHARD EKMAN has been president of the Council of Independent Colleges since 2000. He previously served as vice president for programs of Atlantic Philanthropies and, from 1991 to 1999, as secretary of the Andrew W. Mellon Foundation. From 1982 until 1991, he was a member of the staff of the National Endowment for the Humanities, first as director of the Division of Education Programs, and subsequently as director of the Division of Research Programs. He currently serves as a member of many boards, including the Yale–New Haven Teachers Institute, the National Humanities Alliance, Project Pericles, LSU Press, the Gilder Lehrman Institute of American History, and the Overseers' Committee to Visit the Harvard University Library.

His previous experience includes service as vice president and dean of Hiram College, where he was also a tenured member of the history faculty. Earlier, he served as assistant to the provost at the University of Massachusetts at Boston, and as associate director of the Department of Expository Writing at Harvard University. Dr. Ekman holds a Ph.D. from Harvard in the history of American civilization, the institution from which he also received his A.M. and A.B. (magna cum laude) degrees. He is co-author, with Richard E. Quandt, of *Technology and Scholarly Communication* (University of California Press, 1999).

In his various positions and through multiple publications, JOHN G. FLORES has become a national spokesperson on new classroom technologies and distance learning applications. As a program professor in educational leadership and executive director of business and organizational relationships at Nova Southeastern University's Abraham S. Fischler School of Education, Flores represents a global university focused on the creation, implementation and delivery of quality distance learning educational programs for colleges and universities. In addition, as a member of the board of directors of the United States Distance Learning Association and its executive director, Dr. Flores helps lead a global association focused on the application of distance learning in higher education using varied technologies.

Prior to these positions, Dr. Flores was president and CEO of Global Learning Network, a Seattle-based company focusing on the development and broadcast of educational programming in partnership with the Direct Broadcast Satellite industry. Earlier in his career, he was appointed by Massachusetts Governor William Weld and later Massachusetts Governor Paul Cellucci to serve as executive director of the Massachusetts Corporation for Educational Telecommunications (MCET), a quasi-public state agency focused on the development and application of telecommunication initiatives for all Massachusetts K–12 schools, state colleges, community colleges, the UMASS System, and numerous other state agencies. At MCET, Flores led the development of an award-winning national organization that produced distance learning programming through the Mass Learnpike broadcasting network.

Dr. Flores is a member of the International Society for Technology in Education and also serves as the associate editor for the *USDLA Distance Learning Magazine*, a practitioner-focused research journal for new higher education instructional technologies. Flores also co-edited *Electronic Learning Communities: Current Issues and Best Practices*.

As a distance learning consultant, Dr. Flores has worked with numerous corporations and organizations on new instructional technologies and applications, including Anderson Consulting, Booktech.com, Coalition to Connect Rural America, and the Consortium for Worker Education. Flores also served as a special consultant on distance learning to the World Bank.

Dr. Flores received his B.S. from the University of Massachusetts, Boston, his M.A. from Boston University, and his Ph.D. from the University of Connecticut.

WESLEY R. FUGATE is vice president and chief of staff at Randolph College in Lynchburg, VA. In this position he serves as a strategic advisor to the president, supervises the operations of the office of the president, serves as secretary of the board of trustees, and oversees the communications, marketing, and special events of the college.

Fugate holds a Ph.D. in higher education from the Institute of Higher Education at the University of Georgia. His dissertation explored how liberal arts colleges communicate messages of prestige, legitimacy, and differentiation during the student recruitment process. He was awarded the Alice L. Beeman Research Award for Outstanding Doctoral Dissertation from the Council for the Advancement and Support of Education. Fugate also earned a bachelor's degree from Centre College in Economics and Dramatic Arts and master's degree in Higher Education Administration with an emphasis in institutional advancement from Peabody College at Vanderbilt University.

Previously, Fugate has served as director of program advancement for Kentucky's Governor's Scholars Program; director of events for the

Republican National Committee's victory efforts, where he coordinated events for the President, Vice President, and First Lady of the United States, among other dignitaries; deputy chief of staff for planning and education policy to the Governor of Kentucky; and advisor to the Interfraternity Council at the University of Georgia.

JAMES GANDRE was appointed president of Manhattan School of Music in 2013. Previously, Gandre was provost and executive vice president of Roosevelt University (2007–2013), also serving as dean of Chicago College of Performing Arts (2000–2007), and as interim dean of the College of Education (2006–2007) at Roosevelt.

As a performer, Gandre has appeared as a vocalist with the Cleveland Orchestra, London Classical Players, Philharmonia Baroque Orchestra, and members of the San Francisco Symphony. His professional choral engagements include more than 175 performances with the New York Philharmonic, Aix-en-Provence Festival, Metropolitan Opera Orchestra, Royal Concertgebouw Orchestra (The Netherlands), Israel Philharmonic, Warsaw Symphony, and the San Francisco Symphony. In these performances, he has worked under such conductors as Leonard Bernstein, Zubin Mehta, and Sir Colin Davis.

Gandre is a voting member of the GRAMMYS and serves on the Recommendation Board of the Avery Fisher Artists Program. He has been a writer/consultant for the Peterson's Guides publication, *Professional Degree Programs in the Visual and Performing Arts*, and he has presented numerous panels on issues affecting LGBT youth and college/high school professionals at national and state conferences and is the Founder/former Co-Chair of NACAC's LGBT caucus. Gandre earned his B.Mus. with honors from Lawrence University, his M.Mus. from San Francisco Conservatory of Music, and his Ed.D. from the University of Nebraska–Lincoln.

WILLIAM SCOTT GREEN has been senior vice provost and dean of undergraduate education at the University of Miami since July 2006. In this newly created position, he has overall responsibility for enhancing the quality of the undergraduate experience and strengthening the integration of university-wide undergraduate curricular and co-curricular initiatives. He also holds an appointment as professor of religious studies and senior fellow in the Sue and Leonard Miller Center for Contemporary Judaic Studies. Green previously served as dean of the College at the University of Rochester and Philip S. Bernstein Professor of Judaic Studies. He led the development of Rochester's undergraduate liberal arts curriculum and founded its Department of Religion and Classics. Green earned an A.B. in religion at Dartmouth College and a Ph.D. in religion from Brown University. He has held fellowships from the National Endowment of the Humanities, the American Council of Learned Societies, and the Andrew Mellon Foundation.

ROBERT M. GROVES is a social statistician who studies the impact of social cognitive and behavioral influences on the quality of statistical information. His research has focused on the impact of mode of data collection on responses in sample surveys, the social and political influences on survey participation, the use of adaptive research designs to improve the cost and error properties of statistics, and public concerns about privacy affecting attitudes toward statistical agencies.

Prior to joining Georgetown University as provost in 2012, he was director of the United States Census Bureau (presidential appointment with Senate confirmation), a position he assumed after being director of the University of Michigan Survey Research Center, professor of sociology, and research professor at the Joint Program in Survey Methodology at the University of Maryland.

He is an elected fellow of the American Statistical Association, elected member of the International Statistical Institute, elected member of the American Academy of Arts and Sciences, elected member of the U.S. National Academy of Sciences, and elected member of the Institute of Medicine of the U.S. National Academies.

JULIA BEYER HOUPT is vice president for institutional advancement at Denison University. She received her B.A. from Denison and her J.D. from the University of Southern California. Houpt returned to the college in 2000 and leads the fundraising, communications, and alumni relations efforts. She also serves as a member of the president's senior staff. Prior to returning to Denison, Houpt practiced law in Los Angeles and directed advancement efforts at Stanford University's Southern California office, the University of Pennsylvania, and Friends' Central School in suburban Philadelphia.

LON S. KAUFMAN is vice chancellor for academic affairs and provost at the University of Illinois, Chicago. Kaufman joined UIC in 1985 as an assistant professor after completing postdoctoral work at the Carnegie Institution of Washington's Department of Plant Biology in Stanford, California. He was promoted to associate professor of biological sciences in 1990 and served as the director of graduate studies from 1993 to 1996. He became a full professor in 1995, and served as head of the department from 1998 to 2003. Since 1998, he has also held a position as adjunct professor of bioengineering. His research on the regulation of gene expression, signal transduction, and crop productivity has received continuous federal funding since his arrival at UIC and more recently has also received funding from the Illinois Soybean Growers Association.

From 2003 to 2008, Kaufman served as the founding vice provost for undergraduate affairs. During this time he was responsible for the oversight of several units, including the five UIC Cultural Centers, the Study Abroad Office, the Guaranteed Professional Program Admissions Initiative, and the Office of Campus Learning Environments. During his tenure, Kaufman also oversaw the development and implementation of a several new programs at UIC, including the General Education Program: Setting the Foundations for University Study, the Freshman Read Program, the Summer College Program, the federally funded Chicago Civic Leadership Certificate Program, the NSF funded ASCEND program, and the Undergraduate Research Experience.

In 2008 and until being named as the vice chancellor for academic affairs and provost, Kaufman served as the vice provost for planning and programs and had oversight for the School of Continuing Studies, the US/Asia Executive Development Program, and the Office of International Affairs. Projects included the 2010 UIC Campus Master Plan: *A Framework for the Future*, and the UIC Diversity Strategic Thinking Document: *Through the Lens of Diversity*. He also developed and served as the co-chair of the Academic Directions Task Force charged with assessing the strengths and weaknesses of each academic unit on campus.

MIROSLAVA MEJIA KRUG is senior vice president for finance and administration and chief financial officer at Roosevelt University. As Roosevelt's CFO, Krug is responsible for the finance and administration division of the university, which comprises more than 148 employees, including facilities and operations, risk management, information technology services, budget and financial management and analysis, real estate, financial services, and administrative services. Krug's responsibilities also include support of Roosevelt's Trustee Committees for Facilities, Finance, Audit, and Investment.

Before joining Roosevelt University, Krug was the chief financial officer for the Chicago Housing Authority. As such, she was responsible for financial services and cash management; long-term debt portfolio, including the refunding of $261 million of Capital Fund Revenue Bonds; an operating budget of $1 billion; a capital budget of $1.2 billion; and an asset portfolio of $400 million. Krug also spent ten years in various international finance positions with United Airlines, notably as manager of Finance and Administration. She earned an M.B.A. from Latin America Science and Technology University and a B.A. in accounting from the University of Panama.

MARK B. LAPPING is executive director of the Edmund S. Muskie School of Public Service at the University of Southern Maine. He also served as provost of the university from 1994 to 2000 and from 2007 to 2009. A planner by profession, Lapping was founding dean of the Bloustein School of Planning and Public Policy at Rutgers University prior to joining USM. He has held leadership posts at the University of Guelph (Ontario), where he founded the School of Rural Planning and Development, and Kansas State University, where he served as dean of its College of Architecture, Planning, and Design. Author of several books about higher education planning, he also has written more than 150 articles and monographs and has been on the editorial boards of the *Journal of the American Planning Association; Journal of Rural Studies, Agriculture, and Human Value;* and the *Journal of Planning, Research, and Education.*

Lapping, whose B.S. is from SUNY, New Paltz, and Ph.D. from Emory University, has worked on environmental and food/agricultural issues as a consultant for a number of federal, state, and local governments across the United States and Canada, as well as in Scandinavia, Finland, and Estonia. He also served as interim president of Unity College in 2005–6.

ROBIN MAMLET is senior partner and practice leader in enrollment management and admission at Witt/Kieffer, an executive search firm. As senior partner, she directs search assignments for presidents, provosts, deans, chief advancement officers, and chief public affairs and communications, diversity, student affairs and enrollment officers.

A national leader on access and diversity recruitment, Mamlet came to Witt/Kieffer after twenty-three years in academic administration, most recently as dean of admission and financial aid at Stanford University. She also served as chief enrollment officer at Swarthmore College, Sarah Lawrence College, and The Lawrenceville School. Mamlet has been published in the *Chronicle of Higher Education, New York Times, Wall Street Journal,* and *Washington Post.* Her book, *College Admission: From Application to Acceptance, Step by Step,* published by Three Rivers Press of Random House, appeared in 2011. She holds a B.A. in English from Occidental College.

LINDA A. MCMILLIN served as provost and dean of the faculty at Susquehanna University until 2014, when she resumed teaching after a seven-year term. She has taught at Susquehanna University since 1989 and is also professor of history. McMillin earned her Ph.D. in history from the University of California, Los Angeles. Her undergraduate degree in theology and English is from Loyola Marymount University. She was the recipient of an American Council on Education Fellowship from 2000–2001, during which time she served as special assistant to the president of Bloomsburg University, Jessica Kozloff.

McMillin has authored more than twenty articles, in both English and Spanish, and edited two books, *A New Academic Compact: Revisioning the Relationship Between Faculty and Their Institutions*, with Jerry Berberet (Anker Press, 2002) and *Hrotsvit of Gandersheim: Contexts, Identities, Affinities and Performances*, with Katharina Wilson and Phyllis Brown (Toronto University Press, 2004).

SHEILA MURPHY's thirty years in higher education include serving as the SSAO at Mount Holyoke College, Russell Sage College, and Simmons College. She is now a search consultant in the education practice at Witt/Kieffer, an executive search firm. She is a graduate of Stonehill College and the Harvard Graduate School of Education.

CHRISTOPHER J. NELLUM is a research fellow at the American Council on Education and a doctoral candidate at the Center for the Study of Higher and Postsecondary Education in the School of Education at the University of Michigan.

DAVID W. PERSHING was appointed president of the University of Utah in 2012. Pershing joined the University of Utah as an assistant professor of chemical engineering in 1977. He was named a Presidential Young Investigator by the National Science Foundation in 1984, became Dean of the College of Engineering in 1987, and was named a Distinguished Professor of Chemical Engineering in 1995. In 1998, Pershing was named senior vice president for academic affairs responsible for approximately 1,000 faculty and 25,000 students.

Pershing is the recipient of the University of Utah's Distinguished Teaching and Distinguished Research Awards. He has authored more than eighty peer-reviewed publications, won more than twenty research grants totaling approximately $60 million, and earned five patents. He was named Engineering Educator of the Year by the Utah Engineering Council in 2002 and is a winner of the Governor's Medal for Science and Technology. He was director of the University of Utah's Center for Simulation of Accidental Fires and Explosions, supported by a $40 million grant from the U.S. Department of Energy. Pershing holds a bachelor's degree from Purdue University and a Ph.D. from the University of Arizona, both in chemical engineering.

PENNY RUE is vice president for campus life at Wake Forest University. Prior to her appointment at Wake Forest, Rue had served as vice chancellor for student affairs at the University of California, San Diego, since 2007. Earlier in her career, Rue served for eight years as dean of students at the University of Virginia. She served for five years as senior associate dean of students at Georgetown University and for seven years as Georgetown's director of student programs. She also held student life positions at the University of Maryland and the University of North Carolina at Chapel Hill.

Rue earned her doctorate in counseling and personnel services from the University of Maryland, where her dissertation research focused on building community on college campuses. She also earned a master's degree in student personnel services from Ohio State University and a bachelor's degree in English and religion from Duke University. Rue has regularly addressed important student life issues at national conferences for Student Affairs Administrators in Higher Education (NASPA) and other professional groups. She was named a "Pillar of the Profession" by the NASPA Foundation. Rue taught in the San Diego State University graduate program in student affairs and also taught "College Student Development" at the University of Virginia and "Contemporary Issues in Leadership for Women" at Georgetown University.

JOHN D. SIMON is executive vice president and provost of the University of Virginia and the Robert C. Taylor Professor of Chemistry. He is charged with directing the academic administration of UVA's eleven schools, the Library, the Art Museum, public service activities, university centers, foreign study programs, and the advancement of teaching and research.

Prior to his position at UVA, Simon served as the vice provost for academic affairs at Duke University from 2005 to 2011. In this position, Simon was responsible for overseeing Duke's strategic planning and for nurturing campus-wide academic initiatives to connect the humanities, social sciences, and sciences. He chaired Duke's chemistry department from 1999–2004. Simon received his B.A. from Williams College in 1979 and his Ph.D. from Harvard University in 1983. After a postdoctoral fellowship at UCLA, Simon joined the Department of Chemistry and Biochemistry at UCSD in 1985, and then moved to Duke University as the George B. Geller Professor in 1998.

Provost Simon has earned numerous fellowships and awards for his scientific work, including the Presidential Young Investigator Award, Alfred P. Sloan Fellowship, Camille and Henry Dreyfus Teacher Scholar Award, and the Fresenius Award. He is a fellow of the American Association for the Advancement of Science and the American Physical Society.

After a Biology B.S. (Ursinus College), a Psychology Ph.D., and brain anatomy postdoctoral fellowship (University of Pennsylvania), JAMES R. STELLAR became in 1978 an assistant and then associate professor of psychology at Harvard University. In 1986 he moved to Northeastern University, where he became a full professor and then dean of the College of Arts and Sciences. In 2009, he moved to Queens College CUNY to become provost. His research and teaching has centered on the anatomical and molecular biological basis of reward and motivational processes in laboratory animals as a model for human cocaine addiction. In 2013, Stellar transitioned at Queens to a specially focused vice presidential position to develop an office of Academic Innovation and Experiential Education.

Outside the university, Stellar co-founded and co-directs the Global Institute on Experiential Education that has since 2005 helped more than sixty-five colleges and universities create on-campus experiential education plans. The Institute operates under the World Association of Cooperative Education where Stellar is a board member. Since 2009, Stellar and a team have been writing a blog (www.otherlobe.com) about experiential education, its management by colleges and universities, and the personal transformation such an approach can achieve for students when combined with classical academic excellence.

SURESH SUBRAMANI is executive vice chancellor for academic affairs and a Distinguished Professor of Molecular Biology at the University of California, San Diego. Subramani has been a member of the UC San Diego faculty since 1981. He received his Ph.D. in biochemistry from UC Berkeley and was a Jane Coffin Childs Fellow at Stanford University. He was the recipient of a Searle Scholar Award, an NCI Research Career Development Award, and a Guggenheim Fellowship. At UCSD, Subramani served as the last chair of the Department of Biology (1999–2000) prior to its reorganization as a division, and he served as the interim dean of the Division of Biological Sciences between 2006 and 2007. He is a fellow of the American Academy of Microbiology and the recipient of an NIH MERIT Award. Subramani is the author of more than 100 research articles in international journals.

R. MICHAEL TANNER is chief academic officer and vice president at the Association of Public and Land-Grant Universities. In this position, Tanner leads the association's academic affairs activities, including the Voluntary System of Accountability/College Portrait project. He also serves as senior staff liaison to the Association's Council on Academic Affairs, composed of the provosts and chief academic officers from each of the 215 member universities and university systems.

Prior to this, Tanner served as provost and vice chancellor for academic affairs at the University of Illinois, Chicago, one of the top U.S. universities as ranked by federal research expenditures and including fifteen colleges and schools enrolling almost 17,000 undergraduate and 9,000 graduate students. Prior to joining the UIC faculty and administration in July 2002, Tanner had spent thirty-one years at the University of California, Santa Cruz, as computer and information sciences faculty member and administrator, including six years as executive vice chancellor and three years as academic vice chancellor.

Through his engineering and computer sciences research, Tanner has produced four patents, more than ten referred journal articles, and almost thirty conferences, book chapters, proceedings, and technical reports. His research has focused on codes that protect digital messages against errors introduced in transmission.

GEORGE H. VANDERZWAAG is director of athletics and recreation at the University of Rochester. Prior to this appointment, he served as senior associate director of athletics at Princeton University. VanderZwaag has a strong background in NCAA and Title IX compliance matters; his primary emphasis at Princeton was in regulatory, academic, and student affairs issues. He served as Princeton's coordinator for its Student-Athlete Advisory Committee.

VanderZwaag graduated from Trinity College with a bachelor's degree in economics and earned a master of science degree in sport management from the University of Massachusetts. At the University of Massachusetts, he was a research assistant and worked on revisions to the textbook, *Law and Business of the Sports Industry*, by Glenn Wong and Robert Berry, for the chapters pertaining to the regulation of intercollegiate athletics.

SAUL J. WEINER is vice provost of planning and programs at the University of Illinois, Chicago. Weiner is a graduate of Harvard College, Dartmouth Medical School, and the University of Chicago with board certification in internal medicine and pediatrics. He is professor of medicine, pediatrics and medical education in the College of Medicine. Since 1997 he has served variously as program director of the Combined Residency in Internal Medicine and Pediatrics, division head of General Pediatrics and Adolescent Medicine, vice-head of Department of Pediatrics, and as senior associate dean for educational affairs in the College of Medicine. As senior associate dean, Dr. Weiner led a major curricular reform, aligning the four regional campuses' educational program, introducing learner-centered educational methods, a customized learning management system, and computer-based testing.

Index

academic freedom, 74, 103
academic programs, quality of, 3, 13–15, 19, 99, 104, 106, 113, 117, 168. *See also* curriculum development
accountability, 5–6, 10–12, 24, 40, 47, 84, 111–12, 143, 165; and academic governance, 127; and athletics programs, 3, 181–82, 185–87; and online learning, 114, 117; to students, 15
accreditation, 11, 12, 22, 26; and assessment, 103–4; and co-curriculum, 166
administration, 8, 13, 19, 52–53; and faculty, 4–6, 57, 66–67, 88, 99–100, 137–40
admissions, 157–58, 168, 173, 175, 182–83. *See also* enrollment management
advancement officers, chief, 146–54
age discrimination, 193–94
Alabama, University of (Huntsville), 191
Alexandre, Lourien, 77
Altbach, Philip, 5–6
alumni, 23, 63, 166, 200
American Academic Leadership Institute, 29
American Association for Health Education (AAHE), 61
American Association of State Colleges and Universities (AASCU), 24, 29
American Association of University Professors, 76

American College and University Presidents Climate Commitment, 125
American Council on Education (ACE), 6, 10, 32, 37, 58, 134, 143
American Faculty, The (Schuster and Finkelstein), 61, 71, 73
Anderson, Michael L., 182–83
anti-intellectualism, 75
Antioch University, 74–76, 77
assessment, 5–6, 11–12, 24, 64, 82, 170–71, 185–86; and accreditation, 103–4; and curriculum development, 103–4, 108–9, 114; of learning outcomes, 8, 22, 26, 108–9, 135
Associated Colleges of the Midwest, 24
Associated Colleges of the South, 24
Associated New American Colleges, 60
Association for the Advancement of Sustainability in Higher Education (AASHE), 125
Association for the Study of Higher Education (ASHE), 74
Association of American Colleges and Universities (AAC&U), 24, 160–61
Association of College and Research Libraries (ACRL), 28
Association of Public and Land Grant Universities, 157
athletics programs, 8, 180–87; and academic performance, 186–87; and accountability, 3, 181–82, 185–87; and CAO, 181, 183–87; and experiential learning, 181–82, 184; and mission, 180–81, 187

229